WEiRD ARiZONA

Hello from Sunny Arizona!

STERLING
New York / London
www.sterlingpublishing.com

HERE
LIES

LESTERMOORE
FOUR SLUGS
FROM A 44
NO LES
NO MORE

WEIRD
ARiZONA

by WESLEY TREAT

Your Travel Guide to Arizona's
Local Legends and Best Kept Secrets

Mark Sceurman and Mark Moran, Executive Editors

WEIRD ARIZONA

Published by Sterling Publishing Co., Inc.
387 Park Avenue South, New York, NY 10016

© 2007 by Mark Sceurman and Mark Moran

Distributed in Canada by Sterling Publishing
c/o Canadian Manda Group, 165 Dufferin Street
Toronto, Ontario, Canada M6K 3H6

Distributed in the United Kingdom by GMC Distribution Services,
Castle Place, 166 High Street, Lewes, East Sussex, England BN7 1XU

Distributed in Australia by Capricorn Link (Australia) Pty. Ltd.
P.O. Box 704, Windsor, NSW 2756, Australia

ISBN 13: 978-1-4027-3938-5
ISBN 10: 1-4027-3938-9

2 4 6 8 10 9 7 5 3 1

For information about custom editions, special sales, premium and
corporate purchases, please contact Sterling Special Sales
Department at 800-805-5489 or specialsales@sterlingpub.com.

Design: Richard J. Berenson
Berenson Design & Books, LLC, New York, NY

CONTENTS

Foreword: A Note from the Marks	6
Introduction	8
Local Legends	10
Ancient Arizona	26
Fabled People and Places	44
Unexplained Arizona	64
Bizarre Beasts	78
Local Heroes and Villains	96
Personalized Properties and Innovative Environments	114
Roadside Oddities	136
Roads Less Traveled	168
Ghosts of Arizona	186
Cemetery Safari	206
Abandoned in Arizona	224
Index	248
Picture Credits	253
Acknowledgments	254

Foreword: A Note from the Marks

Our weird journey began a long, long time ago in a far-off land called New Jersey. Once a year or so, we'd compile a homespun newsletter called *Weird N.J.*, then pass it on to our friends. The pamphlet was a collection of odd news clippings, bizarre facts, little-known historical anecdotes, and anomalous encounters from our home state. The newsletter also included the kinds of localized legends that were often whispered around a particular town but seldom heard outside the boundaries of the community where they originated.

We had started *Weird N.J.* on the simple theory that every town in the state had at least one good tale to tell. The publication soon became a full-fledged magazine, and we made the decision to actually do our own investigating to see if we could track down where all of these seemingly unbelievable stories were coming from. Was there, we wondered, any factual basis for the fantastic local legends people were telling us about? Armed with not much more than a camera and a notepad, we set off on a mystical journey of discovery. Much to our surprise and amazement, a lot of what we had initially presumed to be nothing more than urban legends turned out to be real—or at least to contain a grain of truth, which had sparked the lore to begin with.

After a dozen years of documenting the bizarre, we were asked to write a book about our adventures, and so *Weird N.J.: Your Travel Guide to New Jersey's Local Legends and Best Kept Secrets* was published in 2003. Soon people from all over the country began writing to us, telling us strange tales from their home state. As it turned out, what we had perceived to be something of very local interest was actually just a small part of a larger and more universal phenomenon.

When our publisher asked us what we wanted to do next, the answer was simple: "We'd like to do a book called *Weird U.S.*, in which we could document the local legends and strangest stories from all over the country," we replied. So for the next twelve months, we set out in search of weirdness wherever it might be found in the fifty states. And indeed, we found plenty of it!

After *Weird U.S.* was published, we came to the conclusion that this country had more great tales than could be contained in just one book. Everywhere we looked, we found unwritten folklore, creepy cemeteries, cursed locations, and outlandish roadside oddities. With this in mind, we told our publisher that we

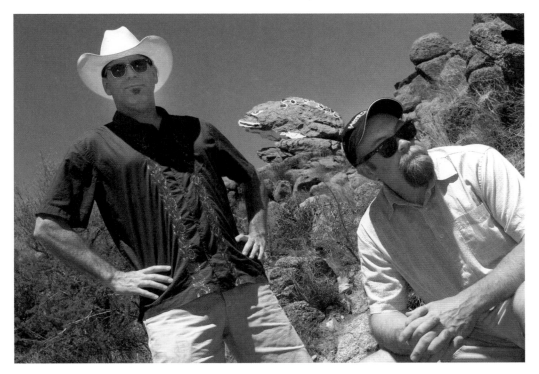

that we wanted to continue our collaboration with Wesley on more book projects. So when we began pulling together material for this *Weird Arizona* volume, Wesley was our go-to guy—hands down.

Why, you might ask, would we choose a roving reporter from Texas to investigate the bizarre tales of the Grand Canyon State? Well, the answer is simple—Wesley had already proved to us without a doubt that he possessed what we refer to as the Weird Eye, which is what is needed to search out

wanted to document it all and to do it in a series of books, each focusing on the peculiarities of a particular state.

One of the first states that we set out to document the weirdness of was Texas, and we found the perfect person to act as our eyes and ears in the Lone Star State in Wesley Treat. Wesley had been traveling around the highways, byways, and back roads for years, chronicling all of the out-of-the-way roadside spectacles and odd goings-on. As soon as we invited him along on our *Weird Texas* ride, we knew we had found a kindred spirit in strangeness. With his talent for seeking out unusual sites, his whimsical storytelling style, and his dynamic photographic technique, Wesley's appetite for odd adventures will be immediately apparent to anyone who shares a similar wanderlust for offbeat attractions.

Even before *Weird Texas* was finished, we knew

the sort of stories we were looking for. The Weird Eye requires one to see the world in a different way, with a renewed sense of wonder. And once you have it, there is no going back—you'll never see things the same way again. All of a sudden you begin to reexamine your own environs, noticing your everyday surroundings as if for the first time. And you begin to ask yourself questions like, "What the heck is *that* thing all about, anyway?" and "Doesn't anybody else think that's kind of *weird?*"

So come with us now and let Wesley take you on a tour of a state that he has come to know very, very well over the past year. Even if you've lived in the Copper State—Arizona's former nickname—all your life, we're certain that there are some stories in this book that will be completely new to you. Some might even seem unbelievable to many Arizonans, but as they say, truth is stranger than fiction—especially in the place we like to call *Weird Arizona.–Mark Moran and Mark Sceurman*

Introduction

When Mark Sceurman and Mark Moran asked me to head west and gather offbeat reconnaissance from the Grand Canyon State, I grabbed the wheel of the first rental car I could find and hit the road. Arizona had found a place in my heart years ago when I first encountered The Thing off I-10, and I was keyed up to explore the state even further. So, with a sack full of clean T-shirts and a bag crammed with camera gear, I zigzagged my way from city to suburb, to high desert and back again, recording all my peculiar encounters along the way.

So it's true I'm not an Arizona native. But with the help of countless willing residents, I quickly absorbed as much local knowledge as I could. I learned what a snowbird is, how to avoid rattlesnakes, and why it's not a good idea to pocket petrified wood. I discovered the proper ways to pronounce Tempe, Casa Grande, and Mogollon. I also learned that one can get along just fine without Daylight Saving Time, that speed limits are just polite suggestions, and that deliberately mispronouncing "butte"—despite such opportune names as Finger Butte and Elephant Butte—loses its humor pretty fast.

My true mission, however, was to uncover Arizona's lesser-known culture, the sort of stuff not typically advertised by the board of tourism. I was sent to find the outrageous, the bizarre, and if I were to come across it, the downright disturbing. Unique roadside displays, localized lore, and people proudly out of step with the norm: These were my goals. I sought stories that were distinctly Arizona, the likes of which are perpetuated through school lunchroom chatter or, in some cases, are swept under the rug entirely for fear of town embarrassment. In short, I was sent to find the Weird.

Now, I'll be honest. I was a little skeptical at first whether I'd be able to find enough oddities in Arizona to fill a whole book. I knew all about the Lost Dutchman and had already been to the Titan Missile Museum (twice), but I was afraid the great undeveloped expanse that covers most of the state would yield little material. Boy, was I wrong. Turns out, the dry southwestern earth makes fertile ground for cultivating Weird. I'd dig up one story, and a hundred more would follow. It was like snagging a single cholla spine and having the whole arm pop off and lunge into my flesh.

In the process, I learned that the old adage about truth being stranger than

fiction certainly applies. With every story, I would investigate the facts as far as my research would take me, and more often than not, the tale would just get weirder. On the other hand, there are legends whose origins are almost impossible to uncover, but I quickly learned that truth is not always essential to a good narrative. Sometimes the story is just about the story.

By the end, I had discovered more material than I could use. Arizona has so much to offer, I was forced to leave some things out of the book purely for lack of room. So, with the help of the Marks and several very valuable contributors, I compiled a diverse selection of what I consider many of Arizona's best stories.

On a side note, I've attempted to include location information for attractions wherever possible. Understand, however, that many sites are inaccessible for various reasons, and we would rather our readers not get hurt, nor do we encourage trespassing. So in many instances, it was either not possible or inadvisable to include specific locations.

Admittedly, there's more Weird out there to be found. Just consider *Weird Arizona* the burning fuse sizzling toward your own explosive search.

Now, hit the gas!

—*Wesley Treat*

Local Legends

he idea of mythology usually brings to mind thoughts of Greek gods or fire-breathing dragons, the sort of things one finds in a history textbook or the pages of a dungeon master's guide. But mythology extends even into our own culture. Stories of lost treasure, bizarre curses, or remarkable deaths—the kind of tales shared over a drink or around a campfire—these are the legends.

Such stories usually develop in areas isolated from everyday traffic. They're connected with sites that are not commonly visited or are simply overlooked. Even when civilization encroaches, these places experience a different kind of isolation, obscured by development or forgotten on some dead-end road. But you can still find them, as long as you listen to the stories they whisper.

La Llorona—The Phantom Banshee

Part sorrowful banshee, part angry spirit, part cursed creature, La Llorona is known to almost every Latin culture. The name, pronounced *la yo-ro-na,* literally translates to "the crier," which is exactly what this spook is said to do for all eternity. There are many different versions of this tale, depending on the region in which it's told, but all of them center around a woman who murdered two children hundreds of years ago.

In one of the more popular versions, a beautiful widow, who lived with her two children in a poverty-stricken town, fell in love with a wealthy man. The man returned her affection, but wasn't interested in being a father and so would not marry the young widow. In her desperation, she led her children down to the river that ran near her town, and in the dead of night, drowned them both.

As the bodies of her children floated away into the darkness, the woman raced to her lover's house to tell him the lengths she'd gone to in order to be with him. The man was horrified and turned his back on her. When she realized the irrevocable act had been for nothing, she went mad. The woman ran back to the river, hoping to save her children, but it was too late. God then condemned her to walk the earth for all eternity, searching for her drowned children.

La Llorona is known to haunt many locations throughout Arizona, as well as the rest of the American Southwest. Two of her most notorious hangouts in this state are along the banks of the Gila and San Pedro rivers. It's said that she steals the souls of living children, and she's often invoked by Mexican mothers to frighten naughty niños. Legend also has it that if you see her, you or someone close to you will die within a week.

The origin of the story is unknown, although some folklorists believe it dates back to Aztec times. Many modern Mexican Americans believe in La Llorona and swear that she still bedevils the living. They say she walks at night, her long, jet-black hair and white dress blowing in the wind. But where her beautiful face should be, they whisper, there is the head of a horse. On moonlit nights, they say, you might glimpse her ghostly form bending over a creek bed or river, her pale arms elbow-deep in the waters, searching for her drowned children.

Launa's Canyon

In northwest Arizona, people say La Llorona's actual name was Launa and she lived with her lover near a canyon about three miles south of Kingman. In this version, the man had already agreed to marry her and had built a cabin for her and the two daughters, who in this case were his. Launa, however, felt the man gave the girls too much affection and became increasingly jealous of the attention he paid them. So one evening she lured the children toward the canyon and pushed them over the edge.

Launa claimed it was an accident, but the children's father was aware of her jealousy and couldn't allay his suspicions that she was responsible. The man's grief and mistrust compelled him to leave her. Launa, now alone, regretted what she had done. Her guilt and anguish led her to end her own life in the same way she had ended the children's, by throwing herself into the canyon's depths.

Launa has been damned to wander the canyon ever since. At night, the woman's cries of despair can be heard echoing along the walls of the caves. Between the hours of midnight and three a.m., she can often be seen drifting through the darkness, clad in a long, white dress. She's said to be desperate for company, and in some accounts will take possession of anyone she finds in her canyon, forcing them to join her in eternal grief.

La Llorona Wants Your Bones

Growing up we heard a lot about La Llorona. Right before my great grandma died, she told me this weird story. One night while she was walking home, she saw a lady in black ahead of her carrying a lamp. (Remember, it was a long time ago and there weren't streetlights.) So she walked up to the lady and asked what was she doing out so late. There was no reply, so she asked again. This time, the lady stopped and looked up at my grandma. She screamed. The lady did not have a human head but that of a horse. At this point, my grandma got the heck out of there, tripping and falling all the way home.

In another variation La Llorona did not have enough cash to feed her children, and not wanting them to suffer, she tossed them off a cliff. Too guilty to live with her sin, she also jumped. When she got to heaven, the lord wouldn't allow her to enter till she found her children's bones (which had been scattered by the river). To this day, she still searches, willing to take anyone's bones, anyone who crosses her path.—*James*

La Llorona Drowned Babies in Tucson

The Tucson version of La Llorona was a promiscuous lady who didn't like to be bothered with children. Whenever she had a baby, she would take it down to the river and drown it.

When she herself died and tried to get into Heaven, St. Peter told her that she couldn't get in unless she brought all her dead babies with her. So now she wanders along the river, wailing for her lost children. Not surprisingly, they haven't come back to her.

Don't leave your baby alone in the dark or let your little ones wander around at night alone, because La Llorona will take them in hopes of fooling St. Peter.—*Maureen*

Woman Without a Face

Once my friend saw La Llorona. I believe him because he never lies to nobody. He said that him and his parents were just driving by and that all of a sudden they saw a lady dressed in white, and once they got closer they got to see her better. But once they saw the front of her they said she didn't have a face and she was carrying a baby all covered in white, but they didn't get to see the baby's face. They said it was like 3 o'clock in the morning. They punched the gas and went faster because they were scared.—*Letter via email*

Apache Leap

At the foot of the Pinal Mountains, rising high above the town of Superior, a dramatic escarpment fills half the eastern sky. It makes for a stunning view, but to those who know the story behind its name, the sight of Apache Leap can be as sorrowful as it is beautiful.

Throughout the 1800s, this region underwent waves of change. Within just a few decades, territorial control passed from Spain to Mexico in a war for independence, then to the United States in yet another intense conflict. Native Americans, meanwhile, fought for their own claims. Tensions ran high, and by the 1870s the relationship shared by the United States and most American Indians, including the Apaches, was not, shall we say, a positive one.

This discord prompted the establishment of several military outposts in an attempt to bring the Apache under control. Among them was Camp Pinal, organized near modern-day Superior. The legend that follows hasn't been corroborated by written record, but given the environment at the time, it's not unlikely the story has a strong basis in fact.

Troops assumed to be from Camp Pinal, as it's told, took the offensive against a band of seventy-five Apache warriors atop the ledge that would one day overlook Superior. As the cavalry advanced, the Apache were driven westward until they were trapped at the cliff's edge. Yet the warriors were too proud to accept defeat at the hands of the army and refused to surrender. Rather than be captured or murdered by their enemy, the men jumped. All seventy-five warriors fell eight hundred feet to their deaths.

When word of the men's fate reached their tribe, their families rushed to the bottom of the cliff. Their wives and mothers wept uncontrollably. The dark obsidian pebbles found in the area today are said to be the tears that were shed by those women, which soaked the earth and hardened into the black, semi-translucent stones known today as Apache Tears.

Curse of the Petrified Forest

It's the Late Triassic, two hundred million years ago, and what would one day be the arid landscape of Arizona is a tropical wetland covered in rich organic mud and scored by an expansive system of rivers and streams. Immense logs, fallen members of huge coniferous forests, are swept up by floodwaters and deposited along sandy floodplains. Over time, layers of silt, mud, and volcanic ash bury the logs as water seeps through the strata and carries silica downward, saturating the timber's cells with minerals. Quartz grows within the logs, replacing organic material and assuming their shape. Epochs later, Arizona reveals its rock-hard wood and legends are born.

Now exposed by erosion and protected in the Petrified Forest National Park, these stone trees look like a scattering of rainbows run aground. Many exhibit the original umber of their mother evergreens or the white of pure silica, but trace minerals that infiltrated the wood also produce shades of green, blue, and pink. Iron oxides generate blazing reds and yellows, producing in some the only fire these trees will ever see.

The trees were petrified at such a minute level that details of the original tissues can still be seen. Sometimes you can see knots or even scars left by ancient insects. Trees that were once as much as nine feet in diameter and nearly two hundred feet tall lie here, now broken into logs, chunks, and shards, fractured due to the frailty of their quartz. Some trunks remain almost complete, laid out as they came to rest, though now divided into nearly equal sections like a party sub sandwich.

The unique beauty of petrified wood has unfortunately been its undoing. Since the first routes were blazed

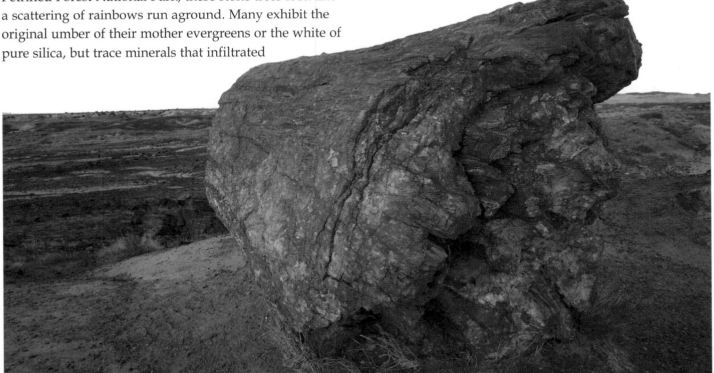

through this region in the mid-1800s, travelers have been carrying off pieces as keepsakes. Specimens were seized by the handful, pocketful, and even the cartful. Today there's a minimum fine of $275 if you're caught pilfering in the park, but that doesn't seem to worry a lot of people. Even though plenty of samples, collected lawfully from private land, are available at the countless rock shops in the area, visitors to Petrified Forest insist on pinching it illegally. Park rangers say people don't think stealing a tiny bit of wood makes any difference, but the park loses between twelve and fourteen tons that way every year.

However, there is one theft deterrent that has apparently been quite effective. Stolen petrified wood, some say, is cursed. Like with the tiki idol in the Hawaiian *Brady Bunch* episodes, bad luck comes to he who possesses it, which has prompted thousands to send the stuff back. For decades, Petrified Forest has received stolen samples in the mail, returned by visitors who regret having taken them.

One visitor described a piece of petrified wood he had taken more than ten years earlier. "It was a great challenge sneaking it out of the park," he wrote. "Since that time, though, nothing in my life has gone right." Another begged, "My life has been totally destroyed since we've been back from vacation. Please put these back so my life can get back to normal!"

Usually visitors return pieces after only a short period, but some people endure their misfortune for a lifetime. Just recently, one piece arrived that was stolen back in 1928.

Does the National Park Service believe in the jinx? Not officially. But they don't deny it either, since anything that prevents people from diminishing the park's beauty is appreciated. Besides, even when petrified wood is sent back, not knowing exactly where the pieces came from removes any scientific value. No matter how much the reformed thieves plead, once the rocks have lost their context, they can't be returned to the park. And that's the real curse.

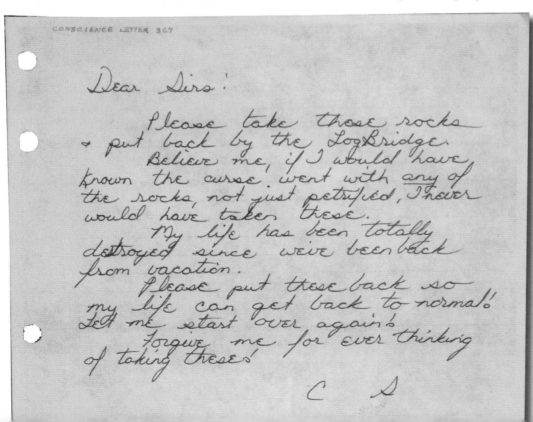

CONSCIENCE LETTER 367

Dear Sirs:

Please take these rocks + put back by the Log Bridge. Believe me, if I would have known the curse went with any of the rocks, not just petrified, I never would have taken these.

My life has been totally destroyed since we've been back from vacation.

Please put these back so my life can get back to normal! Let me start over again. Forgive me for ever thinking of taking these.

C S

Fina's Tree

Trees aren't a big deal in Tucson. You wouldn't expect them to be, with an average rainfall of only an inch a month. That's why the red gum tree on West Congress Street sticks out the way it does, being about eleven stories tall. It's not the world's tallest, sure, but considering most trees in this region reach only about twenty to forty feet, this one is King of the Forest.

That's not the only reason this gum tree receives so much attention. It actually has a story behind it, which sprouted, along with the tree, back in 1910. People say that's the year Tucson was hit by a thunderstorm that felled the gum tree as a sapling. Okay, "felled" may be too big a word for a sapling. "Teetered," maybe. It was teetered.

Anyway, the next day a helpful girl named Delfina Bravo found the young tree lying on the ground. She lifted it, straightened it up, and replanted it. Nearly a century later, it's trumpeted as the tallest tree in the city. An organization called Trees for Tucson even makes it a grand stop on their three-hour, Great Trees of the Old Pueblo van tour every year.

A plotline for a children's book if ever there was one.

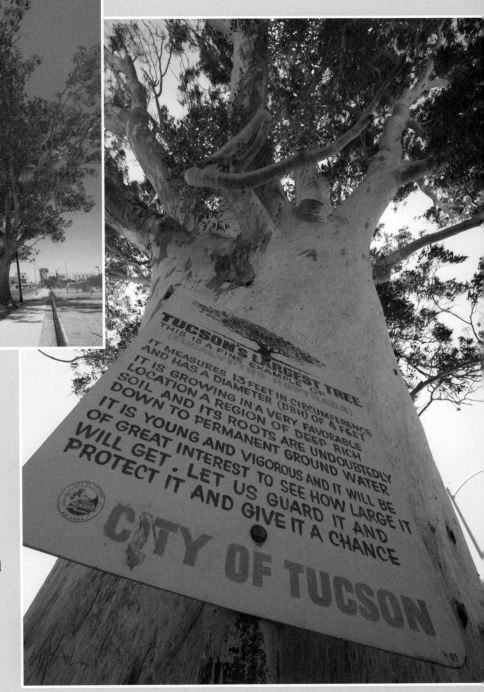

TUCSON'S LARGEST TREE
THIS IS A FINE EXAMPLE OF
IT MEASURES 13 FEET IN CIRCUMFERENCE
AND HAS A DIAMETER (DBH) OF 4 FEET
IT IS GROWING IN A VERY FAVORABLE
LOCATION A REGION OF DEEP RICH
SOIL AND ITS ROOTS ARE UNDOUBTEDLY
DOWN TO PERMANENT GROUND WATER
IT IS YOUNG AND VIGOROUS AND IT WILL BE
OF GREAT INTEREST TO SEE HOW LARGE IT
WILL GET . LET US GUARD IT AND
PROTECT IT AND GIVE IT A CHANCE
CITY OF TUCSON

El Tiradito

At night, a flickering glow fills the secluded court-yard known informally as the Wishing Shrine, radiant with the flames of dozens and dozens of candles. In the daylight, only pools of wax remain, though flowers, crosses, and photographs often stay behind. Either way, the courtyard maintains a serene atmosphere, which is probably due to its location away from the street, tucked between a small Tucson museum and a Mexican restaurant.

Though obviously a place of reverence, this spot in the Barrio Viejo isn't associated with any parish or any saint — at least not one recognized by the Catholic Church. Seen more as a "folk saint," the man for whom this memorial was built actually died an adulterer. His shrine, in fact, is claimed as the only one in the United States dedicated to the soul of a sinner.

The man's name was Juan Oliveras, and his story dates back to the early 1870s when he was working as a sheepherder. Though the details vary, the generally accepted version places him on a ranch outside Tucson, where he lived with his wife and worked alongside his father-in-law. Presumably to avoid the commute, his father-in-law took to boarding at the ranch as well, though his wife chose to stay in the city.

At some point, Oliveras began an affair with his mother-in-law, making trips into Tucson to see her. Living outside the city, his father-in-law was naturally unaware of the liaison, at least until a surprise visit, when he caught the two in flagrante delicto. Enraged, the husband grabbed an axe and chased Oliveras into the street, where he took the philanderer's life in a manner apparently too gruesome to have remained part of the story.

Due to the moral offense that led to his death, Oliveras was denied burial on church grounds. Instead, he was laid to rest on the spot where his father-in-law had tossed his body, which is how the shrine received its official name of *El Tiradito*, "The Little Castaway."

The betrayed husband then ran off to Mexico, and his wife subsequently spent her days lighting candles for her lover and weeping over his grave.

Given that his crime was one committed out of love, women became sympathetic to Oliveras and began praying that he be forgiven. As they too lit candles for him, a small memorial took shape; it grew as the years passed.

The original shrine has been reportedly moved from its original location. Juan Oliveras fell dead near South Meyer Avenue and West Simpson Street, a block away, but when Simpson was expanded, the shrine was relocated west to the 400 block of South Main Avenue. It isn't clear whether the body was moved with it.

The occasional rumor will surface that the cries of Oliveras's lover can be heard, but it seems few come here anymore with the tragic couple in mind or are even fully aware of their story. Instead, the shrine has transformed into a place where the hopeful come to leave their prayers and desires, sometimes in the form of coins representing a need for money or as notes slipped into the shrine's cracks. The practice has even given rise to a new legend, which says if a visitor's candle stays lit until dawn, his wish will be granted.

The JATO Impala

Here's one most of us have heard, thanks to the FORWARD button in our friends' e-mail programs. Over the years, the story has allegedly taken place in both California and New Mexico, but at the height of its fame, it was centered in the good old Arizona desert.

The story begins when a mysteriously charred and partly melted stretch of asphalt was discovered on an unidentified roadway. When the Arizona Highway Patrol was called out to have a look, they discovered what appeared to be an airplane crash on the side of a nearby cliff. Mystified as to what the connection could be between the scorched highway and the airplane debris on the cliff, the police launched a full-scale investigation. What the experts determined was that the remains were not those of an aircraft but were the smoking wreck of a car. The puzzling part was that the impact had occurred one hundred twenty-five feet above the ground.

The investigators' report was astonishing. Apparently, some amateur rocket jockey had managed to get his hands on a JATO unit and strapped it to his 1967 Chevrolet Impala. JATO units are small, solid-fuel booster rockets used mostly to help launch heavily laden aircraft from a short runway. When this Wile E. Coyote hit the ignition, his vehicle quickly hit an estimated 300 mph. From the scorch marks, it seems he tried slamming on his brakes, but they were of no use. They instead melted and blew his tires, launching him skyward. A little over a mile later, the Chevy made contact with the cliff wall and left a crater three feet deep. Among the very few human remains, investigators found fingernails embedded in a chunk of steering wheel.

This story is a goodie and may have a speck of truth to it. According to the folklore site Snopes.com, an issue of *Motor Trend* magazine reported that Dodge actually did attempt this experiment with one of its vehicles in the '50s—but it didn't happen in Arizona, no one crashed, and the car went only 140 mph. Most recently, the whiz kids on the hit show *Mythbusters* simulated the feat via remote control and got similar results.

The best part is that the Arizona Department of Public Safety continues to have trouble convincing people it never happened. Since the story exploded on the Internet in 1995, they've been receiving phone calls from the gullible, nationwide. Their media relations department was eventually forced to issue a press release debunking the myth in detail. Calls still come in.

San Xavier del Bac Mission

Situated a few miles south of Tucson, San Xavier del Bac Mission was one of many erected across the Sonoran Desert by Spanish settlers in the late eighteenth century. The Spanish, who had claimed the land as their own, built the missions in an effort to both establish a stronger presence in what they called New Spain and to bring Christianity to the Native Americans. Unfortunately for Spain, the Apache, who liked their land and their faith just the way they were, attacked and destroyed the intrusive structure.

The Spanish, who wouldn't take no for an answer, enlisted the help of the Tohono O'odham, who were more friendly sorts, and rebuilt the mission two miles away. Construction was finished in 1797, though oddly the building has forever remained "incomplete," in that one

of the domes atop its two eighty-foot towers has always been missing. Although the true reason for the omission is uncertain, rumor holds that the dome was deliberately left absent due to a loophole in the taxation laws at the time, which exempted buildings from property taxes while they remained under construction.

Inside the mission, a somewhat eerie wooden likeness of St. Francis Xavier (patron saint of Navarre, Australia, Borneo, China, East Indies, Goa, Japan, and New Zealand, but not of New Spain, Mexico, or Arizona) reclines in the church's west transept. His wooden head, which from a distance makes him look like a mummy, is smooth from good-luck rubs. Among the many photos, prayers, and locks of hair pinned to his covering are dozens of small *milagros*—charms shaped like arms, legs,

Window Rock

The Navajo call it *Tségháhoodzáni*, or "the rock with the hole in it." The site is sacred in their culture and marks the capital of the Navajo nation. In English, it's known as Window Rock, and it shares its name with the city in which it's located, in northeastern Arizona. The feature forms a sort of natural, two-hundred-foot-tall, sandstone amphitheater, with a distinguishing, forty-seven-foot "negative space" right in the middle.

Legend says the astonishing formation was created by the wind as the world was coming into existence. The Navajo also believe it served as home to a giant serpent who used the gaping exit when hunting. He hasn't been seen for some time, but the threshold widened a bit more when a large chunk was knocked away just a few years ago, meaning that the big snake may still pass this way on occasion . . . and that he's getting bigger.

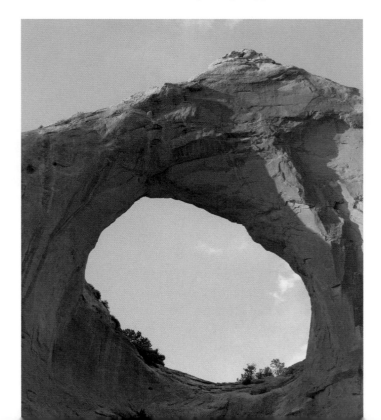

and other body parts, left by those wishing for St. Francis to relieve their afflictions.

Outside, though, is where you'll find San Xavier Mission's strangest detail. Above the front doorway, a badly weathered stone mouse and his feline adversary hide amid the details in the mission's façade. Facing one another from opposite sides of the entryway, each looks as if he's waiting for the other to make a move. As told by the Tohono O'odham, who now own the land on which the mission sits, if the cat ever catches the mouse, the end of the world will be imminent. Armageddon in the hands of Tom and Jerry.

But don't go spending all your savings just yet. Due to recent renovation efforts, Jerry's been concealed behind safety netting and probably will be for a while. Considering that the locals have spent $1.5 million on the restoration, they apparently don't think Judgment Day is likely anytime soon, anyway.

Superstition Mountains

If there's one thing you can say about the hardy souls who first explored this region, it's that they were plainspoken. They called things as they saw 'em. Red Rocks. Round Mountain. Big Black Mesa. There was no time for fancy monikers. If a canyon was grand, that's what they called it.

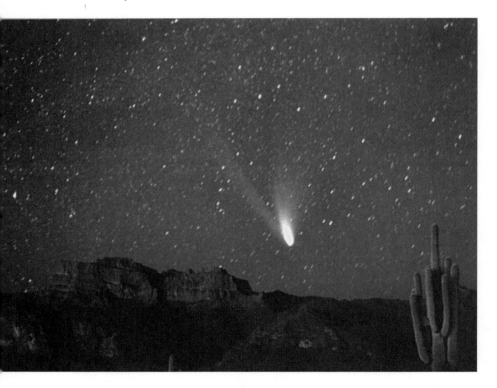

The Superstition Mountains, just east of Apache Junction, are another example. Sure, the name isn't as plainly descriptive as, say, Stinking Springs, but it couldn't be any more appropriate. The Superstitions are home to more strange tales and unusual phenomena than perhaps any other region in the state. For starters, there's the subterranean labyrinth that is said to snake its way beneath their peaks.

Under the Supes, as some call them, there is supposedly a vast system of tunnels that reaches as far as Central America. Many contend these passageways may even be part of a larger, worldwide network. The region is honeycombed with caves and crevices, which serve as either natural thresholds or the perfect camouflage for the labyrinth's artificial entryways. Some who say they've seen the tunnels firsthand have stumbled on them by accident, but many report being taken there by force. Their abductors? An ancient race of lizardlike aliens.

And that's just the beginning. . . .

Homicidal Mania

Unexplained fatalities and murders have for years plagued those who have ventured into these peaks. For every prospector who made it through the Superstitions unharmed, there have probably been just as many who died.

Tales of early Spanish explorers, scouting the area for gold, recount incidents in which the adventurers would find their colleagues beheaded. Many men, usually prospectors, have since been discovered in the same condition. Partners have been said to turn against one another in the mountains, stabbing their trusting companions in the back.

Simple greed may be the motivating factor behind the killings, but some say it's a curse. Others insist there's a secret to be found out there, perhaps the location of the legendary Lost Dutchman Gold Mine, and somebody's determined to protect it. Then again, there might be something about the Superstitions that simply drives men out of their minds, an untold, possibly intentional, force that overcomes some people's rational impulses.

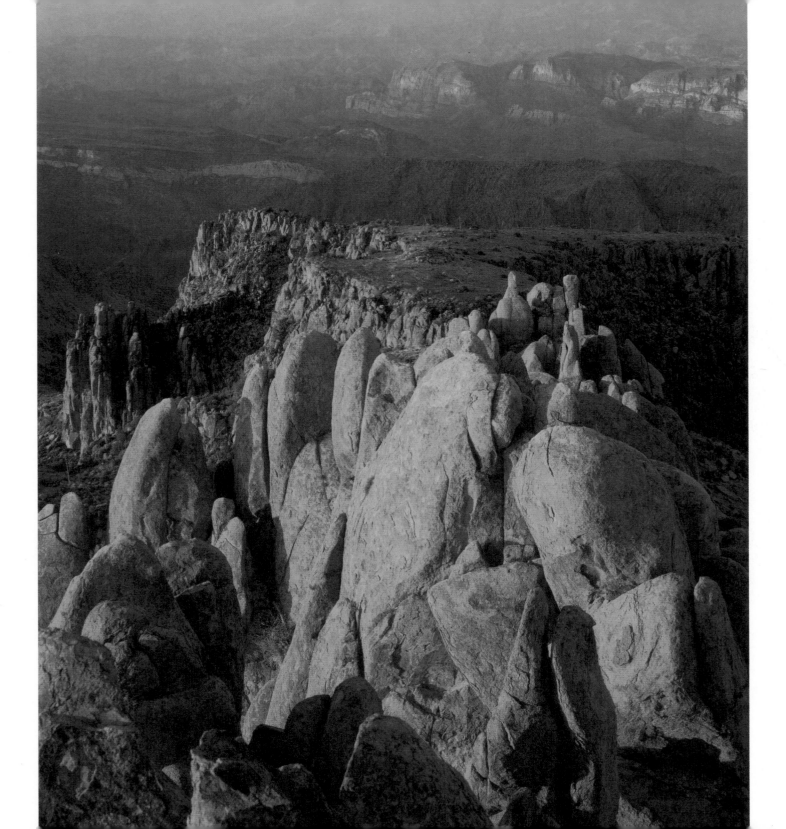

Interdimensional Shifts

More than a few visitors to the Supes have described a loss of time or a conscious displacement in space. Victims who recall the experience report contact with extraordinary beings and visits to unfamiliar places, believing they've been swept through portals to alternate dimensions, a phenomenon often referred to as apportation.

Many believe the line that divides this world from others is exceptionally narrow at this location, making possible trans-dimensional vortexes that some say are even stronger than those widely recognized to exist in Sedona.

Geronimo, the famed Apache warrior who successfully eluded capture by thousands of U.S. and Mexican troops for several months, is thought to have made use of the Superstitions' gateways to escape his pursuers on numerous occasions. His trackers would say it appeared as though Geronimo had stepped into the surrounding rocks and vanished.

Levitation Eddies

One explanation that's been proposed for the Superstitions' strange portals is an unusually intense group of magnetic fields. Investigators have estimated there to be nearly a dozen of these fields, which vary in intensity based on atmospheric conditions and tectonic activity. The iron ore prevalent in the geology, as well as the mountains' layout, theoretically focus the energy created by these natural forces, resulting in intense whirlpools of magnetism.

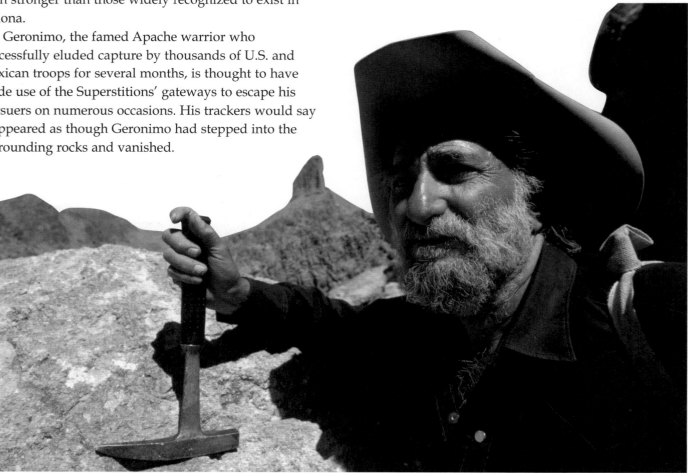

These powerful currents, which are evidently most common following the monsoon season, are believed to produce a sort of temporal shield in which time stands in limbo. Unsuspecting passersby who get caught up in one of these magnetic eddies reportedly experience a sense of tranquillity.

Such events are short-lived, but theorists speculate that if an individual becomes trapped in a strong enough eddy, he can be lifted off his feet and suspended in midair. Victims who succumb to such levitation can find themselves in a fatal situation once the field dissipates, which may explain a number of the mysterious deaths in the region.

A Skeletal Specter

For decades, adventurers camping in the Superstition Mountains have told of a chilling phantom seen wandering the area at night. First witnessed by prospectors, the ghost is said to appear in the unique and unsettling form of a human skeleton.

Witnesses at first notice his lantern flickering in the dark and think the ghoul to be a fellow outdoorsman trying to find his way back to camp. A more careful look reveals the figure to be an astounding eight feet of dry bones and the lantern he's carrying actually floating within his rib cage. Any attempted interaction with the ghoul, including gunfire, goes ignored.

It's anyone's guess as to whom the bones once belonged, but locals generally regard the spirit as that of a long-gone prospector who has refused to give up looking for a lost mine.

That Blasted Bovine, or Cow-Boom!

When someone's ingenuity exceeds his intelligence, the results are usually disastrous, but almost always hilarious.

Take, for instance, the homesteader whose story is told on Groom Creek Ranch in central Arizona. It seems one of his livestock had just about lived out her years and become quite ill. Unfortunately, there wasn't much anyone could do to treat her, so the old rancher decided to put her out of her misery. The problem was, he had run out of ammunition for his shotgun. So, after giving it some thought, he dug up a couple sticks of dynamite he had stashed away for removing tree stumps.

The rancher then led the ailing cow out into a field and carefully tied the dynamite to the poor thing's horns. The cow was completely unaware of what was to come, but as soon as her owner lit the dynamite's fuse, the loud sizzle in her ears took her by surprise. Startled, she headed back to the safety of her barn as fast as her frail legs would take her. The rancher did all he could to stop her, but with a mini stampede on his hands, there really wasn't much he could do.

With the fuse nearing its end, the rancher was forced to head in the other direction. He just hoped the explosion would head the old milker off before she reached home. It didn't. The ensuing blast took out the barn, the sick cow, and three healthy ones.

Ancient Arizona

It's *tough to think of anything* in Arizona as ancient, what with all the golf courses and the shiny new housing complexes going up. Land once considered inhospitable goes for a premium these days. Even the old is new again, as the areas we once thought of as ghost towns become bohemian meccas.

Certainly this state's got a lot of history, but much of what we think of as old dates back only to the turn of the twentieth century. An antique ore cart or a weather-worn cabin, for example—antique, sure; but ancient?

Yet this territory was inhabited by communities we're just beginning to identify, let alone understand. People were building civilizations here before most of the world even knew this land existed. But how they lived and what they intended remain lost in prehistory or encrypted in signs and symbols still undeciphered.

If you delve deep enough, though, and keep an open mind, hints of the unknown can be exhumed; often repackaged as photo opportunities, chronicles of the distant past still lie beneath Arizona's modern landscape.

Casa Grande, Coolidge

Once thought to be the work of the Aztecs, this six-hundred-year-old tower of mud was called the Palace of Montezuma, not to be confused with Montezuma Castle to the north or Montezuma Well even farther away. (Apparently, the Spanish thought this Montezuma guy really got around.) But once it was realized that Native Americans were responsible, the name given to it by earlier discoverers was adopted: Casa Grande, the Big House.

This was the first archaeological site to be preserved by the federal government and has been carefully maintained for over a hundred years. Today it's a national monument deemed worthy of a museum, guided tours, and picnic facilities. And yet, nobody knows what it is.

Casa Grande, which overlooks a two-acre compound that includes several smaller structures, has still to reveal its intended function. Could it have been a fort? Maybe it was a temple or a home for holy men. Some say it was just a place to store grain. Oddly, everyone appears certain that a nearby oval pit was a court for playing some sort of ball game, but they can't decide what Casa Grande itself was for. Even the National Park Service literature admits bewilderment: "Why did the Hohokam build this unique structure? . . . We may never know."

To our knowledge, the Hohokam Indians, who were responsible for this . . . watchtower? museum? . . . never built anything larger. Constructed using thirty-five tons of caliche, it originally stood a full four stories tall. Its lower walls are four feet thick; the doorways had to be accessed using ladders, and it was apparently important enough that it was protected with a seven-foot-high barrier. Still, as far as we know, it may have been a funnel-cake stand.

> **This was the first archaeological site to be preserved by the federal government. . . . And yet, nobody knows what it is.**

Of course, when a prehistoric ruin remains so mysterious, somebody always turns to the default: the astronomical calendar. Frank Pinkley, who served as Casa Grande's custodian in the early 1900s, noticed holes in the building's east wall, through which the sun shone on March 7 and October 7 each year. These, he told visitors, were used to determine the dates of ceremonies. Furthermore, when he noticed more holes in the north wall, he concocted a sacred ritual by which priests would instruct tribal youths to look out through the openings as part of an initiation. According to Pinkley's imagination, the priests would then go outside, hold bowls of water up to the holes to reflect the night sky, and trick the youths into believing the priests had "called down the stars." It was later discovered that these northern holes had been drilled by staff members during preservation work.

Perhaps more amazing than Casa Grande itself is the enormous roof that shades it. Built in 1932, it towers sixty-nine feet high and covers more than eight thousand square feet, making it so imposing that it's practically an attraction on its own—the World's Largest Awning. It was almost replaced in the '50s, when someone invited R. Buckminster Fuller to design a transparent, air-conditioned geodesic dome to encase the ruins, but nothing ever came of that. Today, believe it or not, the canopy is being considered for its own nomination to the National Register of Historic Places.

With its steel construction, its integrated water-drainage system, its grounded lightning rod, and its capability to withstand hurricane-force winds, the roof should outlast the ruins themselves. Perhaps someday, millennia from now, the caliche will have eroded away and future explorers will ponder the ancient purpose of this Umbrella Grande.

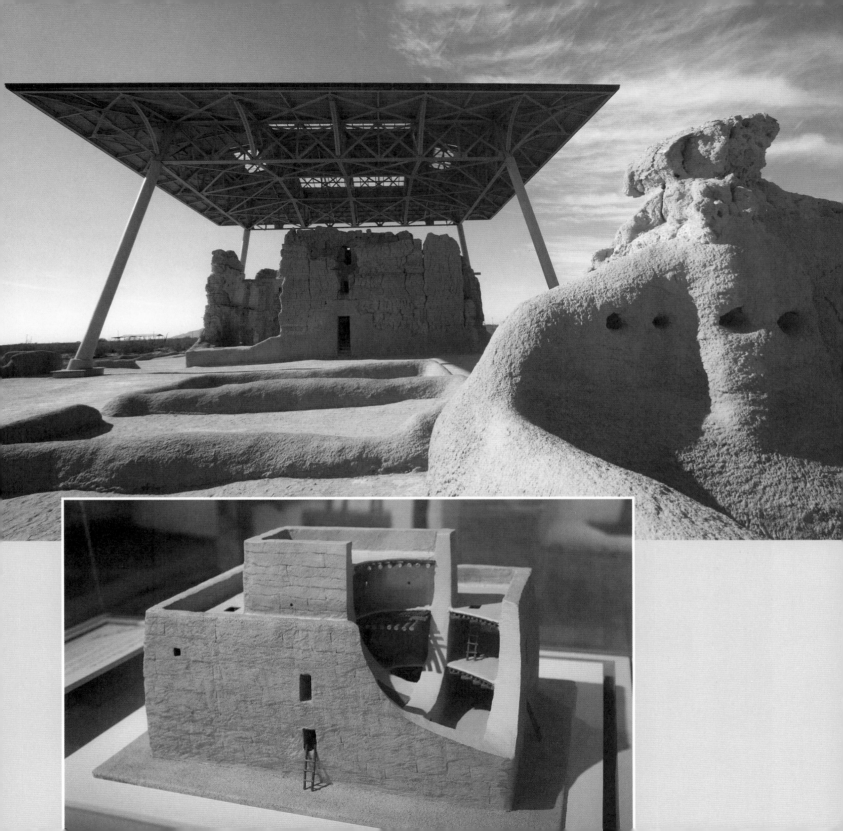

Montezuma Castle: Living the High Life

Slip a fiver to the guy in the funny hat, and it's just a short walk out the back door to one of Arizona's most remarkable perplexities. The postcards in the visitors center provide all the details you're going to see, but catching sight of the real thing still delivers a subtle jab to the optic nerves, not to mention the reasoning centers of the brain.

Lodged in a cranny on the side of a limestone cliff in Camp Verde, Arizona's most staggering housing community teeters about one hundred feet overhead. It's still advertised by the National Park Service as Montezuma Castle, although, as is pointed out in every write-up, Montezuma never lived there nor gave it his celebrity endorsement. Some say it isn't a castle, either, but if a five-story stone refuge atop a sky-high embankment doesn't count as a castle, what does?

This mind-boggling feat of architecture has been attributed to the Sinagua Indians, who lived in this region as agriculturalists and traders. According to the experts, they built this dwelling in the twelfth century, completing it in stages until it consisted of twenty rooms stacked in five layers, totaling a height of about forty feet. When you consider how many tons of rock, mortar, and timber it took to construct these homes, and that the building site was accessible only by a precarious series of ladders, the achievement is incredible. While a cut-away diorama attempts to depict the cliff dwellers as ordinary people, it's hard to think of anyone who cooks breakfast ten stories up

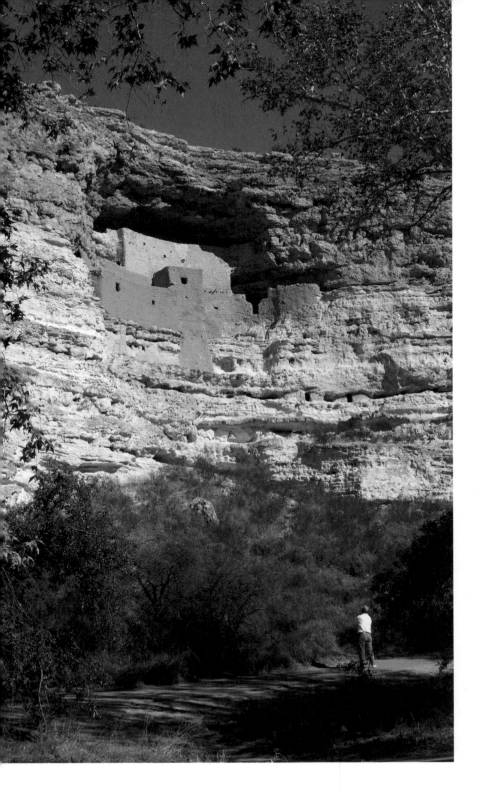

the side of a sheer crag as being run-of-the-mill.

Tours were once conducted through this cliffhanger address; visitors were required to reach it via ladder, as did those who once lived here. Their visits included not only a stroll through the various levels but also the presentation of a glass-encased mummified child that was disinterred during repair work, one of many bodies discovered buried throughout the structure. Due to the damage caused by increasing tourism, however, both the tours and the mummy show were terminated by 1951.

No one's quite sure why the Sinagua chose to settle down on high. Theorists have offered explanations as varied as tradition, utilization of the warm southern exposure, and an appreciation of the view. Being farmers, it's possible they just didn't want to take up any plowing space. Many assume the elevated site aided in defense against invaders, but that makes little sense, since all the enemy had to do was hem the Indians in and wait below till they ran out of food. Perhaps one of the park's volunteer guides had the best explanation: "They kept looking up there at that spectacular cave, and one day one of them said, 'All right, let's get going! We gotta build something up there!'"

Just to cloud the situation a bit more, no one is certain of the former inhabitants' fate. After living on the side of a cliff for about three hundred years, the Sinagua up and left. Again, theories differ as to the reason. Their destination has also remained unknown, though many Hopis claim the Sinagua as ancestors. All we can be sure of is that by 1450, Montezuma Castle sat abandoned, waiting four centuries to be rediscovered.

Hole in the Rock

Papago Park is an eastern Phoenix oasis packed with perfectly pruned palm trees and shimmering lagoons, the likes of which comprise the hallucinations of thirsty crawlers through the desert. The oasis, coupled with the arid landscape and surreal rock formations, looks like someplace the Flintstones might picnic.

The only Stone Age families to leave traces of their presence on this spot, however, are the Hohokam, a Native American tribe that suddenly and mysteriously abandoned much of their homeland six centuries ago. They're believed to have lived atop one of the park's more popular features, known as Hole in the Rock.

Now, if you have trouble understanding why Hole in the Rock has been so named, just imagine a large empty space, say eighty feet high or so, surrounded by a chubby mass of red sandstone. It's a hole . . . inside a rock. For

further clarification, refer to the helpful sign directly in front of the rock, which features a two-dimensional profile highlighting the location of the hole with a purple dot.

Similar holes, technically called tafoni, are not uncommon in the Papago Buttes, but this one forms a complete breezeway that opens into a nice elevated grotto. Made accessible by steps built up the rock's back side, it offers a terrific view of the park, not to mention fabulous Phoenix International Airport. Also visible from the rear is a somewhat smaller, bonus hole located in the rock's peak, which creates a nicely defined spot of sunlight that plays on the surrounding stone.

It's been proposed the Hohokam noticed changes in the spot's path throughout the seasons and began using Hole in the Rock as a natural time instrument. While the winter solstice is observable in the light's interaction with

a seam in the wall, dimples apparently carved in the rock's surface appear to mark the locations of the spotlight on the summer solstice and on both equinoxes. Neighboring boulders are believed to extend the instrument's usefulness.

It seems that the Hohokam, who populated this area until the fifteenth century, were fairly sophisticated when it came to astronomical observation. Evidence suggests they made use of several other Arizona sites in addition

It's been proposed the Hohokam . . . began using Hole in the Rock as a natural time instrument.

to Hole in the Rock to track heavenly objects. The lesser-known ruins on Shaw Butte, twenty miles away in the North Mountain Recreation Area, appear to be an ancient observatory, as does the enigmatic Casa Grande. Sites such as these were probably essential in determining agricultural patterns as well as marking rituals, and may have been sacred to the Hohokam.

Back at Hole in the Rock, it's clear that the site is no longer highly respected, as more modern pictographs have made an appearance. Left by visitors with as big a hole in their heads as the rock they stood on, these markings have been applied with a spray can. We can only hope that all such vandalism will be absent when future archaeologists rediscover this site, lest they forever ponder why the number 420 was so divine or wonder what purpose the place served for the ancient LZBNS.

Sunset Crater

It began with small, intermittent tremors rumbling underfoot, just twelve miles north of what would later become Flagstaff. As the days passed, the shaking grew stronger and more frequent. Then, when the ground could no longer contain the pressure, an eight-mile-long fracture ripped the land apart, belching steam, ash, and flame. Liquid fire raced to the surface, where it sprayed two thousand feet skyward. A column of black smoke blocked the sun as showering lava cooled and fell back to earth, covering the already charred forest in dark cinder.

Years passed, and the violence continued with more earthquakes, smoke, and ash. As the cinder piled up, a cone began to form. More lava exploded into the sky, sometimes hardening into three-foot-thick bombs before striking the ground. New gas vents opened up, discharging noxious fumes and bubbling with molten rock. The cone grew higher and wider. More than once its base tore open and vomited luminous liquid that oozed for miles, sometimes carrying portions of the cone with it.

While volcanoes like this one normally last only around eight months, this beast roared for more than a century. By the end, it had ejected a billion tons of material. Ash, fifteen feet high in some places, covered nearly nine hundred square miles. Lava flows traveled six miles in one direction and covered two square miles in another, accumulating to as much as one hundred feet thick.

At the point of origin, a cinder cone stood one thousand feet tall, measuring almost a mile wide at the base and capped by a crater some four hundred feet deep. A few years later, one last cough topped it off like icing on a cake; vapors reacted chemically with the upper cinders, discoloring the summit to create the reds, yellows, pinks, and whites that would give the peak its name.

The brochures call it Sunset Crater, but the Hopi Indians have named it Palatsmo, "the red hill." The Hopi are the descendants of the Sinagua, the people who lived on this land when the eruption began. As a result, references to the time of *u'wing pangk yama,* or "when the fire came," are prevalent in their tradition, which says the spirit Qa'na, bringer of corn, made the ground erupt because many of the Sinagua were living a life of corruption and immorality. In one legend, Qa'na marries a young Sinagua girl, who is later tricked into committing adultery by a villager in disguise. Qa'na metes out revenge with drought and with the eruption of Palatsmo, which drives many of the Sinagua away and brings famine to those who remain.

In the 1930s, archaeologists found several pit houses abandoned by the Sinagua buried beneath the layers of ash. They found no belongings, nor any human remains, suggesting the inhabitants had not been surprised by the eruption, but heeded the precursory warnings. More recently, researchers exploring an ancient settlement two and a half miles from the lava flows found a stash of more than fifty volcanic rocks featuring corncob casts. It appears the Sinagua made offerings to the volcano by allowing ears of corn to be spattered with lava, then recovered the molds, possibly to be used as charms.

The bubbling fissures where the Sinagua made their offerings have long since fizzled out. There are no more falling ashes or smoldering fractures. The site has been dormant for about eight hundred years, but nature has only just begun to reclaim the land. Charred cinder fields and jagged black lava flows still scar much of the area.

And an eruption will probably happen again. It's come to pass time after time in this region, leaving more than six hundred cinder cones in just eighteen hundred square miles. As the National Park Service says, "Sunset Crater Volcano is the youngest, but not necessarily the last."

Fire and Ice Used to Be Nice

Herbert Hoover brought Sunset Crater under the protection of the National Park Service in 1930 after an outcry by local citizens. The public petitioned for its preservation after a movie company threatened to detonate the volcano with a large amount of explosives to simulate an eruption.

Since then, Sunset Crater Volcano National Monument has allowed visitors to view volcanic formations up close. Most of the fun has been taken out of it, though, in the name of preservation and human safety. The trail that once led up to the crater was closed off in 1973 because years of foot traffic had filed a hip-deep rut in the side of the volcano. An ice cave at the foot of the cinder cone has been closed to visitors, as well. It's part of a lava tube that formed beneath the surface, where cold air settled and froze moisture. Ice is visible year-round due to the insulating properties of the volcanic rock, but a recent collapse in part of the 225-foot-long cave prompted the Park Service to bring an end to access by tourists, lest they be entombed Pompeii-style.

Meteor Crater

The tourism industry in the Grand Canyon State has been blessed with not only one but two enormous holes in the ground. There's that great big one up north for which the state is nicknamed; then a bit farther south there's the gaping void known as Meteor Crater. Mind you, it's not "the" Meteor Crater. Just Meteor Crater—Tonto or Tarzan-speak, like one who hasn't yet grasped the nuance of definite articles: "I drive long way, see Meteor Crater."

It's just thirty minutes east of Flagstaff, off exit 233 and at the end of a six-mile, yet seemingly interminable road extending south into the center of nothing. It sits isolated in the middle of a deserted tableland, a pockmark nearly a mile wide interrupting an otherwise unmitigated horizontality, as if God himself took a melon baller to the Colorado Plateau.

At the rim, which rises one hundred and fifty feet from the surrounding flatland, one can look down from a suspended platform to witness what the absence of roughly eighty million cubic yards of dirt looks like. It's nearly a mile to the other side and well over five hundred feet to the bottom. Though wind erosion has filled in the void just a little in the last few millennia, it appears today very much as it did shortly after its formation fifty thousand years ago, making it the most well-preserved impact crater on earth.

The forces that created the giant pothole were so great that they can be difficult to wrap your brain around. Some 175 million tons of rock were displaced when the meteor responsible hit the planet, scattering debris for over a mile. Limestone boulders the size of houses were blown onto the rim. The compression forces at the moment of impact were so intense—more than twenty million pounds per square inch—that small amounts of graphite present in the meteor were instantly turned into microscopic diamonds.

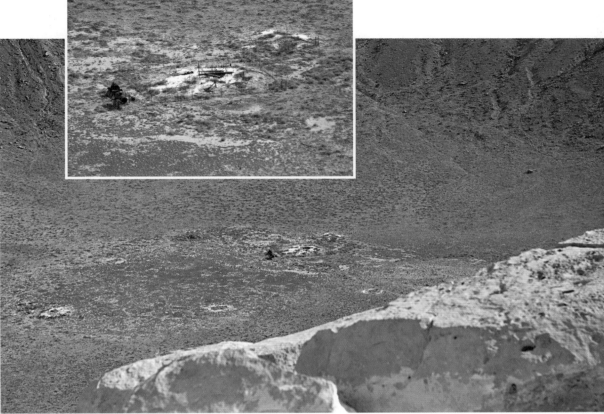

Most of the material melted or vaporized.

All this was done by a mass of nickel-iron that was up to 150 feet in diameter and weighed some 300,000 tons; it is believed to have been traveling almost 27,000 mph upon impact. The resulting blast of energy was equal to that of at least 2.5 megatons of TNT, and some estimates have placed it at 20, or even 40, megatons. In standard measures, that's a ball of 40,000 African elephants traveling from Tucson to Flagstaff in 104 seconds, then exploding with the power of no less than 165 atomic bombs like that dropped on Hiroshima, Japan.

If you're having trouble grasping those figures, don't worry. Even the world's leading scientists only recently worked it out. Until the 1960s, when famed scientist Eugene Shoemaker published his findings, not everyone was convinced the crater was even caused by a meteor. At first, it was dismissed as the result of a steam explosion, and all the meteorites found nearby were said to be just coincidence.

In the early twentieth century, a mining engineer named Daniel Barringer disagreed. Learning that meteorites were mixed with the ejected material, he was positive it had to be an impact crater and he was convinced the meteorite was underground. Calculating its composition at ten million tons of iron, he figured he could make a fortune mining it. Over the next twenty-seven years, he spent the equivalent of $10 million hunting the object, drilling more than two dozen shafts in his search. Finding nothing, he was forced to call it quits in 1929. He died of a heart attack just weeks later.

Yet Barringer's efforts weren't wasted, at least not scientifically speaking. Even though he was wrong about the meteorite still being at the site, the evidence he uncovered in all his years of research and exploration continued to support his impact hypothesis. Though he encountered relentless opposition from those who disagreed, the scientific community eventually accepted his theory, and Meteor Crater became the first proven impact feature on earth.

The Lost Grand Canyon Underworld

In 1909, the *Phoenix Gazette* published a story on what was believed at the time to be the oldest archaeological discovery in the United States. Unearthed by an explorer who was running the Colorado River, the find was described as an extensive series of underground chambers that, according to evidence, may have been the work of ancient Egyptian or Asian colonists.

G. E. Kinkaid, the man responsible for the discovery, had stumbled upon the mysterious land of the lost while on a routine expedition in the Grand Canyon. Traveling downriver, reportedly in search of minerals, Kinkaid noticed "stains" far up the wall of the canyon, and for reasons unexplained in the article, decided to investigate.

When he reached the site, which he said was about two thousand feet above the river and almost fifteen hundred feet below the canyon rim, Kinkaid discovered the mouth of a cave that had been hidden from river's view by a ledge. According to his description, stairs led from the mouth of the cave about one hundred feet down to what he believed would have been the level of the river when the site was inhabited.

Kinkaid entered the cave and followed an evidently hand-chiseled passageway back several hundred feet. There he found a crypt containing an untold number of mummies, each resting on its own shelf. Kinkaid reportedly photographed one of the mummies, then left with several artifacts and made his way downriver to Yuma. From there, he shipped the items to the Smithsonian Institution in Washington, DC, with which he had a long-standing association.

The article suggests that Kinkaid was soon joined by a team of experts from the Smithsonian, who set about investigating the so-called great underground citadel. By the time the *Gazette* published its story, scientists had discovered two more passageways leading from the main corridor, each of which accessed a number of rooms up to thirty by forty feet in size, as well as a "cross-hall" several hundred feet in length. Within the cross-hall was housed a stone idol that, according to Kinkaid's report, resembled Buddha, though the actual identity of the deity could not be verified.

Researchers had followed the main corridor back into the rock nearly a mile to find a "mammoth chamber from which radiates scores of passageways, like the spokes of a wheel," each of which led to even

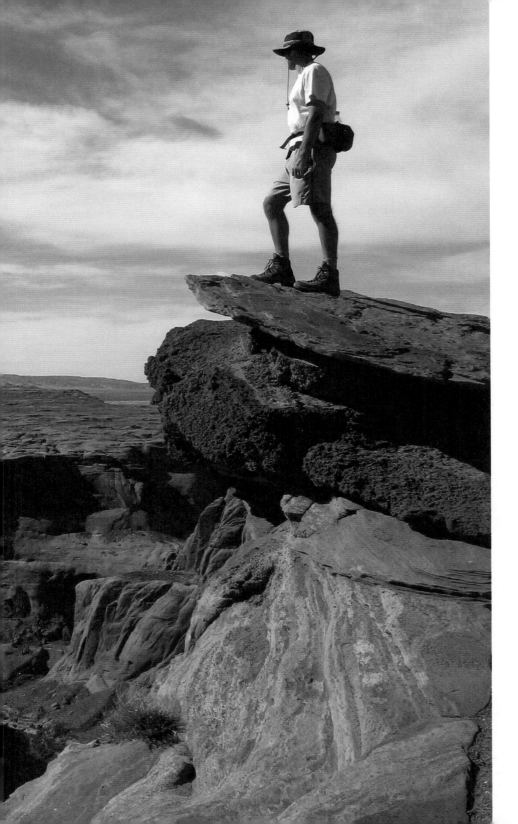

more rooms, hundreds in all. In addition, circular storerooms were found full of seeds, along with a seven-hundred-foot-long room assumed to be a dining hall, and a yet-unexplored chamber that reeked of a "deadly, snaky smell."

The *Phoenix Gazette* apparently never published a follow-up to this story, and no other reports have since been found. Neither has the precise location of the underground city's entrance ever been revealed or discovered. In recent years, investigators attempting to track down further details have only met with dead ends at the Smithsonian, leading many to believe that Kinkaid may have found something Washington was anxious to hush up.

It's hard to say why that would be, since Kinkaid had simply theorized that the inhabitants of the Grand Canyon underworld were the ancient ancestors of Native Americans, who lived underground at a location his report placed somewhere near the confluence of the Colorado and the Little Colorado rivers. An interesting thought when you consider the Hopi legend that the human race emerged into this world from a previous world, which they believe was also underground. More interesting, perhaps, is that the portal through which the Hopi claim mankind passed into this world is a sacred site known as *Sipapu,* which itself is located in a canyon also near the confluence of the Colorado and the Little Colorado rivers.

Signal Hill, Saguaro National Park West

Next time you scratch a sketch of Aqua Teen Hunger Force into a public-phone partition, take a moment and imagine a curious anthropologist centuries from now interpreting your graffiti as a defining aspect of the long-extinct payphone-using subculture. That may be, after all, what certain archaeologists today have unwittingly been doing with ancient petroglyphs: scrutinizing doodles.

Those adorning Signal Hill in Tucson's Saguaro National Park West are a perfect example. Believed to be about a thousand years old, the symbols etched into a pile of boulders there depict what appear to be animals interacting with esoteric circles and spirals. They've been attributed to the mysterious Hohokam or "those who have gone," a title applied collectively to a Native American culture that virtually disappeared around the fifteenth century. The images are assumed to closely represent the people who drew them; yet, after much study, nobody can be sure they actually mean anything.

Experts have speculated on religion, medicine rites, and historical record as influences, but the figures may be just the result of boredom. Pointlessly chipping away at rocks for hours seems a little gratuitous, though, when there are chores to be done—like finding food in the desert, for example.

On the other hand, the petroglyphs' meaning could be hidden right in the shadows. Before his death in 2004, retired technical photographer and Tucson resident Nile Root believed he might have unlocked Signal Hill's secret. After studying the symbols throughout the last years of his life, he concluded that the puzzling pile of rocks was an elaborate timepiece.

A number of sites in Arizona have been proposed as ancient solar calendars, but if Root was right, Signal Hill could trump each of them in complexity, or at least imagination. Upon casual observation, the petroglyphs seem to be applied arbitrarily across randomly scattered boulders. After careful examination, however, it appears

placed a small stone in the inner circle. The subsequent shadow interacts with the lines to track seasons and upcoming equinoxes; it disappears at exactly midday.

The most prominent symbol, a large spiral etched into Signal Hill's tallest stone, appears to link with the site in multiple ways. At noon on the equinoxes, the shadow divides it in half. At sunrise on the summer solstice, a pointed silhouette meets the spiral's center just as the rest of it becomes bathed in light. On the winter solstice, if one stands at the center stone in a small circular clearing, the spiral aligns precisely with the sunrise. Additional icons appear to correlate with the spiral and aid in the tracking of lunar events.

All these phenomena would be virtually imperceptible to the chance viewer or to someone focused on interpreting the glyphs as allegorical characters. Root himself acknowledged it was all just speculation. Seeing his photos, though, is pretty convincing. To see the mechanism in action, you can view Nile Root's Web site, which has been preserved at www.niler.com.

the glyphs were integrated with the natural play of sunlight amid the boulders' gaps and tapers.

For example, Root noticed that during sunrise on the vernal and autumnal equinoxes, two separate glyphs that appear very much like representations of the sun are "pierced" by similar spearlike shafts of light created by adjacent rocks. Another symbol, concentric circles connected by radiating lines, appears to act as a sundial. When Root realized that the boulder on which it's engraved leans at 32 degrees, the site's latitude, he

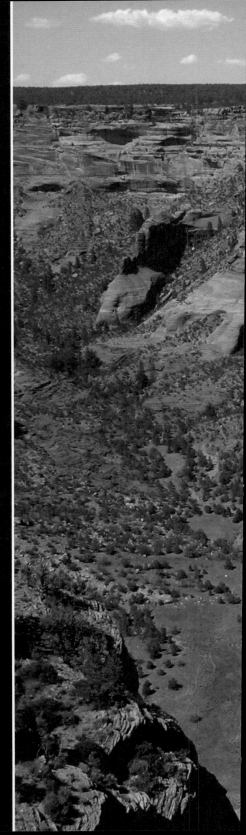

Fabled People and Places

Arizona has some of the most astonishing landscape in the country. It is so vast, so diverse, and so challenging that it has attracted a number of remarkable people whose stories have become bigger than the state itself. Gunfighters, adventurers, and other enigmatic souls who came here looking to make a name for themselves, or sometimes just to make a living, have forever embedded themselves in Arizona lore. Even the land itself has acquired its own mythology, inspiring tales of hidden locations filled with gold, holding strange powers, or infused with a curse.

Explore with us some of these sites. Perhaps you will be the one to uncover a legendary lost fortune. That would make you one of Arizona's fabled people.

Seven Golden Cities of Cibola

Coronado National Memorial, about twenty miles south of Sierra Vista near the Mexico border, is a tribute to Francisco Vásquez de Coronado and what some people deem one of the most important and noble expeditions in the history of the Americas. While that may be a valid rationalization in retrospect, we at *Weird Arizona* know it was based on a wild-goose chase for riches ludicrous enough to be the basis of a Scrooge McDuck comic.

The driving force behind the expedition was the fanciful desire to locate the mysterious Seven Cities of Gold, the lustrous, ungodly rich burgs of lore. Supposedly established by seven bishops who fled Spain in the twelfth century, the cities were said to be built of gold bullion and encrusted with jewels. The inhabitants, who walked on gold-plated streets, possessed wealth so great that even their everyday tools were made of precious metals.

Discounting the ancient tales that fueled the myth, the instigation of this extraordinary fool's errand can be traced to the less-than-reliable reports from four lost conquistadors. The leader of the bunch was Alvar Nuñez Cabeza de Vaca, whose name means "cow's head."

The last survivors of a six-hundred-man expedition to Florida, the four roamed the continent for eight years before wandering into earshot of the Spanish authorities in New Spain, a vast territory that included almost all of the southwestern United States. The men brought with them tales of large cities, multiple stories high and rich with jewels. They also mentioned a prosperous trading center farther north, which they had been assured was the origin of a copper bell they had acquired on their way. From this, the Spaniards presumed that the people of the undiscovered area mined and worked metal, leading them to imagine a wealth of precious elements surrounding fabled cities of gold. All this from a cowbell, which in actuality appears to have had its origins in Mexico.

Nevertheless, gold fever had taken hold. The viceroy of New Spain sent a party, led by Friar Marcos de Niza, to investigate these rumors. What exactly happened on Marcos de Niza's journey is greatly debated, but upon his return, the friar reported seeing one of the golden cities with his own eyes, and he described it as bigger than Mexico City. However, de Niza had seen the city only from a distance, a wise choice since the native inhabitants, the Zuni, had promptly killed the envoy sent ahead of the party to establish relations. Looking from afar, the friar may have mistaken the city's warm-colored adobe walls and the far-off sparkle of embedded silica as gold.

Nevertheless, Friar de Niza's report was enough to convince the viceroy to send Coronado to explore the matter further, supplying him with an army of fourteen hundred men, including the friar, who returned as a guide. The expedition soon discovered, however, that the friar's alleged city of wealth was nothing more than a small pueblo, with no gold in sight. As a result, a member of the party wrote, "such were the curses some hurled at Friar Marcos that I pray God protects him from them."

Somewhat surprisingly, the expedition continued, fueled again and again by rumors of other wealthy cities just over the horizon. The chase went on for two years. In the end, Marcos de Niza returned to Mexico in disgrace and Coronado's expedition was deemed a fruitless failure.

But old legends die hard. The story of the seven cities has become the tale of seven hidden caves scattered around nearby Deming and Silver City, New Mexico. According to hopeful code breakers, petroglyphs strewed about the area impart as-yet-undeciphered clues left by Friar Marcos and leading to secret gold stashes. Is it possible that Marcos located the wealth after all and discredited himself to prevent its discovery?

Spider Rock

One of Arizona's lesser known, but very dramatic, destinations is Canyon de Chelly National Monument, located in the northeast corner of the state. Though it is much smaller than the Grand Canyon, visitors say it can be equally spectacular with its extraordinary ruins and breathtaking features.

De Chelly (pronounced *de SHAY-ee* or, more commonly, *de SHAY*) consists entirely of land owned by the Navajo Nation and still maintains a community of Native Americans who live and farm within the canyon's walls. While sightseers are allowed to explore the chasm's rim freely, visits to nearly all areas within the canyon itself are allowed only with a guide, as many sites are considered sacred to the Navajo people.

Notable among those sites is Spider Rock, a red sandstone survivor of epic erosion. An eight-hundred-foot spire stabbing the air between the canyon's walls, it stands as a sort of unofficial icon of Canyon de Chelly. It's also the address of the mythical Spider Woman, who has chosen its pinnacle as her home.

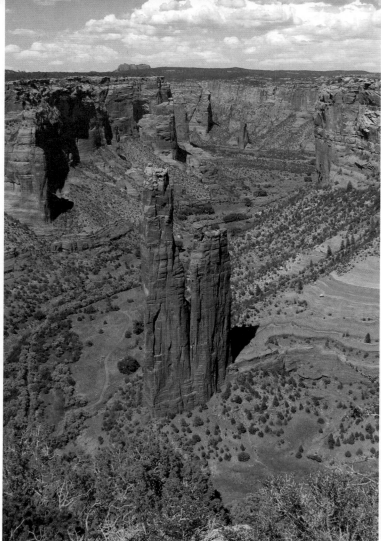

Spider Woman is considered an important deity in the Navajo culture. According to their creation story, when the Navajo people found their way here from the underworld, she gave power to those who destroyed the evil creatures that roamed this land. In addition, she's been responsible for protecting peaceful men who have found themselves in danger from others. In one story, a young Navajo was hunting in de Chelly when an enemy warrior began pursuing him. Chased deeper and deeper into the canyon, the hunter had run out of options until he saw a silklike cord drop down the side of Spider Rock. He tied it around his waist, and with the help of Spider Woman, the young man escaped to the top, where he was allowed to stay until it was safe.

Yet the legend of Spider Woman does have a darker side. Aided by a spirit snitch who resides on the lower, adjacent peak known as Speaking Rock, Spider Woman seeks out those who have been mischievous and disobedient. Whenever she hears of a child who has been badly behaved, she crawls down from her perch, snatches him up, and carries him back to the top to meet his fate. The chalky color that caps Spider Rock is said to be the bones of the Navajo children she has devoured.

Canyon Diablo

Anyone who says Tombstone was the roughest town in Arizona hasn't heard of Canyon Diablo. More men were supposedly killed in Canyon Diablo in one year than in Dodge City, Abilene, and Tombstone combined. Legend has it you couldn't walk a block without crossing the scene of a crime.

The town's name, which translates appropriately to "Devil's Canyon," comes from the gorge on which it was built. As the Atlantic and Pacific Railroad snaked west toward California, it was this gorge that created an impasse necessitating the construction of a bridge. Sections of the new span were to be assembled off-site and shipped to builders at the canyon. But someone misread the plans, and the bridge came up short, halting construction. The delay left the rail workers with time on their hands, and the shack town of Canyon Diablo was born.

The impromptu settlement held only two thousand people, less than that of a Phoenix high school, but had fourteen saloons, ten gambling halls, four brothels, and two dance halls, that may as well have been brothels. Inhabitants had their choice of such establishments as the Last Drink, the Road to Ruin, and the Cootchy-Klatch. Together with a couple of places to get food and dry goods, the mile-long row of mostly tin and canvas buildings formed the only avenue in town: Hell Street.

Crime went unchecked. Robberies occurred hourly. It was fully expected that any train or stagecoach passing through the area would be ripped off. One man got himself hanged when he held up a wagon carrying the workers' payroll. Murder was almost as common. Residents were as likely to be shot in the street as they were to get their boots dusty. The town's graveyard collected thirty-five bodies, although that doesn't account for the many men who were buried where they bled. And God help anyone who tried to clean things up. Wearing a badge in Canyon Diablo was like painting a bull's-eye on your chest. Seven lawmen were bumped off in less than two years.

Work on the bridge eventually resumed after a seven-month delay. It took a year to complete, allowing the first train to cross the canyon on July 1, 1882. No sooner did the first locomotive vanish over the horizon than Canyon Diablo dried up and blew away. The hired hands moved on, and with them went the prostitutes and the barmen. A shovelful of coal, and everybody was gone.

Canyon Diablo lingered as a flag stop between Winslow and Flagstaff for many years, but little remains today. At last report, only a single grave marker denotes the existence of the cemetery. The plot is

said to hold the remains of Herman Wolf, the only man to have died peacefully in Canyon Diablo. That's probably because he passed away in 1899, after the shantytown had fizzled out. The largest ruins are those of a trading post once run by Fred Volz, a Navajo Indian who lived there from 1886 to 1910. But, again, this was well after the town's heyday. Actually, the only remnants from Canyon Diablo's era of bloodshed and debauchery are the masonry stanchions from the original bridge that started it all. They poke up from the base of the canyon, some 255 feet below the bridge's contemporary replacement.

There were talks a few years ago of restoring the town and creating a Tombstone-like attraction, but the only modern additions to be found are a few abandoned vehicles rusting nearby. If old stanchions and trading posts are your thing, though, you can take Interstate 40 east of Flagstaff and head north up the path from exit 230. Just be sure you do it in a 4x4.

A Canyon Diablo Tongue-Lashing

Even though the Atlantic and Pacific Railroad completed its crossing of Canyon Diablo in 1882 and resumed its steam-powered push west, travelers continued their much slower crawl into the new territory via wagon. The road they followed passed through pretty much the same terrain as the rail line near Two Guns, east of Flagstaff. However, travelers were forced to cut northward at the canyon, where the gorge dissolved into flatland and allowed passage to the other side.

The crossing was located near the future site

of Leupp, about twenty-five miles northwest of Winslow. This made the closest patch of civilization at that time the town of Canyon Diablo. Remote and sparse with traffic, the trail made for a perilous journey.

In 1888, one unfortunate soul seeking life beyond the chasm found out just how dangerous the route could be. Discovered just short of the crossing, the lone traveler had evidently been ambushed by highwaymen. The contents of his wagon were strewn about the ground, and his animals either stolen or let loose. The wagon's tongue, the pole that met up with the horses' hitch, had

been propped vertically. And from it hanged the man himself. He had been strung up from his own conveyance, left to swing from a makeshift gibbet, alone in the desert.

The traveler, whose identity officials were unable to determine, was buried on-site. His assailants were never discovered. Neither was the reason why they executed their victim in such a troublesome manner, when a simple bullet would have done just as well. Exactly what transpired there at the end of the canyon remains an unknown. It's a Wild West murder mystery that has never been solved.

Geronimo

Leader of the Chiricahua Apache and one of the most recognizable Native Americans in history, Geronimo was not only a fearless and determined warrior but, as many believe, may also have possessed abilities reaching well beyond the average man.

Legend says that Geronimo, who became a powerful medicine man, received protection from harm following the murder of his family by Mexican soldiers. As he grieved, a voice spoke to him and told him that no gun could ever harm him and that he would never be killed by any weapon. It was a divination that held true, demonstrated by the warrior in later years when he revealed the astounding number of bullet wounds in his body and exclaimed, "Bullets cannot kill me!" Geronimo affirmed he could impart his power of protection to others if he willed it so.

More astounding was Geronimo's apparent capacity to hold back daylight. In one instance, as he and his people crossed a wide valley under cover of night, dawn threatened to expose them to enemy soldiers hot on their trail. Geronimo's voice, however, was enough to suppress the daylight long enough for the Apache to reach the safety of the mountains. As one of his followers explained years later, "[He] sang, and the night remained for two or three hours longer. I saw this myself."

Geronimo many times demonstrated a faculty for clairvoyance, as well. Once, while traveling through Mexico, he surprised his fellow warriors by revealing the unknowable fact that they were being trailed by Mexican soldiers. As a result, the Apache were ready and waiting when the soldiers arrived at the exact time and place Geronimo predicted. In another instance, witnessed firsthand by a relative, the great leader, startled, stood up from a fireside feast and declared, "Men, our people we left at base camp are in the hands of the U.S. soldiers." What he said had indeed

FRANK LESLIE'S ILLUSTRATED NEWSPAPER

No. 1,618.—Vol. LXIII.] NEW YORK—FOR THE WEEK ENDING SEPTEMBER 25, 1886. [Price, 10 Cents.

TEXAS.—THE APACHE CHIEFS GERONIMO AND NATCHEZ, WITH THIRTY-TWO BUCKS AND INTO SAN ANTONIO ON THE 10TH INST.
FROM A SKETCH BY W. DAVID HART—SEE PAGE 90.

A CAPTIVE WHITE BOY IN AN APACHE CAMP.

GERONIMO.   NATCHEZ.
IN ORDER OF BATTLE

GERONIMO.   GERONIMO AND NATCHEZ.

GERONIMO, HIS SON, AND TWO PICKED BRAVES.   GERONIMO.

THE HOSTILE APACHES.—Photographed by C. S. Fly, Tombstone, Arizona.—[See Page 266.]

APRIL 24, 1886.

HARPER'S WEEKLY.

taken place, although how Geronimo saw it from one hundred and twenty miles away remains unexplained.

Some say Geronimo could even walk without leaving footprints and was reportedly seen by his pursuers stepping into surrounding terrain and vanishing altogether, alleged talents that may explain his extraordinary, final rebellion against the United States. Before his surrender to U.S. troops in 1886, Geronimo took nearly forty of his people and fled across the Arizona Territory. Under his leadership, the renegade band of Apache continuously evaded followers. Despite the fact that five thousand U.S. troops, as well as an additional four thousand Mexican soldiers, took pursuit, they were unable to capture or kill a single Apache fugitive under Geronimo's protection for over five months.

In his later years, Geronimo became something of a celebrity, traveling with Wild West shows and selling pictures of himself. He lived to a fine old age, eventually dying of pneumonia—not a gunshot—in 1909.

Lost Dutchman Gold Mine

Arizona is home to one of the most intriguing legends ever to come out of the Great Southwest, perhaps one of the greatest in all of American folklore. It has more twists than a mile of barbed wire and just as many sticking points. More than a century after its birth, the tale of the Lost Dutchman Gold Mine has become so convoluted, it's impossible to separate the truth from fiction. For every facet of the story, there is a contradiction. For any piece of evidence that surfaces, there's another that refutes it. And considering the number of people who still search for the fabled cache of gold, many of the so-called clues revealing its location must be intended to throw the rest of us rubes off the trail.

The one thing we know for sure is that the story begins with a German immigrant by the name of Jacob Waltz, who had been saddled at some point in his life with the erroneous nickname "the Dutchman." He came to Arizona in the 1860s, seeking his fortune in the state's mineral-producing geography. Following his arrival, he worked as an employee of at least one established mine, the Vulture in Wickenburg, but eventually set out on his own.

Records indicate Waltz filed a number of mining claims around Prescott, but none apparently produced any valuable ore. Sometime in the 1870s, however, he showed up in Phoenix carrying several bags filled with gold. Buying rounds of drinks as though there were no end to his fortune, Waltz drunkenly boasted about the mine he had uncovered in the Superstition Mountains to the east, though he wisely kept the exact location to himself. He spent the next several years living off his supply of gold, taking to the mountains regularly whenever his funds ran low. Of course, he was always careful not to reveal the source of his riches to anyone,

going so far as to drag blankets behind his pack mules each trip to sweep away any tracks others might follow.

The Superstitions were especially dangerous at that time, as the local Apache were notorious for attacking anyone who trespassed on ground they considered sacred. So Waltz joined with fellow immigrant Jacob Weiser, and the two took turns standing guard while the other collected gold. Unfortunately, the pair became lax in their vigilance when Waltz went to town alone to retrieve provisions. When he returned, he discovered their camp destroyed, the animals gone, and Weiser's shirt, sans Weiser, torn and bloodied. Though Waltz claimed he found evidence the Apache were responsible, rumors persist he had murdered Weiser himself.

Weiser's wasn't the only demise to cast suspicion on the Dutchman. Several deaths were recorded around that time, in fact, and many of the victims had been looking for Waltz's mysterious pot of gold. Notable among them were two men who had turned up in Pinal carrying bags of ore, which they claimed to have found in a mine near Waltz's stomping ground. The pair soon set out to retrieve more, but were later discovered dead, their bodies mutilated—two more in a long series of homicides. And yet Jacob Waltz always managed to emerge from the Superstitions unscathed.

In light of these deaths, a large number of people believe there may not have been a mine at all. Many contend Waltz was probably just a bandit. He knew the mountains intimately and could have easily robbed other prospectors, left them for dead, and taken off. Still others think there was a mine, but Waltz never laid eyes on it. Historians point to the wealthy Peralta family of Mexico. They say the Peraltas mined the area intermittently during the early 1800s and carried packsaddles full of gold back to their country via mule train. In what would be termed the Peralta Massacre of 1848, Apache warriors reportedly attacked the last of the gold shipments, killing the miners and stealing most of the mules. The warriors presumably stripped the animals of their gold-filled saddlebags, which the Apache had no use for, and disposed of them. It's said that Waltz may have stumbled across the discarded bags twenty years later and that these were the true source of his wealth. Lending credence to this theory is the story of two prospectors who, in the 1850s, cashed in $37,000 worth of gold they claimed to have found strapped to the remains of three burros, which probably ran from the Peralta ambush.

Regardless of how Jacob Waltz came across his gold, thousands believe the surplus is still out there. Before he died in 1891, Waltz reportedly revealed the mine's location. As he lay on his deathbed, he muttered a patchy description to Julia Thomas, his caretaker in his final hours, and to Rhinehart Petrasch, a man said to be Thomas's adopted son.

Following Waltz's death, Julia Thomas, Rhinehart Petrasch, and Rhinehart's brother Hermann spent many years searching for the mine without success. After sixty years of frustration, Rhinehart reportedly put a gun to his head. Hermann died a few years later. Thomas gave up much earlier, having quickly exhausted all her money on the search. She granted an interview in 1895 to the *San Francisco Chronicle*, and the resulting article, though considered by some as full of embellishment and misinformation, sparked a widespread search for the mine that persists to this day.

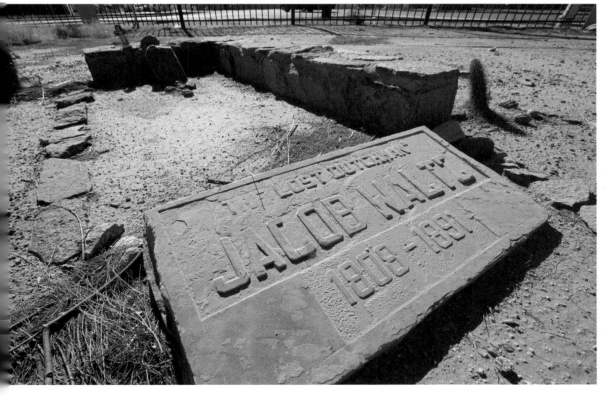

There's far more to this story than what's been covered here. If we were to follow every fascinating tangent leading to the Lost Dutchman Gold Mine, there would be no room in this book for anything else. Suffice it to say the tale is either one of the most alluring mysteries in history or, thanks to Jacob Waltz's cunning ambiguity, the best practical joke of all time.

If you'd like to ask him yourself, Jacob "the Lost Dutchman" Waltz is buried in Phoenix's Old City Cemetery at the corner of South Fifteenth Avenue and West Harrison Street.

Buried Treasure

If even half the state's alleged misplaced riches really exist, then Arizona's soil holds treasures more valuable than all the gold bricks in Fort Knox. That's why, even after more than a century since most of it was supposedly lost, so many adventurers still comb the hills looking for elusive fortunes. Armed with maps and metal detectors, every one of them hopes to be the lucky fellow who unearths the prize. If you too would like to be that lucky chap, here are a few treasures you might start with.

Cannon's Diamonds

Many of the meteorite fragments scattered for miles around northern Arizona's Meteor Crater contain minuscule diamonds that were created when the huge rock struck the earth. Though most of the diamonds hold no value, reports suggest that some of the material that was higher in graphite content produced larger stones of fair quality.

Adolph Cannon, a prospector at the turn of the twentieth century, had evidently discovered this fact and spent the latter part of his life scouring the region for valuable stones. For thirty years, he lived in the caves within Canyon Diablo and was frequently seen collecting meteorites. He must have been fairly successful because, although his buyer was unknown, Cannon always had lots of money when he stopped in Winslow for supplies.

In 1928, a skeleton was found along the Little Colorado that proved to be Cannon's. He had died an estimated ten years earlier, leaving behind what was believed to be one or more sizable diamond stashes somewhere in the area. Not long after the skeleton's discovery, a wounded man with a pocketful of raw diamonds wandered into town claiming to have found one of Cannon's caches. He said he and his partner had fought over it, resulting in his gunshot injury and his partner's death. The stranger died before he could relay the diamonds' location, and neither they nor the body of his partner have been found.

Canyon Diablo Loot

Many men who saw Cannon searching for diamonds near Canyon Diablo assumed he had been looking for a different kind of treasure. Loot stolen from the Atlantic and Pacific Railroad just a few years earlier was believed to be in the same area.

On March 21, 1889, the railroad's number 7 train was stopped at the nearby Canyon Diablo station for water when a band of four outlaws ambushed the engineer and emptied the onboard safe. Money in hand, the thieves then raced south along the canyon before doubling back and heading for Utah, where they were eventually captured and sent to Yuma Territorial Prison.

Although they got away with nearly $150,000 in cash, gold, and jewelry, the foursome was apprehended with only $100 between them. So what happened to the rest?

A PROSPECTOR AT HOME IN ARIZONA

According to one of the prisoners, they had stopped somewhere along the canyon after their getaway and divided up the loot. The men then stashed their piles, along with their rifles, somewhere in the canyon not far from Two Guns. The exact location of the burial has been lost to time, but hopeful hobbyists still search for it.

Juanito's Silver Stash

Cerro Colorado, southwest of Tucson, is now just a crumbling ghost town, but from the 1870s through the 1910s it was an active mining community. Charles Poston, the "Father of Arizona," organized operations in the area to extract the abundance of silver discovered there.

The venture was chugging along successfully until the outbreak of the Civil War stirred up trouble. Troops stationed in Arizona to keep the peace were called away, leaving Cerro Colorado vulnerable to Indian attack and to plunder from the Mexican laborers hired to work the mines. Even Poston's foreman, Juanito, was caught stealing silver. Charles Poston's brother, John, who had been left in charge, decided to make an example of Juanito and executed the thief.

But his death only caused further chaos, as other workers began stealing from the mine and deserting back to Mexico. The miners who hightailed it back south told others about the silver Juanito had attempted to steal, plus much more that Poston didn't know about.

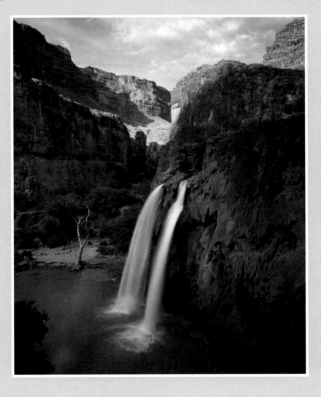

Rumor had it that Juanito had accumulated about $70,000 worth of stolen ore and buried it near the mine. Mexican bandits, upon hearing about the cache, rode to Cerro Colorado, where they led the remaining miners in revolt. The miners subsequently turned on Poston and brutally killed him. The renegades never found Juanito's buried silver, though, and it's presumed to lie there still.

Waterfall of Gold

"Long Tom" Watson was one of countless prospectors searching the Grand Canyon for riches at the onset of the 1900s, but he was among the few to actually find them. However, Tom's discovery didn't come from the swing of a pickaxe, but from the slice of a letter opener.

While using some old papers to light a fire, Tom came across an unopened letter that had evidently never reached its addressee. In the letter, a man wrote to his brother about the gold he had discovered in the Grand Canyon. He also explained how he had stashed the gold one evening after spotting two men following him earlier in the day, a wise decision since the men ambushed him later that night. The man shot and killed both of his attackers, but not before he was seriously wounded himself. The man was able to make it to safety with the help of a passerby, whereupon he wrote the letter in his final hours. As for the gold, the man explained, it was hidden behind a waterfall.

He included a map to help his brother find it.

Thankful he hadn't burned the letter with the rest of the papers, Tom set out to find said waterfall. After some trouble, he located the falls in a side canyon, and to his surprise, the gold was still there! As he stepped out from behind the cascade, however, he slipped on a rock, broke his leg, and hit his head, dropping the sack of nuggets into the water. Amazingly, another passerby was on hand to help Tom out of the canyon. He recovered but unfortunately was never able to find the waterfall again. Neither, apparently, has anyone else.

Lost Opata Tomb

There are those who deny it, but many people insist the Jesuit priests who ran the eighteenth-century missions in southern Arizona amassed great wealth by mining precious metals from the surrounding terrain. Believers also say that the missionaries employed the Opata and Pagago Indians, whom they intended to convert to Christianity, to do their mining for them and that much of the priests' wealth is still sealed within those mines.

The most bizarre story related to these supposed fortunes recounts the horrifying actions by one group of Indians working a silver mine near Tumacácori National Historical Park. According to the tale, all the extracted silver ore was amassed in a large room that was dug adjacent to the mine. In addition to using it as a secret storeroom, the Indians also found the room to be an ideal spot to conduct their ceremonies, hidden from the Jesuits' certain disapproval.

During one of their rituals, a kidnapped Indian princess was allegedly strapped down atop the pile of ore to be sacrificed. She had refused to marry the tribe's chief, and the tribe intended to poison her. Jesuit priests walking nearby heard the commotion and rushed inside to put an end to the ritual, but they were too late. The woman was already dead. Horrified, the holy men sealed off the mine, entombing the princess's body along with the fortune in silver. When the Spanish king ousted the Jesuits in 1767, the location of the tomb, along with the other mines, was lost forever.

Gunfight at the O.K. Corral

The most famous event to occur in Tombstone is comparatively trivial in the grand scheme of American history, but the notorious gunfight at the O.K. Corral remains the most renowned incident in the entire chronicle of the Wild West. The name of the site, as well as the names of those involved, are recognized around the world, and have been immortalized in countless books, films, and TV shows.

Unfortunately, the precise details of the shootout that took place October 26, 1881, are mostly uncertain, as there was much disagreement in the testimony of both eyewitnesses and those involved, not to mention Hollywood's numerous convolutions since. What we do know is that two parties met in an armed confrontation fueled by blame, loyalty, and ego. On one side were Doc Holliday and brothers Virgil, Wyatt, and Morgan Earp. On the other side were Billy Claiborne, brothers Ike and Billy Clanton, and brothers Frank and Tom McLaury.

The nine men faced off following an escalating series of run-ins that began hours earlier. Doc Holliday had provoked Ike Clanton the night before, probably concerning an old disagreement about a stagecoach robbery. After the dispute ended with the help of the Earp brothers, Clanton angrily threatened both Holliday and the Earps. The next day Clanton staggered around town fully armed, drunkenly announcing he was looking for any one of them. Virgil Earp, who was city marshal, and Morgan Earp, a deputy, found Clanton that afternoon, pistol-whipped him, and took him to court for

illegally carrying firearms within the city limits.

Shortly thereafter, Wyatt Earp had his own run-in with Tom McLaury, Clanton's cohort. Wyatt accused McLaury of being illegally armed and tried to provoke him into drawing the hidden pistol Wyatt believed he was carrying. McLaury never revealed a pistol, and the clash ended with Wyatt Earp pistol-whipping Tom McLaury. Wyatt was not able to arrest him, however, as Wyatt was not officially an officer of the law.

Having heard about the troubles, Billy Clanton and Frank McLaury arrived in town intent on backing up their brothers. Both were armed, and as such were required to deposit their weapons at the first hotel, saloon, or stable they came to. Hearing about their arrival, Virgil Earp sought them out, supported by his brothers and by Doc Holliday, to make sure they did so.

By the time Billy and Frank were found, however, the two had been joined by Tom McLaury, Ike Clanton,

were Morgan and Virgil. Still, it's believed the victims held a grudge with the Earps to begin with and were deliberately looking for a fight.

Visitors to Tombstone can visit the site made famous by the incident, which stands on Allen Street as it did in the 1880s. Be aware, however, that the shootout didn't actually take place there. In reality, the whole thing occurred on a section of vacant property out back, along Fremont Street. The O.K. Corral just made for a better title than *The Gunfight on Block 17, Lot 2*. Visitors can also witness a re-creation of the event, played out by a cluster of short, stiff dummies, or a more animate reenactment featuring live stunt actors. The latter is the real draw. (Pun fully intended.)

As an alternative, try visiting the block at the corner of Fremont and Third streets at night, where some people say they've had apparitions of men dressed in dusters and cowboy hats approach them before vanishing in the darkness.

and Billy Claiborne. Words were quickly exchanged. And so were bullets. No one can say for sure who fired first, but in less than thirty seconds, Holliday and Virgil and Morgan Earp stood injured. Billy Clanton and both McLaurys lay dead.

While popular history remembers Holliday and the Earps as the good guys in the dispute, there are those who believe Clanton and the McLaurys had been unjustly killed in a blatant abuse of power. The Earps insisted the victims had been illegally armed, but detractors say that was just an excuse for murder. Some argue that Frank McLaury and Billy Clanton hadn't yet had a chance to deposit their weapons as required, and disparities in testimony make it difficult to determine whether Tom McLaury had actually been armed as Wyatt believed him to be. Plus, Doc Holliday and Wyatt Earp would have been guilty of illegally carrying weapons themselves, since neither one was an officer of the law, as

The Disappearance of Glen and Bessie Hyde

In the winter of 1928, two young newlyweds, teamed in a daring bid for immortality, mysteriously vanished from the depths of Arizona's Grand Canyon. They left little evidence as to what fate befell them, only a question that becomes ever more captivating as the years roll by: What exactly happened to Glen and Bessie Hyde?

Their legend began when the pair met off the coast of California, aboard an overnight passenger ship bound for Los Angeles. Glen, a farmer from Idaho, had recently taken up the sport of river running and fancied himself an adventurer. Bessie seemed more of a romantic, an art student who worked in a bookstore and wrote poetry. When the two struck up a conversation, romance blossomed, and they were married just a few months later.

It wasn't long before the duo combined their talents in a grand bid for immortality. Glen decided he would employ his newly acquired boating skills and ride the rapids of the Colorado River. Moreover, he would take Bessie with him, and together they would be the first man-and-woman team to run the Colorado through the Grand Canyon. With Bessie's gifts for writing and illustration, they would publish a book of their adventure, tour the lecture circuit, and enjoy fame and fortune.

The couple started out from Utah. As transport, Glen constructed a twenty-foot-long, five-foot-wide, flat-bottomed scow, which one local referred to ominously as a "floating coffin." On October 20, 1928, the two jumped into the vessel and set out for Arizona, spending the next few weeks floating down the Green River to the Colorado.

By mid-November, the Hydes arrived at Lee's Ferry, considered the official Grand Canyon starting point for the Colorado River. While there, an experienced river runner who was concerned for the couple's safety encouraged them to purchase a pair of life jackets before continuing on. Glen, however, refused, intent upon completing the journey without such safety equipment, perhaps to render their feat just that much more daring.

The couple next arrived at Phantom Ranch, near River Mile 88 (or eighty-eight miles downstream from Lee's Ferry). There they tied up their scow and hiked up Bright Angel Trail to the South Rim, where they could replenish their food supply. Their stop also gave them a chance to confirm for the world they were still alive and had traveled over four hundred miles from Green River in record time.

Emery Kolb, famed Grand Canyon photographer, met the couple at the rim and captured their arrival on film. As he photographed them, Kolb, himself an experienced boatman, insisted they take his life jackets before returning to the river. Once again, Glen refused. He turned up his nose at what he called "artificial aids" and swore he was going to conquer the Colorado "without life jackets, or else." It was a surprising attitude, considering he and Bessie had both been thrown from the scow by rapids upstream, each barely making it back aboard without drowning.

Bessie had also displayed unusual behavior during their stopover. It was evident to those around her that the weeks on the river had taken their toll on the young woman. While visiting Emery Kolb's studio, Bessie gave away some of her best clothes to Kolb's daughter, remarking as she stared at the shoes included with the gift, "I wonder if I shall ever wear pretty shoes again."

The couple had agreed that in exchange for some supplies they would take a tourist, Adolph Sutro, to Hermit Camp, just a few miles downstream from Phantom Ranch. Sutro would later comment on Glen's preoccupation with the fame their trip would bring them, while Bessie seemed less than eager to continue on, even to the point of fear. According to Sutro, Bessie bore a look of "stark terror" as the couple shoved off after leaving him at Hermit Camp. It would be the last time the Hydes were ever seen.

A month later, when the honeymooners failed to arrive as scheduled in Needles, California, the concern of Glen's father prompted a search of the river. Despite efforts by the National Park Service and a host of volunteers, no trace could be found of either Glen or Bessie, though their boat was located. The scow, trapped in an eddy at River Mile 237, was completely intact and still held nearly all of the Hydes' belongings, including their coats. The only other evidence anyone turned up was an abandoned camp upstream near River Mile 212, where there was a food jar with a marking from Idaho, Glen's home state, and near Mile 217 Rapid, Glen's footprints.

Despite continued search efforts, neither Glen nor Bessie could be located. Whatever happened to them remained a complete mystery. Had they drowned? Had their scow gotten away from them, forcing them to hike out of the canyon? Or had Bessie tried to escape the expedition, leading Glen on a chase and getting them both lost?

Notches that Glen had carved into the scow to mark each day of their journey placed the couple still in their boat on November 30. Bessie's diary, a simple record of river conditions they encountered, supported that date and indicated their last probable position to be about River Mile 225. Interestingly, a search party organized for an unrelated drowning victim more than two years later would discover, near Mile 225, an inscription in an unused cabin that read, "Glen and Bessie Hyde, November 31st, 1928." The author probably meant December 1 rather than the erroneous November 31. Assuming the inscription was genuine, it confirmed the Hydes' last known date and location.

Still, what happened to them? The search team's best guess was that Glen and Bessie had collided with the rocks at Mile 232 Rapid, were thrown into the water and drowned. Yet their scow showed little wear and their equipment remained onboard. So was there another explanation?

After Emery Kolb, the photographer who tried to convince Glen Hyde to take his life jackets, passed away in 1976, men clearing out his studio at the South Rim made a bizarre discovery. Hidden in a small boat were a bundle of clothes dated to about the 1920s, along with a man's skeleton. The skull had a bullet hole in it. Instantly, theorists proposed this to be the body of Glen Hyde. Rumor had it that Emery Kolb had disappeared for a short time after the Hydes left the South Rim. It was suggested that Kolb, in another attempt to convince the Hydes to take life jackets, hiked down to Diamond Creek, where the abandoned camp had been found. There Glen and Kolb got into a confrontation that ended with Glen's death. Kolb and Bessie then hiked back out, Kolb returning later for the body and Bessie departing to start a new life.

But it gets even stranger. One of the Grand Canyon's most notable characters was a woman named Georgie White, a daredevil white-water rafter who ran death-defying, often unnecessarily dangerous, passenger rafting trips for more than forty years. She was always one to tell a fantastic story, especially about herself.

Yet her life was no more interesting than the mystery that surfaced upon her death in 1992. When an employee dug up Georgie's birth certificate in preparation for her funeral, he discovered her real first name was Bessie. Plus, found in Georgie's dresser were a pistol and a marriage certificate for Bessie Haley and Glen R. Hyde. Even more interesting was the well-known fact that Georgie held an enormous grudge against Emery Kolb, the man rumored to have killed Glen Hyde. She reportedly hated him with a passion and refused even to be in the same room with him, though no one knew why. A few already suspected Georgie of being Bessie Hyde, and for them, the new evidence confirmed it.

As for the skeleton in Kolb's closet, forensic specialists determined that the trajectory indicated by the bullet hole did indeed point to murder, though the bones were unlikely those of Glen Hyde.

And so, the intrigue of the couple's disappearance continues. The fact is, we may never know what became of Glen and Bessie. It's sad to think they may have simply drowned, especially when you realize Bessie was just forty-five miles from being the first woman to run the entire Grand Canyon. Then again, would her name be remembered nearly as well?

Strange

Strange things can happen in the desert. Take a wrong turn down a rutty back road, and you might find yourself stranded without another soul in sight, marooned among the unknown forces that drift across the lonely stretches of the Southwest—desolate regions where one experiences abnormal visions, startling noises, and unsettling sensations difficult to explain. Chalk it up to the heat, if you will, or an imagination run out of control.

Yet often these peculiar phenomena take place in populated areas, where they're witnessed by too many people to be dismissed so easily. Mysterious lights gliding over the capital or ethereal formations in the twilight sky have been seen by thousands. Such spectacles defy what our common sense tells us is possible. They defy pure, scientific rationalization and challenge us to consider alternative explanations.

The Phoenix Lights

On March 13, 1997, Arizonans witnessed what is perhaps the most intriguing UFO encounter ever reported. Passing through the night sky, an unmistakable pattern of lights drifted across the state and hovered for as long as twenty minutes above the state capital. The event was witnessed by hundreds, if not thousands, of residents, some of whom captured the lights in video footage that's become a standard in UFO studies. The National UFO Reporting Center (NUFORC) in Seattle has said the sighting "may rank as the most dramatic UFO event in the past 50 years." Even a decade later, it remains one of the most publicized paranormal events on record.

According to reports, the lights first appeared shortly before eight p.m. mountain time over Henderson, Nevada. A man there described a V-shaped object made up of six lights, which traveled southeast toward the Arizona border. About twenty minutes later a former police officer saw a similar object fly over Paulden, Arizona, some one hundred and sixty miles away. He observed the lights through binoculars for several minutes, describing them as reddish or orange in color, before they disappeared over the southern horizon toward Prescott.

At this point, calls started pouring into Seattle's NUFORC. Witnesses in Prescott offered accounts of a triangular craft moving silently across the sky. One caller, who had been driving along Highway 69 just south of Prescott, said the object took up so much of the sky that he could hold out his fist at arm's length and still couldn't block it out. An experienced pilot, the caller estimated its altitude at only one thousand feet and its speed as much slower than a conventional aircraft would fly.

The most dramatic observation was soon to follow.

Just minutes later, at 8:23, the lights arrived in Phoenix, where a family living about two thousand feet up in the city's northern mountains received a spectacular, close-up view. Tim Ley, his wife, his ten-year-old son, and his thirteen-year-old grandson all saw the lights approach from the north; they said they were arranged in an arc pattern. As the lights got closer, they appeared to slow down and assume the V shape described in previous reports. Interestingly, witnesses in Prescott had seen the

V-shaped lights transform into an arc before they sped away toward Phoenix.

As the lights slowed down, they passed directly over the Ley family, only one hundred to one-hundred-and-fifty-feet above their heads. Tim Ley said the craft reminded him of a carpenter's square set at about sixty degrees. Though few details on the dark object were visible, the space between the lights blocked out the stars above, making evident the craft's two arms, each of which appeared to be at least a couple of blocks long. Ley said the area between the arms—where one would find the horizontal bar in a capital letter A—gave the stars a sort of wavy appearance that he described as "almost like a video projection." At least one other witness would later report observing the same phenomenon.

Heading south at what some called "blimp speed," the lights passed over the intersection of Indian School Road and Seventh Avenue, where they reportedly hovered for four to five minutes. In a call to NUFORC several hours later, a man identifying himself as a pilot at Luke Air Force Base said that two fighter planes had been dispatched and reached the object as it hovered over the intersection, at which point the pilots saw the lights dim and disappear from sight. Though the existence of the planes couldn't be corroborated, the apparently defensive action by the lights was later substantiated by witnesses on the ground.

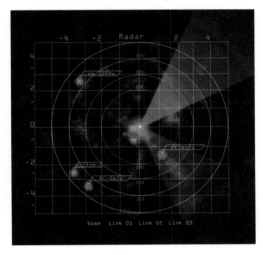

The pilot radioed the control tower for confirmation, but he was informed that nothing could be seen on radar, even though personnel in the control tower reportedly also saw the lights.

The lights reappeared at Sky Harbor Airport, where a pilot preparing for takeoff spotted them overhead. According to a news report, the pilot radioed the control tower for confirmation, but he was informed that nothing could be seen on radar, even though personnel in the control tower reportedly also saw the lights.

Around 8:30, the lights reached the southern edge of the city, where they were seen passing near the eastern edge of South Mountain Park. From here, the timeline becomes a bit confused. At 8:45, the lights were seen arriving in Tucson. Around nine, however, several witnesses saw them again in Phoenix, where the object allegedly flew low over a neighborhood and emitted a beam of light, which a nine-year-old girl told her mother had passed through her bedroom. At about the same time, lights were reported in Oracle, thirty miles northeast of Tucson.

The simultaneous sightings suggest that more than one object had been buzzing Arizona that night. Though far from proof, witnesses' varying descriptions of the lights' appearance and behavior support this inference. The number of lights reported averages seven, though they vary from five to as many as ten. Also, while most people said the lights appeared to be in a locked formation, at least one observer said they moved slightly relative to one another. The lights near Oracle were said to scatter and head in different directions. One group described the object with all its lights turned off, revealing a bluish black surface and windows with humanoid silhouettes.

Yet the most prominent and remarkable display remains the string of lights witnessed directly above Phoenix. Perhaps that's why, in an attempt to squelch conjecture regarding their source, the U.S. Air Force organized a demonstration near Phoenix involving air-dropped military flares. The air force insisted that the lights people saw were simply the result of an aircraft training run in which parachute flares were released between 9:30 p.m. and 10 p.m. over a bombing range southwest of the city. For some, the repeat exhibition closed the case. For most, however, the flares were a pathetic substitute that could never account for at least two hours of sightings across the state.

In a more transparent act of denial, spokesmen at Luke AFB insisted they heard nothing about the lights and received no calls from supposed witnesses. Many of the callers to NUFORC, though, said they were given the center's number after phoning the desk at Luke, and witnesses' phone records have shown that numerous calls were indeed made to the base.

But what should one expect? Even the state government refused to take the sightings seriously. Governor Fife Symington announced his request for the department of public safety to look into the incident on June 19, but held a press conference to announce their results just four hours later. Their "findings" were presented in the form of a DPS

officer dressed up in the costume of a bug-eyed alien.

Independent researchers and UFO buffs, however, continue to delve into the intriguing episode. And March 13 isn't the only day Arizona has been visited by unexplained lights; UFOs appear rather frequently, according to witnesses, especially near the Superstition Mountains to the east of Phoenix. So if we hope to find out just what the heck is going on up there, Arizonans need to keep their eyes on the skies. As a leading advocate for research on the Phoenix lights put it, "I don't know *what* they are, but I know *that* they are."

UFOs in the Arizona Skies

I have been living in Arizona for a period of four weeks and let me tell you something, I have seen some pretty weird stuff in the sky. I have been working on the computer almost every night and one night when nobody was home, all the dogs in the area began barking at the same time.

I stepped out of my front door to see what all the commotion was and there in the sky was an object. It must have been about one mile off and about five hundred feet or so from the ground. I watched as the object moved across the sky in a slow but steadily southern movement. It was round in diameter and it was totally red. It moved slowly across the night sky and then disappeared behind some mountains that are just south of us.

I don't know what it was and I am not sure I want to know, but it did not have any blinking lights like an airplane, and there was no sound to speak of. I have had people tell me about the strange lights in the sky, but until you actually see one, you never quite believe it. I kind of hope to see another one soon, but not too soon.

—DarkDante

Dreamy Draw Dam

According to those "in the know," an alien craft rocketed through earth's atmosphere in October 1947, dove for the American Southwest, misjudged its landing, and made an unscheduled—and permanent—stop in lower Arizona. Apparently, the ship's pilots overestimated their altitude, encountered mechanical failure, or simply fell into hyperspace hypnosis, and slammed headlong into the desert.

One version of the story has the craft plummeting into a landfill in Cave Creek, but the more popular account states that it plowed into the sandy base of Squaw Peak, just outside downtown Phoenix.

What's more, two four-and-a-half-foot creatures were reportedly recovered from the wreckage, held briefly in cold storage inside a local screwball's freezer, then promptly collected by the men in dark sunglasses. After the pair of extraterrestrials was retrieved, the government, in typical fashion, covered the whole thing up—with infrastructure.

Dreamy Draw Dam, which can be seen from East Northern Avenue as you enter Dreamy Draw Recreation Area, was supposedly built on the site of the alien crash to conceal the wreckage. Rather than smuggling the vessel out, the army Corps of Engineers simply hauled building material in and heaped it atop the craft. According to UFOlogists, the dam is entirely unnecessary and exists solely to conceal the extraterrestrial debris.

Why not load the spacecraft into the back of a semi and transfer it to a secret lab somewhere? The military already had one just like it, of course, that had been dropped in their laps three months earlier outside Roswell, New Mexico, and hidden in Area 51. (Dreamy Draw Dam, by the way, lies immediately to the south of HIGHWAY 51—coincidence?)

Accounts of the episode are difficult to come by, so it seems the men in dark sunglasses weren't doing their job. Even maps of the area that illustrate the dam's location are hard to dig up, not to mention signs of any kind in the park with the word "dam" on them. You will, however, find plenty of NO TRESPASSING signs threatening fines and imprisonment. But, of course, you don't hide a spaceship by inviting everyone to see where it's buried.

The real kicker, though, is that Maricopa County is adamant in its claim that the dam wasn't built until 1973. Obviously, the conspiracy runs deep!

The Hum Beneath the Dam

I was wondering if you had heard anything about a place called the Dreamy Draw Recreation Area. It's in Phoenix off SR 51 and Northern Avenue. The place has kind of a funny name, so I searched on Google to try and learn about it. Boy, was I in for a surprise!

There is a wild rumor that the Dreamy Draw Recreation Area was the site of a UFO crash in October of 1948, approximately three months after the famous "Roswell crash." The story goes that locals recovered a pair of 4.5-foot-tall carcasses from the spacecraft, which were stored in a local man's freezer until the authorities could arrive.

The government supposedly took over the investigation and later built the Dreamy Draw Dam on top of the crash site. Some speculate that it was not needed for flood control purposes at all. Do I believe the story? Not entirely. But is it weird? Hell, yeah!

So I went to check this place out after school. It's Monday afternoon; hardly anybody is around. I'm pedaling around on my bike, and I find the dam. It's fenced off pretty well and there are LOTS of NO TRESPASSING signs everywhere. Pretty high security for an earthen dam with no water behind it!

I take some pictures, look around, and I see the outfall of the dam buried in the bushes. I ride around to the other side and hike down into the low area. There's a large concrete box with a fence on three sides. As I am getting down toward the bottom, I hear this steady, low-pitched humming noise. I can't figure out what it is! Is there really a UFO buried beneath this thing? As I glance around to see if anyone's watching, a plane crosses the sky.

The place is not TOO far from the airport, but it's still close enough to hear jets taking off. That's probably what I heard. But I got some pictures if you'd like to see what I'm talking about. The lesson is that you'll never realize how much weird stuff is out there until you start looking!—*Trevor Freeman*

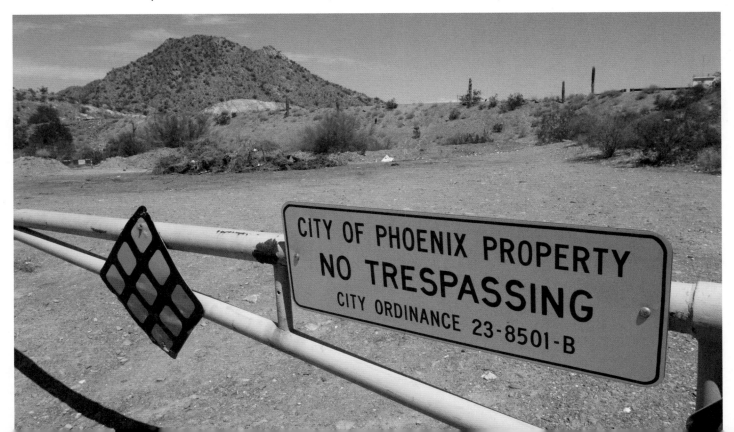

Red Rock Vortexes

Sedona could easily be regarded as the prize gem in Arizona's scenic treasure box. Spires, cliffs, and mesas as tall as a thousand feet overpower the landscape, their bright, warm hues and sheer size mesmerizing onlookers. While there may be larger formations in the state, few are as awe-inspiring, especially at sunset.

But there's more to these sedimentary sentinels than their beauty. As well as being some of the most visually powerful creations on earth, Sedona's Red Rocks are also considered to be some of the most spiritually charged. Native Americans have been drawn to them for thousands of years, and people continue to flock here even today, though most are of the new age persuasion.

Since the 1987 "Harmonic Convergence"—a gathering of spiritualists intended to ring in an era of universal peace—Sedona has been the destination, and increasingly the home, of metaphysical believers. They come to experience the location's power, which is considered to be in high concentration due to the site's mystifying "vortexes." Described as whirling masses of energy, the vortexes purportedly affect anyone who comes within a quarter mile of them.

The energy contained in a vortex, it's said, is similar to that inside every human being. Coming in contact with one causes a resonance that visitors often describe as a faint vibration or a sudden whoosh. Those who experience the phenomenon report being overcome with tranquillity or rejuvenation, as if they've had their batteries recharged. Skeptics, or even those who've never heard of the vortexes, come back from Sedona's hiking trails with stories of emotional outbursts, or at the very least, a subtle yet bizarre feeling they find too puzzling to explain.

Visitors also report other, more tangible effects. Strange lights often materialize in the area, and sounds like that of bells or muted thunder emanate from the rocks. The vortexes appear to influence the natural environment, as well. Local juniper trees frequently develop a warped spiral formation, their branches and growth lines twisting and curling.

So far, the vortexes elude scientific explanation. Authorities on the subject habitually describe them as "electrical" or "electromagnetic," but tests have revealed nothing conclusive in

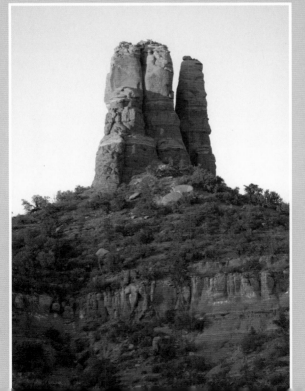

that regard. Interestingly, however, researchers report that earth's intrinsic electromagnetism normally resonates between three and six hertz, which falls in the range of the human brain's delta waves. When a test subject's brain is stimulated at these frequencies, hallucinations can result, meaning that any EM field present at the Red Rocks could feasibly have an effect on visitors' psyches.

Some proponents theorize that the area's geology might amplify this effect. They say the iron and silicon in the Red Rocks act as an induction coil that focuses the energy, possibly harmonizing with the same minerals naturally present in the human body. A number of researchers dismiss the geological aspect, however, as Sedona isn't the only location on earth known to produce this effect. Stonehenge in England, the pyramids in Egypt, Machu Picchu in Peru, and Easter

Island are also considered power points. These sites all purportedly lie at intersections between "ley lines," a grid of energy meridians said to crisscross the planet. Ancient civilizations, evidently more in tune with the earth, felt drawn to these spots just as metaphysically "sensitive" groups are drawn to Sedona today.

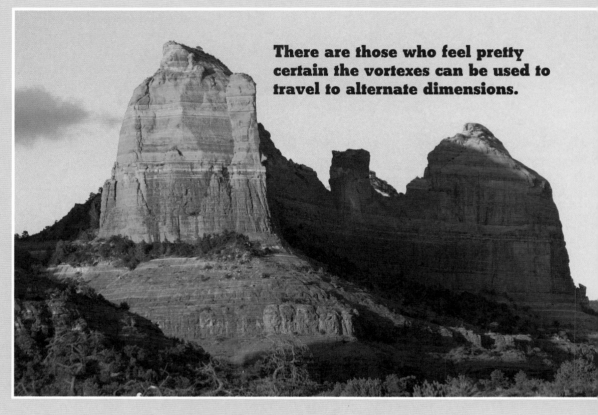

There are those who feel pretty certain the vortexes can be used to travel to alternate dimensions.

Of course, if these hypotheses don't stroke your aura, there are plenty of other vortex-related notions to ponder. For example, there are those who once believed, and some who probably still do, that Bell Rock is hiding a giant crystal and will someday open up to reveal a spacecraft. Then there are those who feel pretty certain the vortexes can be used to travel to alternate dimensions, but only if your psychic centers can resonate at the correct frequency. According to the entity Zoosh, as channeled through Robert Shapiro in *Feeling Sedona's ET Energies*, the vortexes' effect is merely caused by equipment left behind by visiting aliens in the 1960s.

Vortexperts disagree on exactly how many vortexes exist in Sedona, citing as few as five or as many as twenty, but four sites invariably make the list. Bell Rock is known as a place of intensely revitalizing energy as well as frequent UFO sightings. Cathedral Rock is a site for lovers and the perfect place for stress reduction. Airport Mesa is considered the hub of the vortex sites and a good place for opening one's chakras or just admiring the view. Lastly, Boynton Canyon, often considered the most powerful site, is filled with numerous vortexes that aid in renewing one's motivation. (Guides warn, however, that Boynton Canyon is the focus of the Yavapai creation story and, to avoid an unpleasant experience when visiting, one must pay respect to both Kachina Man and Kachina Woman.) Other sites typically include Schnebly Hill, Courthouse Butte, and the popular Chapel of the Holy Cross. To get the full experience, though, you should sign up to take a tour with any number of vortex guides or "shamans" who have set up shop in Sedona. Just be prepared to be . . . open-minded.

Aura Photography in Sedona

Orgone energy, élan vital, Prana, Brahman, Odic force—whatever you want to call it, the idea of a "life energy" has been a tenet of religious and metaphysical beliefs for centuries. Sometimes considered the basis for what many call a soul, this energy purportedly explains the driving force behind living organisms beyond simple biomechanics. From microbes to human beings, it supposedly permeates every living thing on the planet.

Many believe this life force is quantifiable and can be stored or transferred. Holistic practitioners employ various energy-influencing methods to heal the sick, believing an imbalance in one's personal energy to be the root cause of illness. Others have taken it even further, allegedly capturing a life force for use in "scientific" endeavors like those of psychoanalyst Wilhelm Reich, who developed an energy gun in the 1950s in an attempt to influence the weather.

Whatever its usefulness may be, a large number of those who believe in the universal life force also believe it can be directly perceived, the most commonly recognized manifestation being the aura. Apparent as a nebulous field of color emanating from one's body, the aura has been explained as a "luminous cocoon" that reflects a person's spiritual and emotional condition.

Previously, only psychics with extrasensory abilities or those who have undergone special training have been able to see auras, but in Sedona, where one of the nation's largest concentrations of new age devotees continues to grow, auras enjoy retail accessibility. Technological advancements, it seems, now enable even the layman to view them. At alternative depots like the Center for the New Age, anyone can sit down for a personal aura photo session.

Utilizing biofeedback sensors designed to pick up a person's "bioplasma," a specially designed camera measures the subject's electromagnetic field and projects it onto film. The procedure is based on a photographic technique developed by Semyon Kirlian in 1939, the results of which are still debated and, for many, still not fully explained. With his method, Kirlian was able to capture distinctive halos radiating outward from living matter like a glowing "fingerprint." Kirlian's most intriguing result was an image of a leaf that, despite being torn in half, still projected an outline of its complete shape.

With the modern version, subjects are allowed to view their energies as a perceptually sensitive "reader" would see them. An aura's colors and shape, which change measurably according to the subject's emotional state, are recorded like a psychic Polaroid. The phenomenon, as with most paranormal issues, is scientifically unclear. However, if the camera reflects what each of us is putting out there, the results pose some interesting questions about how our personal state of mind just might be affecting our surroundings.

Ring of Mystery

Perhaps the most inexplicable occurrence to take place in the Arizona skies is an almost forgotten anomaly that appeared over Flagstaff more than forty years ago. Moments before the sun set on the last day of February 1963, residents stepped out onto their lawns to observe an extraordinary nebulous ring hanging above the city. It appeared to be dozens of miles in diameter and gleamed with a silvery luster—a big bright loop delineating the city. It was as if the gods had circled Flagstaff for destruction on their celestial Telestrator™.

Drifting slowly across the sky, the enormous halo continued to glow for nearly half an hour after the sun disappeared. Witnesses described it as having a fibrous, somewhat "wood grain" texture and, from certain perspectives, demonstrating an iridescent quality that shone with greens, blues, and pinks. Some described its shape as resembling a horse collar: more an oval than a circle. The more macabre spotters said it looked like a hangman's noose.

The mystery of the ring grew as eyewitness accounts came in from locations hundreds of miles away. Reports arrived from Tucson, two hundred miles to the south. Accounts from Colorado and New Mexico followed. A man as far removed as Juárez, Mexico, reported seeing the ring.

The distance from which it was seen meant the circle must have hovered at an astonishing altitude. Extensive analysis of amateur photographs placed the ring at almost twenty-seven miles above sea level and showed it to be around fifty miles wide. Though researchers at first believed the feature may have been a meteorological phenomenon similar to the stratospheric clouds found above the earth's poles, the object was too high by several miles. The ring was so high in the atmosphere, in fact, that it lay in a region in which water can't form drops or ice crystals to even create a cloud.

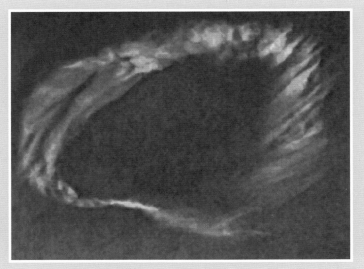

James McDonald, at the time senior physicist for the University of Arizona's Institute for Atmospheric Physics, investigated several possibilities for the event but was unable to explain it conclusively. He considered airplane condensation trails, but the highest a contrail could have formed that day was about fifteen miles. McDonald also considered both nuclear and conventional explosions at testing facilities upwind of Flagstaff, but no tests had been performed that day. A satellite launched earlier from Vandenberg Air Force Base in California self-destructed after experiencing complications, but data that may have connected it to Flagstaff's ring were questionable. Besides, the rocket's destruction wouldn't have accounted for a second, smaller ring that was later seen to form and dissipate northwest of the first. For as much as anyone could tell, the earth was just a square in an interplanetary game of tic-tac-toe.

One man did, however, claim to have the answer. According to the Reverend William Branham, Flagstaff's mysterious circle was no less than a sign from God. Branham, a preacher who was known by his own claims to experience frequent visions, miracles, and visitations, said he was in the mountains outside Tucson when he felt a "blast" so powerful it caused boulders to roll

down mountainsides.
Seven angels then appeared
before him in a V formation
and told him it was time to
reveal the secrets locked in
the Book of Revelation; these
included the destruction of
America and the return of
Christ by 1977. Allegedly,
a ring-shaped cloud then
appeared over him, grew in
size, and floated up into the
sky, though apparently no one
else noticed it before it traveled
two hundred miles north to
Flagstaff.

The Reverend was no
stranger to halo-shaped
apparitions, as he himself was
photographed with one above
his head while he preached a
sermon in Houston in 1953.
Proof that the much larger
vision that hung in the Arizona
sky was a sign from God came
when Branham was studying
a picture of the ring from *Life*
magazine. A voice told him to
turn it clockwise, whereupon
he saw the face of Jesus. And
just as Revelation 1:14 had
predicted, *His head and his hairs
were white like wool.*

For the rest of us,
Flagstaff's ring remains one of
Arizona's great mysteries.

A Rain of Stones

The Berkbiglers' new Tucson home wasn't finished yet, but in September 1983 Richard, his wife Mary, and three of their five children decided it was time to move in, regardless. The trailer they had all been living in for the last year was starting to feel just a little too cramped. They decided they could do without carpet for a while; they just needed some space.

They never imagined things could get worse. Shortly after taking up residence in the unfinished home, the family found themselves under attack. Rocks slammed into the outside walls and against the family's van. It was as though someone next door wanted them off the block. Problem was, there wasn't anyone next door. Their home was surrounded by nothing but brush and cactus.

It appeared the Berkbiglers had attracted a poltergeist. Such behavior, after all, is not unheard of from mischievous spirits. Rock throwing tends to be the activity of a specific type of poltergeist—a vocational specialty of sorts—but a large number of cases have been reported worldwide. Rocks and pebbles pelt the walls of a target's house or rain down on the rooftop. They often create little more than noise, but sometimes cause serious damage. The projectiles are frequently thrown with incredible accuracy, striking the same point again and again or passing repeatedly through a hole in a window broken by a previous throw. In some extraordinary cases, victims witness the stones' changing direction in mid-flight or materializing out of thin air.

The Berkbiglers' phantom wasn't that creative, but it was relentless all the same. The attacks reportedly occurred about the time Richard arrived home from work and would continue for hours. Five or so rocks, usually fist-size, would hit the house in quick succession. After a pause, another volley would arrive. They struck the roof, walls, and doors. People sometimes became targets as well, including visiting news reporters and law-enforcement officers, or the Berkbiglers themselves. At one point, stones beat the family's side door for two whole hours. The only way to make the onslaught stop each night was to turn off all the lights.

The Berkbigler family suspected the perpetrator was a local homeless man who might have been living in the unfinished house before they moved in, but if so, he had to be extraordinarily elusive. Even with help from friends, reporters, the sheriff's department, and a helicopter pilot, the tormented family was unable to spot the source of the throwing, which went on for weeks. Quoted by the United Press, Mary Berkbigler offered another explanation: "Maybe we've built over some sacred burial ground or something."

Bizarre Beasts

Despite *Arizona's* seemingly exponential urban sprawl, most of the state remains unspoiled—millions of acres of pristine, uninhabited America. Uninhabited by humans, at least. With so much of Arizona's landscape rarely seen, or even fully explored, it doesn't seem too far out of the realm of possibility that the state could play host to creatures not yet understood. Barren desert, dense pine, gorges, peaks, and caverns all provide more than enough hiding places for critters unknown to any zoological texts.

Of course, you'd have to be a hardy sort just to survive in such harsh geography. That may be why there are reports filled with such creatures as flying dinosaurs and hirsute monsters. After all, a dark forest and a dry, unforgiving wasteland are just the sorts of environments

where you'd expect to find goblins, shape shifters, and vicious bloodsuckers. Really, where else would they live?

And you thought you only had to worry about rattlesnakes.

Mogollon Monster

The Sasquatch has for decades served as front man for the peculiar field of cryptozoology, the study of unknown animals, or unknown to mainstream science. Sasquatch has trudged his way, enormous step by enormous step, into popular folklore, with sightings of the beast surfacing with regularity in widely separated spots around the globe. The Yeti pops up among the Himalayas, the ever-popular Bigfoot emerges frequently in the Pacific Northwest, and Texas has reported numerous encounters with its Big Thicket Wild Man. Yet few know that a member of this brotherhood of hairy hominids makes a home here in Arizona. He's known as the Mogollon Monster.

The reclusive creature is described as being at least seven feet tall, hairless in the face but otherwise covered with a long, thick coat of either dark or reddish brown hair. He travels with a wide, inhuman stride, sometimes leaving footprints measuring twenty-two inches in length.

Those who say they've crossed paths with Mogollon regularly describe an eerie silence prior to their encounter, an appreciable stillness in the woods that generally surrounds predatory animals. Even more common are reports of a strong, very foul stench, which has been described as that of dead fish, a skunk, decaying peat moss, or — by someone with an apparently exceptionally keen sense of smell — the musk of a snapping turtle.

Most sightings of the Mogollon Monster, as suggested by the name, occur in and around the Rim Country. The lumbering giant reportedly covers territory stretching from Prescott north to Williams, east over to Winslow, and south down to the Heber area, but most agree he generally sticks to the vicinity of Payson, near the Rim's edge.

It was near Payson that the creature was spotted by cryptozoologist Don Davis, whose run-in is generally accepted as the first known encounter with the Mogollon Monster. Davis said he witnessed the tall hairy beast during a Boy Scout trip in the mid-1940s, when he was about thirteen years old. He and his fellow Scouts were camping near Tonto Creek when something in the night woke him up as it rummaged through the boys' belongings. Davis called out to the noisemaker, thinking it to be a fellow Scout, and the figure approached him and stood near his bed. Later, he described what he saw:

> There, standing still less than four feet in front of me was a monster-like man. . . . The creature was huge. Its eyes were deep set and hard to see, but they seemed expressionless. . . . His chest, shoulders, and arms were massive, especially the upper arms — easily upwards of 6 inches in diameter, perhaps much, much more.

Yet, an even earlier report has surfaced from a 1903 edition of the *Arizona Republican,* in which a visitor to Arizona by the name of I. W. Stevens recounts his confrontation with a creature he referred to as the "wild man of the rocks." His encounter occurred farther north, within the Grand Canyon, and the story may be one of the earliest written records of such a sighting.

Stevens described the wild man as having "long white hair and matted beard that reached to his knees." When he approached for a closer look, Stevens saw that the creature "wore no clothing, and upon his talon-like fingers were claws at least two inches long." He also noted that "a coat of gray hair nearly covered his body, with here and there a spot of dirty skin showing." While this is not a traditional description of the beast we've come to know, we could infer that Stevens had run across an elderly Sasquatch, possibly suffering from a touch of the mange.

Stevens went on to tell how the canyon dweller threatened him with a large club and "screamed the wildest, most unearthly screech" he had ever heard, after Stevens discovered the beast drinking the blood of two young cougars that he had just beaten to death.

Attempts to explain the origins of the Mogollon Monster vary in detail, but for the most part implicate a tormented Indian bent on revenge. One variant tells of a prehistoric tribe which, for untold reasons, exiled its chief. The chief called upon the spirits and was transformed into a hirsute bogeyman, which enabled him to scare away his former clan. He lives on today, continuing to defend his territory.

Further variations identify the Mogollon Monster as a pioneer who was the victim of an Indian attack; he escaped into the woods, but was cursed by the spirits and went insane. In a more modern incarnation of the story, Dolan Ellis, Arizona's Official State Balladeer, portrays the monster in song as an environmentally conscious being that only eats children who litter.

In comparison with his kin, however, the Mogollon Monster enjoys scant notoriety. He's sort of Bigfoot's loser cousin. Unable to hack it as a legitimate cryptocritter, he ekes out a living performing at conferences and children's parties, hoping one day to get some consulting work.

Besides, he really isn't seen that often. Sightings that approach legitimacy are few and far between. Then again, he may not be around much. It's possible he treks down here from the Northwest only for the winters . . . the Abominable Snowbird.

El Chupacabra

El Chupacabra is yet another beast that continues to elude science but has dropped enough puzzle pieces to leave even the skeptical wondering. Its very name, which means "goat sucker," is disturbing, a reflection of the practice for which the creature is known. According to believers, it feeds off the blood of hapless livestock.

Tales of the beast originated in Puerto Rico but quickly spread throughout Latin America and up through Mexico, leading some to believe Chupy is on the move. In recent years, reports have started coming in even from the southwestern United States. One of the first reportedly came from a Tucson resident named Billy Nubian, who was awakened in the middle of the night by the panicked bleats of the two goats he kept. When the man ran out to see what was happening, he found what he described as a large "ratlike creature" in the goat pen, pinning one of the animals to the ground. Nubian said that when the beast noticed him, it turned to face him and let out an inhuman shriek before disappearing into the dark.

A few years later, in 2003, another Tucson resident reported a similar experience. The girl, who wished to be identified only as Sarah A., recalled a "half-man, half-ape looking thing" squatting in her front yard. As she walked outside toward her mother's car, she and the creature startled one another. Crouching "frog style," the beast leaped toward her, made a hissing noise, then ran away. According to the girl's description, the frightening creature had big piercing eyes, large hind legs, and an arched back covered in spines.

Unfamiliar with the Chupacabra legend at the time, Sarah discovered only later that what she saw agreed with others' accounts of the blood-sucking monster. The kangaroo-like legs, large eyes, and spiked back all matched. Some witnesses say its oversized eyes glow red in the night.

Stories of the beast, when compared to those of other elusive creatures like the Mohaves' Amaypathenya or the Mogollon Monster's Bigfoot brethren, are rather new, dating back no further than the 1950s or '60s. This has led many to believe the Chupacabra is nothing more than a regional superstition. But that leaves little explanation for the thousands of mutilated, blood-drained animals that continue to be discovered in the areas that it's said to inhabit. The victims, mostly goats, cattle, and chickens, are discovered after having been attacked sometime in the night. The animals are found emptied of blood, with peculiar, well-defined puncture wounds in either the neck or the hindquarters, though with no evidence of external bleeding.

These disturbing crime scenes also commonly lack any tracks, as one would expect from a normal animal attack. But this absence of footprints may support yet another unusual feature sometimes assigned to the Chupacabra—various witnesses report seeing Chupy bare his leathery wings. One Arizonan told us he spotted something about the size of a small ape crossing his path along Interstate 19 as he was on his way from Phoenix to Nogales. Somewhere near the border, the creature, which bore all the signs of the Chupacabra, flew into his headlights and upward into the night sky.

As yet, no humans have been assaulted by the blood-thirsty being. But if the Chupacabra really has moved into Arizona, it's only a matter of time before it tires of dining on javelina and starts looking for larger game.

Small World After All

It has been observed that fairies, by one name or another, have existed in the lore of every known culture. There is scarcely a region in the world where stories of small mysterious beings do not exist. Arizona is rich in such history, boasting a host of diminutive hominid creatures and the mighty powers attributed to them.

Tribes in the Numic language group, such as the Paiute of northern Arizona, tell stories of the Ninimbe, who appear as tiny elves, anywhere from two inches to three feet tall. They have tails and large heads, short legs and small feet. They lurk around wells, bushes, and rocky places, and are said to be cannibals. A tail also appears in Hopi and Zuni depictions of the Kokopelli, who also can be recognized by his exaggerated nose and hunched back. Images of this tailed, gnomelike spirit appear on Hohokam pottery dating back 1,000 years.

Pima Indian tradition tells of the Vipinim, hideous little entities who were said to live below a certain pool or spring south of Sacaton. Vipinim are closely related to water babies or, more ominously, water monster children. These evil manifestations resemble children but are covered in green or black hair and have webbed hands and feet. They mimic the cries of drowning babies to lure victims out into the water, where they drown them. Some may represent the ghosts of drowned infants, but most simply seem to be malicious monsters.

Are these just the tales of a superstitious people? Perhaps not. In 2004, archaeologists discovered hard evidence of a three- to four-foot-tall species of early human who appears to have shared the earth with *Homo sapiens* as recently as 18,000 years ago. Now some scholars speculate that there might be a connection between the mythic races of little creatures described by people worldwide and some ancient "Hobbit" species. However, if you happen to hear a tale of the Ninimbe or Vipinim while on a scenic hike across the desert, they won't seem like something out of the distant past. They'll seem vivid and contemporary, and might be just around the next rocky bend in the trail.—*Joe Durwin*

Skinwalkers

Skinwalker tales, like those of El Chupacabra, are not native to the Anglo-American culture of the United States but over the last few decades have been reported by people of all ethnic backgrounds. In traditional Navajo culture, the skinwalker, or *yenaaldlooskii,* is a dangerous practitioner of witchcraft who wears the skin of various animals, morphing into a coyote, wolf, bear, owl, or whatever other creature strikes its fancy. Sightings of skinwalkers have been reported by non-Indians since at least the 1960s but have become a subject of greater interest since the publishing of Tony Hillerman's novel *Skinwalkers* and the subsequent television movie based on it.

Skinwalkers are usually described as half-human monstrosities who run on two legs—and do so at extreme speeds. A Flagstaff woman claimed that one night while she was driving across Navajo reservation land at about 60 mph, one of these apparent shape-shifters started running alongside her car, tapped on her window, then darted in front of her car and disappeared off the road. A man said that he had a virtually identical experience while driving near Sedona. This type of roadside encounter, which has also been reported around Winslow and Window Rock, is by far the most commonly recorded form of modern skinwalker account. Frequently, they are said to let loose a volley of screeching laughter as they torment motorists.

Skinwalkers are usually described as half-human monstrosities who run on two legs—and do so at extreme speeds.

It is hard to say what lies behind the skinwalker phenomenon, because it is very difficult to get good information from those who know the most about it. There is a strong taboo in Navajo culture against talking about witchcraft. It is thought that to say too much about skinwalkers is to draw their attention, and that can be disastrous. In traditional Navajo lore, *yenaaldlooskii* not only travel at incredible speeds but also rob graves, steal livestock, and commit murder. As one Navajo commentator remarked, "Navajo witchery is the essence of predatory criminality. No law-enforcement agency of any kind intrudes into the matter of traditional Navajo self-defense when this extremely ancient evil threatens one's very health and life."

Do these dangerous mischief-makers really prowl the land? Just to be safe, it might do to consider the advice of a Navajo student interviewed in 1977: "If you ever see the skinwalker, just stand up to him. If you show him you're scared, man, he'll kill you. If you stand up to him and stare at him, he won't hurt you."
—*Joe Durwin*

The Missing Thunderbird

One of the great mysteries of modern times has its roots in Arizona; it involves a photograph of a so-called Thunderbird, a mysterious creature that was said to have been captured near the town of Tombstone.

The story goes that in April 1890 two cowboys sighted an enormous flying creature in the desert. The beast had the body of a serpent, immense wings, two clawed feet, and the face of an alligator. The men got as close as their skittish horses would allow and then chased the bird on foot. It took off and landed a few times, and the cowboys opened fire with rifles and killed the monster.

The enormous wingspan of the creature was said to have been 160 feet, and the body was more than 92 feet long. It was smooth and featherless, more like a bat than a bird. The cowboys cut off a piece of the wing and brought it with them to Tombstone.

Or at least that's the story that was told in an April 1892 issue of the Tombstone newspaper, the *Epitaph*. Though it seems to have all the appearances of the tall tales that were often written in the western newspapers of the era, this story has given rise to an odd modern legend.

The tale of the Thunderbird was revived in 1930 in the book *On the Old West Coast,* by Horace Bell. Thirty-three years later, a writer named Jack Pearl mentioned the story in the sensationalistic men's magazine *Saga.* Pearl went one step further, though, and claimed that in 1886 the Tombstone *Epitaph* had "published a photograph of a huge bird nailed to a wall. The newspaper said that it had been shot by two prospectors and hauled into town by wagon. Lined up in front of the bird were six grown men with their arms outstretched, fingertip to fingertip. The creature measured about 36 feet from wingtip to wingtip."

Then, in the September 1963 issue of the magazine *Fate,* a writer named H. M. Cranmer would state not only that the story was true, but that the photo was published and had appeared in newspapers all over America. Perhaps succumbing to some sort of photo hysteria, the editors of *Fate* even came to believe that they may have published the photo in an earlier issue (the magazine started in 1948). However, a search through the archives failed to reveal it. Meanwhile, the original *Epitaph* story, which mentions no photograph, was revived in a 1969 issue of *Old West,* further confusing the question as to whether the photo was real or not! The *Epitaph* itself stated that the photo did not exist or, if it did, it had not been published in their newspaper. An extended search of other Arizona and California newspapers of the period also produced no results.

So is the photo real? If not, then why do so many of us (myself included) who have an interest in the unusual claim to remember seeing it? Just recently, in the late 1990s, author John Keel insisted, "I know I saw it! And not only that—I compared notes with a lot of other people who saw it." Keel also remembers the photo in the same way that most of us do—with men wearing cowboy clothing and the bird looking like a pterodactyl or some prehistoric winged creature.

During the 1990s, the search for the Thunderbird photo reached a point of obsession for those interested in the subject. A discussion of the matter stretched over several issues of Mark Chorvinsky's *Strange* magazine. Readers who believed they had seen the photo cited sources like old books, western photograph collections, men's magazines, and beyond. As for myself, I combed through literally hundreds of issues of dusty copies of *True* and *Saga,* but could find nothing more than the previously mentioned article by Jack Pearl.

So how do we explain this weird phenomenon of a

photograph that so many remember seeing and yet no one can seem to find? Author Mark Hall believes that the description of the photo creates such a vivid image in the mind that many people who have knowledge of and an interest in curious things begin to think the photo is familiar. It literally creates a "shared memory" of something that does not exist. We think we have seen it, but we actually have not.

To be honest, I can't say for sure if I agree with this or not. I can certainly see the possibility of a "memory" that we have created from inside our own overcrowded minds, but then again, what if the photo does exist out there, just waiting to be discovered in some dusty garage, overflowing file cabinet, or musty basement? I, for one, haven't given up quite yet. And I have a feeling that I am not the only one who is still out there looking!—*Troy Taylor*

Killer Cacti

It isn't only the humanoids, quadrupeds, and bizarre winged beasts that terrorize the desert landscape. The flora, as it turns out, can assault the unsuspecting just as well as the fauna.

The cholla cactus, for example, is routinely accused of leaping right out and grabbing its victims. Rather than wait for passersby to make contact themselves, the cactus allegedly takes the initiative, springing to life and gouging random targets with whole, banana-size stems covered in barbed spines. The plant's quarry regularly insist that they were nowhere near their attacker when speared. Many of them testify they actually saw the thing bound into the air and attach itself. Such allegations have earned the cholla the nickname jumping cactus.

More fearful, however, and far more underestimated, is the mighty saguaro, which can weigh thousands of pounds when mature. Left alone, the saguaro is just harmless scenery. Rub it the wrong way, though, and you could earn yourself more than a few lethal pricklies. Death by cactus has become eerily common in recent years. One might speculate that, in response to increasing saguaro rustling, vandalism, and mutilation, the so-called sentinels of the desert have turned against us in murderous self-defense.

In 2002, a student ran his car off a Scottsdale road, subsequently colliding with a saguaro, which flipped the car, then toppled, crushing the vehicle and its passenger. A similar incident occurred with a Phoenix woman in 1990. Both victims were killed.

A twenty-three-year-old man was involved in a near miss in 2001 when the forty-foot-tall saguaro in his front yard keeled over of its own accord and totaled his Camry. Said the vehicle's owner, "I grew up with [the cactus] and I was always throwing things at it. I guess it got back at me."

The most bizarre incident, however, was a 2005 mystery of a Scottsdale hotel guest. The thirty-four-year-old man's body was discovered about one hundred yards away from the hotel. The cause of death wasn't apparent, but police found blood in his hotel room, and the only apparent injuries to the dead man, as reported by a detective, were "wounds from running into a cactus."

Cactus Attack!

A few years ago I visited a friend who had moved from New Jersey to Phoenix. While I was there, he suggested that we spend a day fishing at a lake not far from where he lived. It sounded funny to me, a lake in the middle of that arid desert region, but he assured me that the water really was there. When we arrived, I could see that not only did the lake exist, but it was actually quite picturesque—a glistening body of fresh water smack-dab in the middle of the parched, sun-baked desert landscape.

As you might imagine, a rare oasis like this was a pretty popular spot among the locals. My friend and I decided to try to find a secluded place, away from the rowdy rabble, where we could cast our lines and fish in relative peace and solitude. We parked our car on a high embankment and began to hike down a fairly steep hillside to the water. As we descended the

slope, my friend called back to me, "Keep an eye out for the jumping cholla!"

"The jumping cholla? What the hell is a jumping cholla?" I asked. I stopped dead in my tracks and looked around at the dry scrubby vegetation at my feet. In my mind, I was picturing this "jumping cholla" as some sort of venomous flying lizard or giant hairy hopping tarantula.

"Cholla is a cactus," my friend informed me. "But it has spiny pears that it can eject off the plant at you if you get too close."

We proceeded down the sandy slope toward the lake, with me being careful not to brush up against any cacti, jumping or otherwise. A few moments later an incredibly sharp pain struck me in my lower right leg. The sensation was so acute and excruciating that I actually shouted out loud. Before I looked down, I had myself convinced that I had failed to notice the coiled diamondback rattler that had just dug its fangs into the back of my calf.

When I did look, I was shocked to see not a scaly poisonous serpent, but something that looked more like a Chia Pet clinging to the flesh of my bare leg. It was the dreaded jumpy cholla!

Okay, you got me, I thought. Yes, it hurts, but I'll just pull it out and be on my way, no big deal.

But that's where the truly sinister nature of the jumping cholla comes into full effect. First of all, the entire pear, which is about the size of a human fist, is covered in hundreds of inch and a half–long quills, so there is no place to grab it to pull it off. Then, if you do manage to get a handle on it somehow without skewering your hand, upon trying to extract it, you discover that the end of each of those spikes has a porcupine-like barb that is imbedded in your skin. Pulling the critter straight out is almost impossible, no matter how much force you use or how much pain you are willing to inflict upon yourself. The other diabolical feature of this sadistic little plant is that its needles do not all go in one direction, but are rather like a complex cross-hatching of

torturous impaling spikes. This means that if you try to pull it out in one direction, you are actually forcing more points into your flesh from another.

I made several failed attempts at extracting the vicious cholla from my leg, grimacing and muttering profanities all the while. Then I decided to try to fling the thorny little thing off me using my Swiss army knife as a catapult. I inserted the blade through the needles between my skin and the cactus. Then, steeling myself, I pulled the knife away from my leg with all my might. With this, a wave of pain washed over me as the cholla dislodged itself from my leg in one spot, only to roll slightly downward and deeply imbed its hideous barbs into another. I screamed an overture of obscenities. My fishing buddy could hardly catch his breath, as he was doubled over from laughing so hard.

I'd decided I'd had enough. I was determined to get this biting little pit bull off me once and for all. Again I dug my knife underneath it and pulled away with all my might, as if tearing off a very well-stuck Band-Aid. My screams echoed across the water and faded into the vast wasteland of the desert beyond. Then I opened my tearing eyes to see that the cholla was gone! Sure, I was still feeling like a pained pincushion and bleeding like a stuck pig, but the cholla was off me—and for that I was thankful.

It's a funny thing—I never even saw the cactus that this spiny ball had come from, nor do I believe that I ever came in direct contact with it. I know that some people won't accept the idea that certain plants have it in for more mobile creatures, such as man, but to this day, I am convinced that that cactus knew what it was doing when it launched its spiky projectile at me. So to all of you reading this, I say beware, lest you fall prey to this shrewd and remorseless desert sniper that lays quietly in wait for its next unsuspecting victim. Beware the jumping cholla!—*Mark M.*

Sacred White Buffalo

A time of great peace may be upon us, and the evidence lies in northern Arizona. According to Native American belief, the appearance of a white buffalo is a sign of abundance and rebirth in troubled times—an exceptionally uncommon occurrence that has taken place at Spirit Mountain Ranch twenty miles north of Flagstaff.

The Lakota Sioux tell the legend of *Ptesan-Wi,* the White Buffalo Calf Woman, who appeared to their people ages ago in a time of strife. She bestowed on them the *chununpa,* the peace pipe, holiest of the Lakota symbols, and taught them the seven sacred rituals that would lead them to a life of harmony. When she left them, the spirit woman explained that she would someday return and would once again establish serenity in a troubled time. As she walked away, she took the appearance of a white buffalo calf—the form in which it is said she will return.

On April 30, 1997, Miracle Moon, a white buffalo, was born. She was not the first in recorded history, but considering that the odds of a white buffalo appearing are approximately 10 million to 1, she was extraordinary. What made her truly remarkable, however, was her delivery three years later of Rainbow Spirit, another white buffalo. Then a year after that, she gave birth to Mandela Peace Pilgrim, her second white buffalo. You're more likely to win The Pick jackpot than for Miracle Moon to be born, let alone for her to have two more like herself.

There had been some controversy over whether Miracle Moon was the true sign of *PtesanWi*'s return, as another white buffalo preceded her, a similarly named bison called Miracle, born in Wisconsin. Some versions of the White Buffalo Calf Woman's story say that the spirit transforms into buffalo of different colors before her departure, becoming yellow, red, black, and brown before turning white. As Miracle aged, her coat cycled through these same colors, darkening over the years, before she died in 2004. Certainly a significant correlation to the legend.

Yet Miracle Moon's achievement can't be ignored. After all, it could be argued that her two offspring represent the coming of the new accord, as Miracle Moon's blessings persisted. In 2002, she gave birth to her third white calf. Then, in 2004, Mandela Peace Pilgrim produced her own. Five days later, Rainbow Spirit had one, as well. Three generations of white buffalo. A 1-in-10-million delivery six times over. But Miracle Moon wasn't through. In 2005, she gave birth for the fourth time. Once more, her calf was white. Seven sacred rituals, seven white buffalo.

Oatman Burros

Should you decide to take a leisurely drive along historic Route 66 and down through Oatman, don't be surprised if your journey comes to a sudden halt, thanks to some stubborn jackass in the middle of the road. The town is full of them.

I'm not talking about the people, of course. I'm talking about burros. And they're the reason most visitors stop in Oatman to begin with. Sure, Oatman's got a gold mine tour, Wild West shootouts, and an annual egg-frying contest, but it's the braying beasts of burden everybody comes to experience. Come to think of it, it's probably the only vacation spot tourists flock to in order to be surrounded by asses entirely on purpose.

The burros, though they've gotten quite comfortable among humans, are actually wild. It's estimated there are about six-hundred feral burros meandering between Kingman and Lake Havasu City, and about a dozen of them enter Oatman on a daily basis. They come down from the Black Mountains and invade the town as though commuting to work. When the shops begin to close and the tourists start to leave, they head back out again.

The burros are direct descendants of pack animals that were once used in local mining operations. When the federal government shut the mines down in the 1940s, the workers simply let the little beasts go. They never really left, though, and due to their obstinate charm, Oatman has just barely escaped becoming a

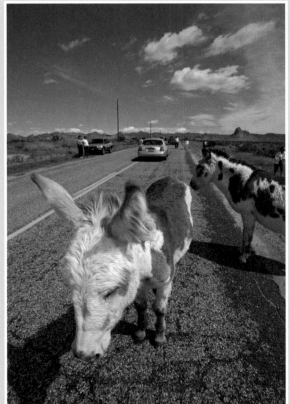

ghost town. As a nearby sign admits, IF IT WERE NOT FOR THESE BURROS, IN ALL PROBABILITY, NEITHER YOU NOR THIS PLAQUE WOULD BE STANDING HERE TODAY.

These days the burros willfully amble among Oatman's small collection of storefronts, planting themselves along the shoulders and walkways. They persistently beg for handouts, which come in the form of carrots sold in many of the town's shops. The animals aren't subtle about it either. They head-butt their way into car windows and wander directly into the shops to get what they're looking for. Tourists who neglect to have treats on hand are sometimes chased down the street. Those with an ample supply quickly find themselves outnumbered and drowning in donkey slobber.

Oatman insists the burros are friendly but still advises visitors to beware. The more zealous of the bunch have been known to mistake fingers for carrot sticks. Kicking isn't unheard of either. And the locals recommend that you leave pets at home, as some of the pack tend to see dogs as furry soccer balls.

Donkeys Rule in Oatman

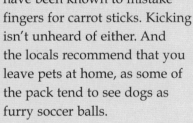

There is a little town northeast of Bullhead City called Oatman. It's on old Route 66. The road is narrow, twisty, and pot-holed. The town is an old gold and silver mining town with lots of character and weird history. Many donkeys roam the streets and they have the right of way. I'm sure that this place is rife with weird stories .
–Ken Karnes

Between Benson and Willcox Is "The Thing"

With *seemingly endless desert* miles separating Arizona's roadside businesses from ready consumerism, the key to economic survival is advertising. More specifically, billboards. Extending innumerably to the horizon, highway signboards advertise things the average person wouldn't normally buy had they not been billed in eight-foot type. RATTLESNAKE EGGS . . . MOCCASINS . . . OPAL JEWELRY . . . APACHE TEARS. The messages bombard motorists relentlessly, tunneling through the daze of highway hypnotism and comforting city folk with reminders of civilization.

The least subtle of these shoulder campaigns, stretching all the way from California to Texas, is the bright yellow series of billboards calling attention to The Thing. Their furtive delivery teases drivers with the unknown like a sideshow barker:

The Thing? A Wonder of the Desert …

The Thing? Mystery of Arizona …

The Thing? Have You Seen It?…

The Thing? Don't Miss It!

Shameless taunting it may be, but the I-know-something-you-don't-know tactic works. Every day hundreds of visitors passing between Benson and Willcox give in and take Exit 322 to discover just what this enigmatic Thing really is.

It takes only a dollar to find out. (Seventy-five cents if you're under nineteen.) Just pay the cashier, then step through the mysterious doorway and follow the yellow footprints. Within a handful of sheds, you'll discover a farrago of unrelated junk—old cash registers, bear traps, and disturbing driftwood sculptures. Over there,

something labeled PIECE OF MAMMOTH'S FRONT LEG. Up front, a Rolls-Royce BELIEVED TO HAVE BEEN USED BY ADOLPH HITLER, though admittedly IT CAN'T BE PROVED. As implied by the big blue question mark in the attraction's logo, indeterminate credibility is part of the gimmick.

Finally—past hand-carved figures both miniature and life-size, past gold-dust scales and cracked pottery—you see it. Encased in cinder blocks and guarded by what

can only be described as Emperor Bigfoot Horsehead, lies the end to your anticipation. The mystifying . . . the remarkable . . . the unknowable . . . THING.

What is it? Is it real? Where did it come from? For a moment, you ponder the mystery of the object before you and wonder whether a dollar was an appropriate admission price.

On your way out, as you pass a few more driftwood sculptures and an anticlimax of antique surreys, you contemplate what you've seen. Your curiosity has been allayed, but you feel less than satisfied, left with what some refer to as Dorito Syndrome—you've consumed an entire bag of cheesy goodness but feel strangely unsated.

True satisfaction, however, is soon to come. You realize that knowledge of The Thing brings the empowering ability to irritate your friends, to withhold its secret until you can goad them into their own unfulfilling road trip.

Mystery of the Desert . . . Solved?

It's difficult to discuss The Thing without giving at least some idea of what it is, so if you want to preserve your uncertainty, skip ahead. Otherwise, we'll try not to reveal too much.

Around 1965, a purveyor of the weird, a former lawyer named Thomas Binkley Prince, opened an attraction just east of Benson, right alongside Interstate 10, and placed The Thing at the top of the bill. It's unclear at what point Prince acquired The Thing, but it's likely the item originated in the workshop of one Homer Tate, who ran his own curiosity museum in Phoenix. Tate's exhibits consisted of shrunken heads and various beasties like those he termed the "wolf boy" and the "bamboozle bat," all of which he had fabricated himself, from papier-mâché, human hair, and the hides of dead animals.

Not only does the timing coincide, but experts on the subject—and they do exist—will attest that the quality of The Thing matches that of Tate's other work. It's hard to say exactly how it came into Prince's possession, but as Tate distributed his creatures worldwide via mail order, it's likely Prince simply ordered it from a catalogue.

Thomas Prince passed away in 1969, leaving his wife, Janet, to run the business. Janet has since moved away and leased The Thing to Bowling Travel Centers. Today a portion of the money brought in by The Thing goes to a University of Arizona College of Law scholarship in Prince's name.

When I saw the first billboard for The Thing, I blew it off. With the second one, I began to wonder. After the third one, I started to obsess. What was The Thing? What was it doing in Arizona? Whoever crafted the path to The Thing at its rural gas-station location was a master of suspense.

The old cars on display were filled with cobwebs . . . and doom. I walked farther down the passageway and began to sweat as I spied ancient firearms and bizarre art. Finally I reached the container of The Thing. After taking a moment to steel myself against the unknown, I looked inside.

Hmm. How about that. Well, that sure is . . . some Thing.

—*Craig Robertson*

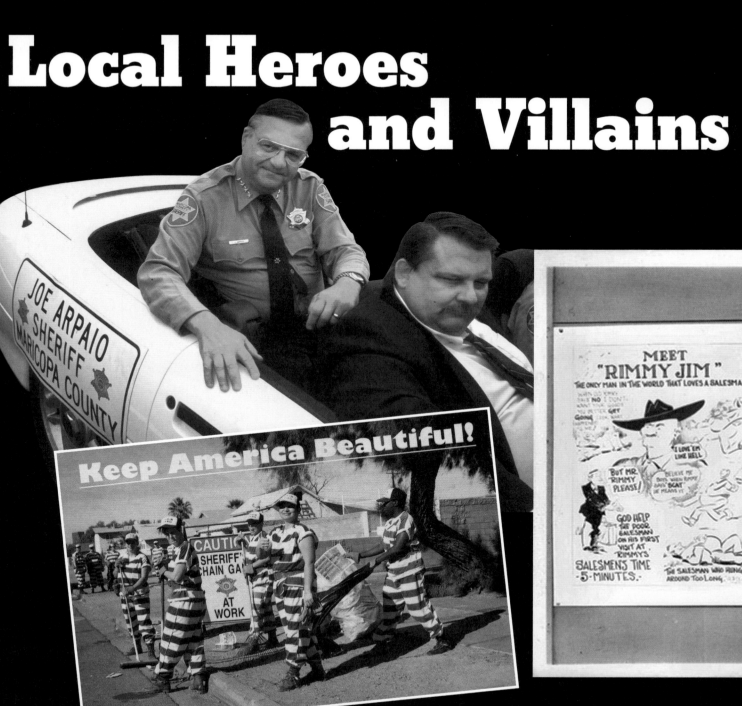

Local Heroes and Villains

JOE ARPAIO SHERIFF MARICOPA COUNTY

Keep America Beautiful!

CAUTION SHERIFF'S CHAIN GANG AT WORK

MEET "RIMMY JIM"
THE ONLY MAN IN THE WORLD THAT LOVES A SALESMAN

The variety of characters in Arizona is truly amazing. The particular strain of people who gravitate here isn't easily identified, like those, for instance, from the East Coast or the Deep South. This state's residents are too diverse, too assorted. It's like a grab bag of personality.

From corner to corner, Arizonans have proved to be some of the most far-out, friendliest, and sometimes most peculiar people we've had the pleasure of meeting. Many, sad to say, passed on long before we

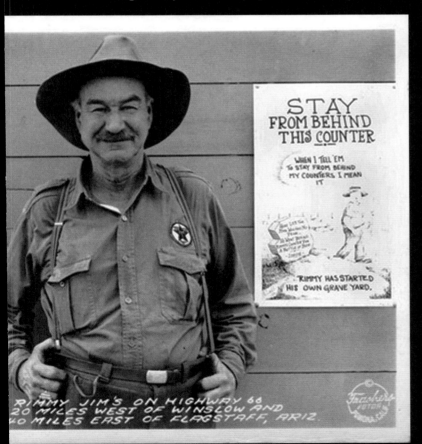

RIMMY JIM'S ON HIGHWAY 66
20 MILES WEST OF WINSLOW AND
40 MILES EAST OF FLAGSTAFF, ARIZ.

arrived, but left behind their epic personal tales. Then, of course, there are those we're glad are gone — those of dubious or downright criminal character — but whose legends we've savored nonetheless.

So many interesting people have cropped up in our research that we couldn't fit all of them into one chapter. But we hope we've assembled a crowd that demonstrates what a truly weird and wonderful group Arizonans are.

Tombstone's Only Lynched Man

Boothill Graveyard is full of the unfortunate, though often worthy, recipients of death who made the mistake of setting foot in the Town Too Tough to Die. The regularity with which violent killings occurred in and around Tombstone earned this Wild West town a reputation as one of the most treacherous in history. Stabbing, shooting, suicide, Indian attack—all were likely ways of meeting one's maker. On occasion, someone would actually live long enough to meet his end by legal means, with a proper hanging at the courthouse. Yet surprisingly, only one man was ever put to death by a mob.

It was the winter of 1883, and a band of six men had ridden into Bisbee, a mining town twenty miles south of Tombstone. They were acting on a rumor that several thousand dollars in miners' payroll had been delivered to the vault at the local general store, and they were intent on taking the money for themselves. Much to their embarrassment, however, they got there too early. So they took what they could and got on their horses.

Something must have gone very wrong at that point, because the men shot four residents before getting away. Among them were a deputy and a pregnant Bisbee woman. When the men were caught, they were found guilty for the murders and sentenced to hang. It was an execution turned festival, with one man building bleachers and selling tickets for the event.

The criminals were hanged simultaneously on a gallows built specially for the occasion. Only five of the six men wore nooses that day, however, as one was already dead. The public had been so outraged by the thieves' monstrous killings that a posse from Bisbee had marched to the courthouse, yanked the gang's alleged leader from his cell, and strung him up from a telegraph pole at the corner of First and Toughnut. It's said that every citizen who was there ceremoniously laid his hands on the victim's noose before it was all over. John Heath thus became the first and only man ever to be lynched in Tombstone.

Despite there being a photograph of Heath's swinging corpse, with his executioners posing nearby, the cause of death was recorded as "emphysema of the lungs—a disease common in high altitudes—which might have been caused by strangulation, self-inflicted or otherwise."

George Warren

While on a scouting mission in the late 1870s, a lieutenant with the U.S. Army discovered precious metals in southeastern Arizona. Unable to abandon his mission, however, Lieutenant Jack Dunn enlisted the help of a prospector named George Warren, in whom he confided his discovery. As his partner, Warren would stake claims in the area on Dunn's behalf, and they would share the riches together.

Rather than fulfilling his end of the bargain, though, Warren proceeded to have a few drinks with some buddies, as he was apt to do, and soon struck a new deal. Dunn was left out in the cold, and Warren filed all the claims in his own name. In a later whiskey binge, however, Warren's karma would come back to bite him. Putting one of his mining claims up as ante, he made the drunken bet he could outrun a horse in a two-hundred-yard dash. The mine he lost became Bisbee's famous Queen Mine, one of the most productive copper mines in history.

Regarded as one of the state's most eccentric characters, George Warren now appears on the official Arizona state seal.

Rattlesnake Bill

Folks at the Arrowhead Steakhouse in Congress still talk about old Bill Esenwein, better known in these parts as Rattlesnake Bill. A writer and a prospector, Bill earned the nickname as a result of his unusual rapport with poisonous reptiles. He rescued them, cared for them, even lived with them. Apparently, he was a regular Dr. Doolittle of diamondbacks.

Back when the Arrowhead still had a roadside zoo, Bill used to drop by to check on his friends in the snake pit. Often, he would complain that the snakes weren't getting enough to eat, then head into the kitchen, where he'd mix a batch of raw hamburger meat and eggs. Bill would then leap into the pit, pick up the snakes, and force-feed them through a tube. He'd stay in there until they were all nice and full.

Sometime in the '50s, workmen installing a septic tank for a nearby ranch discovered two rattlers in the pit they had been digging. When none of the men proved brave enough to remove the vipers, they called on Bill. Helpful as ever, Bill hopped on the end of a chain and was lowered down to the snakes. One at a time, Bill picked them up—about eight inches behind their heads as he always did—then brought them to the top, gave them a friendly stroke, and set them free.

It was nothing out of the ordinary for Bill. In the cabin where he lived, rattlesnakes slinked about like slithery roommates. They were both his pets and his security guards. Whenever Bill went out, he'd put all his possessions on a table in the center of the room, shepherd all the snakes into the middle, then corral the lot with chicken wire.

As far as we know, no thief ever ventured into Bill's place.

To the end of his life, Bill maintained he had never been bitten. He was once rushed to the doctor when someone noticed he was ill and his arm was swelling, but when people suggested the injury was the result of a snakebite, Bill got upset. He insisted no snake would do such a thing, and he demanded to be taken home. The doctor concluded the snake had simply brushed its fangs against him by accident.

You can still see what remains of Rattlesnake Bill's cabin, a former powder magazine for local mining operations, just off Stanton Road north of Congress. It sits near the Octave Mine at a place now known as Rattlesnake Haven.

Rimmy Jim

Little, it seems, has been written about the late "Rimmy Jim" Giddings, but tales of his escapades continue to drift in from the old alignments of Route 66. He was a notorious practical joker and dealer of abuse, making the trading post that bore his name almost as much an attraction as the meteor crater just to the south.

Photos from the 1930s show Rimmy Jim to be a real-life caricature, idling around in front of his outpost sporting suspenders and a mischievous grin. He bore a slight resemblance to Elmer Fudd, but with a mustache. His rumpled cowboy hat and the Texaco star sewn to his baggy shirt gave him the appearance of a genial small-town sheriff—the deceptively nonthreatening sort who sat on his porch tossing around "how-do's" until a bad element wandered into town.

Only two types got under Rimmy Jim's skin. Second on the list were pretentious tourists from the East Coast. First were salesmen from anywhere. The former he simply tormented with lively pranks, while the latter he terrorized with death threats. His customers received their fair share of ribbing too. It's been told that when any of his regulars drove by without stopping for their coffee in the

morning, he'd charge them double on the way back.

Eastern women were special targets for Jim. When a particularly high-and-mighty specimen stopped to use the facilities, he would forget he had indoor plumbing and send her to the outhouse. After enough time had passed for the woman to get comfortable, Jim would announce from a speaker hidden under the seats that he wasn't finished painting down there and asked that the lady please move to the other hole, which would invariably send her screaming out the door.

Number one on Rimmy Jim's hit list, however, was

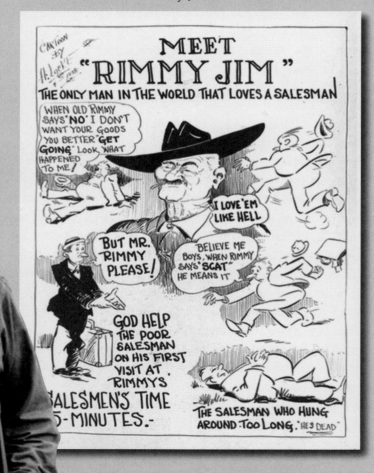

RIMMY JIM'S ON HIGHWAY 66
20 MILES WEST OF WINSLOW AND
40 MILES EAST OF FLAGSTAFF, ARIZ.

the traveling salesman. SALESMEN'S TIME—5 MINUTES was clearly posted next to an illustration of a lifeless peddler, THE SALESMAN WHO HUNG AROUND TOO LONG. HE'S DEAD. He even erected a few headstones on the property to drive the point home. Few solicitors who pulled up to Rimmy's even bothered to get out of the car.

Decades have passed since those days, but Rimmy Jim's sense of humor plays on. Perhaps as an inside joke, or possibly a tribute, maps today still present a waypoint at exit 233 north of Meteor Crater that bears his name. But Rimmy Jim is gone now and so is his shop.

God's Man of Faith and Power

Located a few miles southeast of Sierra Vista is a town named Miracle Valley, where visitors can drive on such inspirational streets as Faith Avenue and Deliverance Way. There isn't much here, but if you pop in to the cemetery next to the Miracle Valley Bible College, you'll find the grave of the town's founder, A. A. Allen.

Allen was considered by many to be one of the great evangelists of his time. He toured the country with his tent revivals and broadcast his sermons via the radio. Working at first with the Assemblies of God, Allen was forced to withdraw his association with that Pentecostal denomination after he was arrested for drunk driving, an incident that Allen reportedly blamed on a glass of sour milk he drank at a café. According to an associate, when Allen pulled over, he was met by police officers, the media, and several denominational pastors, whom Allen believed set the whole thing up to stop his increasingly popular church assemblies.

After this, Allen went independent and established his own ministry through which he sold revival recordings, "miracle tent shavings," and prayer cloths anointed with "miracle oil." Not to mention that, for $100, Allen would perform a laying on of hands and bestow upon believers a "power to get wealth."

In his revival meetings, Allen claimed to heal the sick, including a "fat sister" who lost two hundred pounds and visibly shrank in front of him. Yet his most profound claim was the ability to raise the dead, an assertion he quit making when too many people reportedly began shipping dead family members to him.

Allen's own death came in 1970, though true believers refused to accept it. That's no surprise when you take into account Allen's prerecorded radio broadcast that aired days after he was found dead in a hotel room: "This is Brother Allen in person. . . . People, as well as some preachers from pulpits, are announcing that I am dead. Do I sound like a dead man?"

The Juan and Only

If you're ever anywhere near Seligman, you've got to stop at Delgadillo's Snow Cap. This roadside café is a true, one-of-a-kind Route 66 experience.

Here the legacy of the eatery's late founder, Juan Delgadillo, lives on in what can be summed up in one word: cheese. Not the cheese that comes on their "Cheeseburgers With Cheese," but the kind that can make you laugh and shake your head at the same time. Ask for mustard, and the man behind the counter squirts yellow string at your shirt from a squeeze bottle. Request a straw, and you'll get a bail of that stuff they feed cattle. The gags have been flying here for so long, there's little you could say that doesn't already have a wise-acre response.

Juan built the Snow Cap in 1953 and worked hard to make his customers laugh for the next fifty years. The whole place reflects his absurd sense of humor, starting with the SORRY, WE'RE OPEN sign out front and the decoy doorknob on the wrong side of the door. The outhouses in back have real toilets, as well as phones and TVs, and there's kitsch everywhere you look.

Anyone who asked Juan for his card got one that read MY CARD. He'd fill an order for a small ice cream with a tiny, three-inch cone. Correct him by asking for a whole cone, and you'd get a cone with a hole in it. One of the few serious bits of decor in the place is a sign that reads THERE IS NO HIGHER RELIGION THAN HUMAN SERVICE.

Juan passed away in 2004 at the age of eighty-eight. His sons John and Robert continue to operate the Snow Cap just as their father did, with a welcoming smile, good food, and that fake bottle of mustard.

The Man Who Killed Santa Claus

There's been a lot of talk in recent years about the dilution of Christmas (a.k.a. the holidays), but back in the '30s, the season of goodwill was still going strong. Unfortunately, the economy was not. The Great Depression was taking its toll, and the joy of giving and receiving was on the decline. No surprise, then, that the holidays weren't shaping up to be too happy for merchants in the town of Mesa.

So, in 1932, when it came time for Mesa's annual Christmas parade, John McPhee, editor of the *Mesa Journal-Tribune,* concocted a plan. What Mesa needed was a gimmick, he decided, a publicity stunt to attract the crowds and get them in the buying mood. Seeing that aerial stunts were popular at the time, McPhee's idea was to launch Mesa's parade with a fitting performance. Santa Claus himself would parachute in! McPhee would hire a professional skydiver, dress him in red, and drop him over downtown, where jolly old St. Nick would glide in and kick off the big procession. The crowd would subsequently be filled with excitement and holiday spirit, ready to open their pocketbooks.

Naturally, things didn't go as planned. When the big day arrived, Santa Claus showed up drunk. There was no way he could ride in the parade, let alone jump from a plane. So McPhee drew up a new plan. He would dress a mannequin in a Santa suit, strap a parachute to it, and drop that from the plane instead. When the dummy landed in a nearby field, McPhee would ride out in the recovery truck, switch places with the mannequin, then join the parade himself.

The strategy would have been flawless if only the dummy had known how to pull a ripcord. Santa leaped from the plane, began to fall . . . continued to fall . . .

fell some more . . . then hit the ground with a hollow thump. Onlookers, who had been cheering in excitement, suddenly gasped in horror. Women screamed. Children cried.

The crowd was no longer in the mood for a Christmas pageant, let alone shopping. The sidewalks cleared in a hurry. It was the saddest parade in Mesa history. And although John McPhee would live for another quarter of a century, Mesa would never let him forget that day. When his own newspaper publicized his death in 1958, the headline referred to him as the Man Who Killed Santa.

Sheriff Frank J. Wattron

Six feet tall and thin, with dark, deep-set eyes, Frank Wattron made an imposing lawman. The first elected sheriff of Navajo County, he was known to be fearless and frequently ill-tempered, the former quality underlined by the sawed-off shotgun he always carried

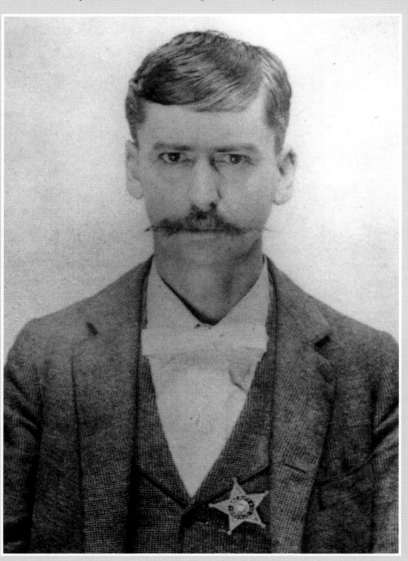

beneath his black overcoat, the latter most likely triggered by his notorious opium addiction. Yet the way Sheriff Wattron carried out justice revealed a keen, although somewhat acerbic, sense of humor. In one instance, when he was serving as justice of the peace in Holbrook, Wattron presided over a case in which a man was arrested for disturbing the peace. The fellow admitted his transgression, paid a fine equal to whatever he had in his pockets, and took off. Afterward, as Wattron was making a record of the case, he asked the arresting officer what the man's name was. "Dam'f I know," came the reply. Steadfast, Wattron scrawled, "*Territory of Arizona vs. Damfino*, defendant."

The sardonic sheriff's most unforgettable breach of legal etiquette, however, came with the sentencing of one George Smiley. Smiley had blamed his foreman for shorting him a day's pay and avenged himself by callously shooting the man in the back. For this crime, Smiley was condemned to death by hanging.

By law, Frank Wattron was required to send out invitations to the execution to all of Arizona's sheriffs, certain territorial officials, and various legal witnesses. Since this was Navajo County's first legal execution, the exact nature of the invites was up in the air, and Wattron's friends had a great deal of fun at his expense, ribbing him about how he would word them. So, employing what some might call a strange sense of humor, Wattron made up cards looking very much like wedding invitations and printed them like so:

Holbrook, Arizona, *December 1ˢᵗ* 1899.

Mr. *J. M. Pratt.*

You are hereby cordially invited to attend the hanging of one

George Smiley, Murderer.

His soul will be swung into eternity on December 8, 1899, at 2 o'clock p. m., sharp.

The latest improved methods in the art of scientific strangulation will be employed and everything possible will be done to make the surroundings cheerful and the execution a success.

F. J. WATTRON,
Sheriff of Navajo County.

Revised Statutes of Arizona, Penal Code, Title X., Sec. 1849, Page 807, makes it obligatory on Sheriff to issue invitations to executions, form (unfortunately) not prescribed.

Holbrook, Arizona, *1/7—* 1900.

Mr. *J. M. Pratt*

With feelings of profound sorrow and regret, I hereby invite you to attend and witness the private, decent and humane execution of a human being; name, George Smiley; crime, murder.

The said George Smiley will be executed on January 8, 1900, at 2 o'clock p. m.

You are expected to deport yourself in a respectful manner, and any "flippant" or "unseemly" language or conduct on your part will not be allowed. Conduct, on anyone's part, bordering on ribaldry and tending to mar the solemnity of the occasion will not be tolerated.

F. J. WATTRON.
Sheriff of Navajo County.

I would suggest that a committee, consisting of Governor Murphy, Editors Dunbar, Randolph and Hull, wait on our next legislature and have a form of invitation to executions embodied in our laws.

Within a week, the invitations' irreverent phrasing made international news. Picked up by Albuquerque's *Daily Citizen*, whose printing department turned out the cards, the story appeared in newspapers across the country, as well as in London, Berlin, and France. Newspaper editors accused Wattron of perpetuating a bad image of the West, and even President William McKinley complained to the governor of the Arizona Territory. The governor responded by granting George Smiley a thirty-day reprieve.

Sheriff Wattron, irritated by the response, sent out a revised version announcing the execution's rescheduling. This time, he had the cards and their envelopes printed with a somber black border, but worded the invitations with no less sarcasm. In fine print, Wattron explained with condescension that Arizona statutes make it "obligatory on Sheriff to issue invitations to executions, form (unfortunately) not prescribed" and added, "I would suggest that a committee, consisting of Governor Murphy, Editors Dunbar, Randolph and Hull, wait on our next legislature and have a form of invitation to executions embodied in our laws."

Wattron waited until the day after Smiley's execution to drop the revisions in the mail.

Back on the Chain Gang with Sheriff Joe Arpaio

By Mark Moran

Outspoken lawmen like Sheriff Frank Wattron are by no means a thing of the past in Arizona. As a matter of fact, one of the most controversial figures in the state today is Maricopa County's sheriff, Joe Arpaio. It seems that just about everybody in the county and even outside it have strong feelings about the sheriff—some

see him as a hardnosed crime fighter who is tough on criminals. Others view him as a cruel and inhumane self-aggrandizing windbag. Both camps just might be right.

What sets Joe apart from other elected law officials is not only his views on how to run his county jail but the fact that he has managed to put many of his strange ideas into practice. One of the more unusual aspects of Joe's jail is his extensive use of chain gangs (not only for men, but also for women and children), which are as uncommon these days in the penal system as thumbscrews or the iron maiden. Another unconventional practice is his Tent City jail, where 1,500 convicts while away their days and nights surrounded by an electrified razor wire fence and with nothing but the canvas of army surplus tents to shelter them from the brutal Arizona desert climate.

As if this weren't torture enough, Sheriff Arpaio bans all entertainment and luxury that most prisoners elsewhere take for granted: No dirty magazines are allowed, no cigarettes, no cable television (except a few "educational" channels like the Weather Channel and Food Network), no movies (except G-rated), no weights to lift—not even coffee is allowed in Joe's jail. "Under my watch, prisoners are treated like criminals and not like guests at the country club," he states on his Web site, reelectjoe.com.

Sheriff Joe has a long career of chasing bad guys. He began his career as a cop in the '50s in Washington, DC, and later Las Vegas. Joe says his biggest bust was in 1957, when he arrested Elvis Presley for speeding. He then spent twenty years working with the DEA tracking drug smugglers around the world. After moving to Arizona, where he became head of the state's DEA, he ran for and was elected to the office of sheriff of Maricopa County in 1992. He's been reelected four times since then—in 2004, by a landslide.

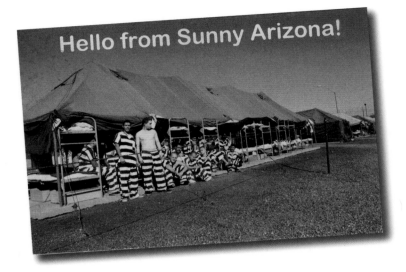

Hello from Sunny Arizona!

"I do have the support of the people," he told us. "So, when I do things, I get away with it. I've been investigated by the Justice Department, Amnesty International, the Civil Liberties Union—but I'm still here."

Some of the policies he has instituted, though unquestionably tough, seem like radically reasonable ideas. For example, he started what he calls Hard Knocks High, the only accredited high school program in jail, where young offenders can get a high school education while behind bars. He has instituted various drug rehabilitation programs. He runs a Web site that posts pictures of deadbeat parents along with their last known addresses.

We were fortunate enough to meet Sheriff Arpaio for an interview one summer day. First, though, we had to report to the Maricopa County Jail at five thirty a.m., just as the sun was coming up over the Sonoran Desert, because we were going to hitch a ride with a female chain gang out to the road where they would be performing their work duty that day.

When we arrived at the jail that morning, the temperature outside was already 114 degrees. At six a.m., the doors of the women's cell were unlocked and the inmates, chained together at the ankle in groups of five, formed ranks and began to shuffle down the hallway with a military-style cadence. The jangling of their steel chains dragging on the floor echoed down the long concrete corridors as they made their way to the waiting buses.

When we reached our destination, a blazing hot stretch of Arizona asphalt, the inmates were let off the buses and, still shackled together, began picking up litter from the sides of the highway. Soon Sheriff Joe Arpaio arrived in his car and took over the show. A stout man with short salt-and-pepper hair and wire-framed glasses, Arpaio was surprisingly spry for a seventy-four-year-old as he swaggered toward us, hand outstretched to shake.

"Hi, I'm Joe Arpaio, sheriff of Maricopa County. Welcome to hot Arizona. A stupid time for you to pick to come down here, but. . . ." he said, dressed in a full suit and tie, despite the heat. It was instantly clear that the sheriff would be taking control of the situation and he meant business. Joe's business is to promote Joe, and he clearly loves his work.

Weird Arizona: Sheriff Arpaio, we've heard that you're the toughest sheriff in America.

Sheriff Joe Arpaio: In the world.

WA: As a matter of fact, you actually wrote the book on being tough (*America's Toughest Sheriff: How We Can Win the War Against Crime*, by Joe Arpaio and Len Sherman). So what makes you so tough?

SJA: Well, I just use common sense, number one. I have a philosophy, when you're convicted and doing time, you should be punished . . . PUNISHED. I take away your privileges, take away your nice things.

One way Joe shows his toughness is to work his inmates seven days a week and feed them only two meals a day—without the luxury of such fancy condiments as salt, pepper, and ketchup, or even a cup of coffee. Joe says pulling coffee from the menu saves him $150,000 a year and serving bologna sandwiches instead of a cooked meal slashes another half million from the annual budget. According to one CNN report, "Arpaio makes inmates pay for their meals, which some say are worse than those for the guard dogs. Canines eat a dollar ten worth of food a day, the inmate ninety cents." Arpaio claims that this is not true, stressing that he feeds his inmates for thirty cents a day, not ninety. And he is very proud of that.

It is ironic, however, given all of the sheriff's pride for his cost-cutting efforts, that a variety of lawsuits against the county has cost taxpayers millions (e.g., wrongful death of an inmate settled for $8.5 million, $1.5 million for an inmate who died because he was denied medical treatment, and so forth). Still, this sort of thing doesn't seem to deter Sheriff Arpaio, and the chain gangs march—or rather shuffle—on in Maricopa County.

Chain gangs had been abolished in most states for decades, but in the 1990s Sheriff Joe rode the get-tough wave of prison reform and joined states like Alabama in passing laws to restore them. By 1999, even Alabama had given up the idea under public pressure. Still Joe forged ahead, this time adding women and children to the list of the shackled.

SJA: (*addressing a group of women chained together at the ankle cleaning up roadway litter*): You have made history. There has never been a female chain gang in history, around the world. You are part of history. Eight years ago I put the women on a chain gang. You know why I did it?

Female Inmate: Why?

SJA: Because we should never discriminate against women. We put men on the chain gang, why should you not have the opportunity? I am an equal opportunity incarcerator.

So how does Sheriff Joe get away with using a punishment that much of the rest of the country considers barbaric? Believe it or not, he gets his inmates to volunteer for the chain gang.

SJA: When they violate our policies—they spit on my officers or smuggle cigarettes in—we put them in a lockdown with three others, four others. The only way they're going to get out is volunteer for the chain gang. Everyone, the male chain gang, the female . . . I also have the only juvenile chain gang in the history. They all volunteer.

After our visit with the chain gang, Sheriff Joe escorted us back to his beloved jail for a tour of another of his accomplishments that he takes obvious pride in—Tent

City. It looks like a military camp in the desert. Korean war–era army tents sleep 1,500 minimum security prisoners—men and women in separate units, and juvenile males in units called pup tents—all surrounded by electrified razor wire fences. A blinking neon motel sign placed high on a tower above the encampment glows VACANCY, just to let everyone know that Sheriff Joe always has room in his jail for one more guest.

SJA: Land is expensive. These tents were free, free from the army. And no need for air-conditioning. How's that for a money saver?

But just how hot is it inside one of Sheriff Joe's Tent City tents? we wondered. To find out, we pulled out a digital thermometer we had smuggled into the jail with us. Holding it up to the level of the upper bunk of one of the prisoners' beds, we took a reading.

WA: It's a hundred and thirty-seven degrees in here!

SJA: Well, you're in front of the fan. That's cooling it off.

WA: Cooling it off? It's a hundred and . . ."

Joe once told his inmates who complained about the Tent City temperatures, "It's a hundred and twenty degrees in Iraq, and our soldiers are living in tents too, and they have to wear full battle gear, but they didn't commit any crimes, so shut your mouths!"

Sheriff Joe walked across the burning gravel to a tent, where he was surrounded by a group of inmates. Oddly, they did not gather around him and begin beating him to the ground, as we had feared they might. Instead they were clamoring for his autograph! The sheriff is actually treated something like a rock star whenever he makes these occasional visits inside the electrified razor wire to mingle with his subjects (most such sojourns are made when some sort of media attention is involved), and he

clearly revels in the celebrity. Sheriff Joe joked casually with the men and signed his name on postcards for them—postcards provided by the jail for the inmates to send home to their loved ones, each bearing a different image of Joe himself. Most of the cards also bear a funny slogan about just how tough Joe is and how miserable he makes life for his prisoners.

One of the sheriff's more shocking practices is his choice of underwear for his prisoners.

WA: Sheriff, we've heard that you force the inmates, both men and women, to wear pink underwear. Why is that?

SJA: Because they don't like it! That's the reason I did it, because if they liked it, I probably would not do it. But they don't like it. That's why I do it.

Strangely, though, the prisoners seem to really like this man and share a kind of Stockholm syndrome camaraderie with him. He ambles through the crowded, sweltering tents barking his tough rhetoric at the overheated inmates. Now and then a witty retort will echo back from somewhere in the crowd.

WA: Sheriff, you seem to have a good rapport with the prisoners here—almost like a father figure. We can almost see you putting them to bed and reading them a story at night.

SJA: I do.

WA: You do? How do you do that?

SJA: I film myself in a beautiful room with a fireplace and the Mr. Rogers sweater on. I have a German shepherd at my side, and I make a videotape to show on the jail's TVs. "Hi, inmates, it's the Bedtime Story Hour with me, your host, Sheriff Joe. For the next thirty to forty-five minutes, you will be treated to a literary treasure. Good night, see you tomorrow."

Hmm, maybe Sheriff Joe ain't so tough after all.

Mother Goose

Guess what, kids! Your favorite storyteller, that masterful mistress of nursery rhymes, Mother Goose, lives right here in Arizona! Well, actually, she lives in an RV and travels the country most of the year, but when she's not working the Renaissance-festival circuit, she sets up home just east of Phoenix.

Out of costume, she goes by Nancy Townsend, although we here at *Weird Arizona* suspect that might just be a cover. After all, Nancy really does live with geese— three of them, in fact—and a duck. And they're more than just pets; they're part of the family. Maggie, Lucy, Mimi, and Cricket (the duck) live and travel with Nancy and her husband, Alan, sharing the household more as children than as pets. They think they're people.

The whole thing started when Alan was fishing in a lake a few years ago. He saw a duck that was drowning— the second leading cause of death in ducks, believe it or not—and fished the poor thing out with his net. He brought it home, where he and Nancy kept it in the backyard. Well, one December, Nancy thought it would be "country-Christmas charming" to bring the duck into the house, but to do so would require some kind of duck diaper. So she invented one. "The more I thought about its," she says, "that's the only reason they weren't house pets." Now she markets the diapers online.

Nancy adopted the fairy-tale persona when the local children saw her walking her duck on a leash and started calling her Mother Goose. She liked the idea so much, she made a costume, got herself a goose, invented a goose diaper, and volunteered at the local ren-faire. When the gaggle drew huge crowds, the fair offered them a contract, and other festivals followed suit. Nancy has since become the all-out authority on waterfowl as pets. She's written a book on the subject, *Duck! There's a Goose in the House!*, and people from around the country write to her for advice.

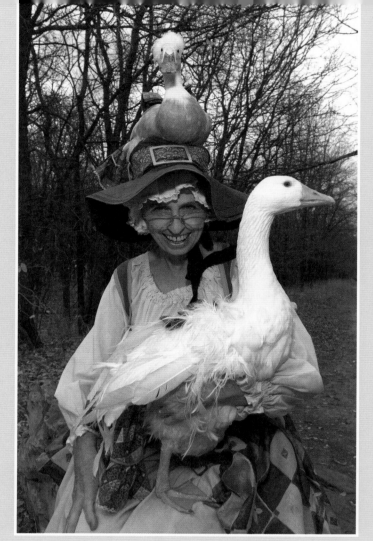

Nancy's birds are surprisingly affectionate and love to share hugs by wrapping their necks around people's. They'll also nibble ears and give little kisses. They're consciously gentle with babies and even possess an inexplicable ability to draw reactions from otherwise unresponsive mentally disabled children. Especially susceptible to their charms, however, are grown men. Nancy says, "We've had Hell's Angels mumbling baby talk for an hour."

What's the best part, though, about being the mother of a goose? Alan holds up an egg bigger than his fist. "When was the last time your cat gave you breakfast?"

Dr. Constantine Slobodchikoff or Dr. Doolittle?

It may be quite some time before we see Prairie Dog as a Second Language, but the work of one Northern Arizona University professor could certainly make it a possibility. Dr. Constantine Slobodchikoff, of N.A.U.'s department of biological sciences, understands the animals' language. That's right—he communicates with prairie dogs.

Slobodchikoff has studied the tunneling rodents for more than two decades and says he's uncovered a surprisingly advanced vocabulary. In fact, prairie dogs may possess one of the most complex languages in the animal kingdom. Take that, dolphins.

The good doctor first learned that prairie dogs' alarm calls varied in regard to different types of predators. When threatened, the animals emitted a sort of high-pitched bark, alerting others in their colony of impending danger. A bark warning of a hawk, for example, differed audibly from that of a coyote, and the barks remained consistent.

Since then, Slobodchikoff has been able to distinguish the use of adjectives and verbs. He says prairie dogs can describe movement, size, and shape. In an experiment in which he had people walk through colonies wearing different-colored clothes, he found that prairie dogs could distinguish between blue shirts, green shirts, yellow shirts, and so forth. They could even discriminate between a tall person and a short person and describe what they were doing. Introducing geometric shapes had similar results, indicating they were able to invent new words to describe new things. Different colonies even have different dialects.

Two-way conversations are still under development, though. Apparently, it's tough to master the accent. "I used my best prairie dog imitation to say 'coyote,'" Slobodchikoff said. "They just looked at me in disgust."

If we here at *Weird Arizona* are smart, we'll get in on this from the ground floor. In ten years, we could break the prairie-dog market with *Weird Burrows*.

Digging Orville Mickens in Dos Cabezas

He's like Indiana Jones, but with suspenders and a different kind of hat. "Arizona" Mickens they call him. Okay, they don't really, but they should. Orville Mickens is his name, and he's one of the most productive amateur archaeologists you'll ever meet.

Mickens has hunted for lost tidbits of history for more than sixty years, collecting just about anything that's older than he is. Bullets, farm implements, toys, opium paraphernalia, you name it. He's scoured ghost towns, abandoned forts, canyons, mines, cabins, and anywhere else someone might have dropped something interesting. He's even done a little gold panning, just for fun.

By 1981, Orville had accumulated so much tangible history, he opened the Frontier Relics Museum, less than two hours east of Tucson in Dos Cabezas (that's Two Heads, for you monolinguists). He's packed six decades of found items in under one thousand square feet. It's almost all from the late 1800s and almost all from Arizona. Some of it spills over to other times and places, like the prized 1950 Cadillac he keeps in back—"That's when they made good cars," he says—or the unopened can of World War II rations—"That has a cookie and some other stuff in it."

He says a lot of people who come by stay for just a few minutes--they scan the place and leave. If you linger a while and let Orville show you around, though, he can tell you a story about nearly every article in the place. At least part of one, anyway.

He picks up a bullet. "These are what they killed the Indians with." Pointing to a miner's helmet, he says, "That's crushed. That came out of a mining tunnel that caved in on the old boy." Orville moves on, pulling something from a shelf. "I don't know the age of that, but it's pretty old."

Some things have a more exciting history. "That's the biggest snake I ever killed. I think he would've got my dog and maybe me too, but he had a cottontail rabbit in his mouth. He couldn't strike or anything else, so I shot his head off." Understandably, certain items aren't on display, like a bit of munitions he keeps in another room. "This here came from where Pancho Villa had his revolution on the border. It's a rocket, and it's still loaded. It's supposed to go off when it hits. And I'm kind of afraid of it, so I keep it back here. Chances are it won't go off . . . but you never know."

Orville always asks permission from the landowners before collecting. He's proud to tell you that everything he got, he got legally. Due mostly to his age, he doesn't explore much these days. He says he doesn't step too high. "I could almost trip over a toothpick," he jokes. He's more than willing to amble with you through the museum, though, which you can find fifteen miles down Highway 186 from Willcox. Just pull up in front and honk your horn. He'll come and get you.

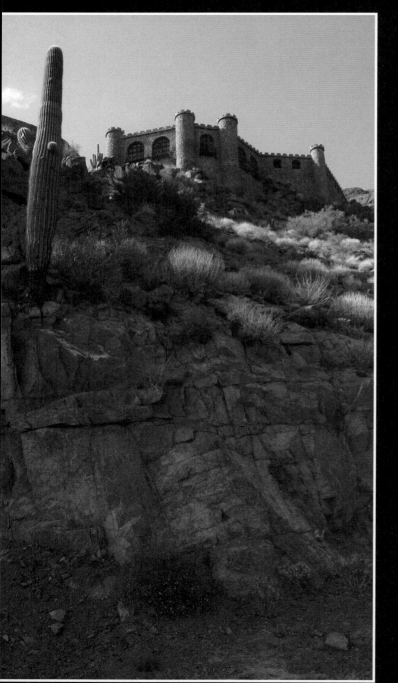

Personalized Properties and Innovative Environments

Stucco, stucco, Mexican tile, stucco, swimming pool, stucco, Mexican tile. So goes a drive through suburban Arizona. Save for the occasional golf course, the stretches of middle-class domestication can be mind-numbingly conventional.

If you take enough left turns, though, you might drive past the abode of one of the few homeowners to rub the khaki haze from his eyes and shirk the conformist covenant. Though rare, these are the people who understand the purpose of individual housing: to be individual.

Such creative souls are the ones *Weird Arizona* wishes to honor in this chapter—people like Louis Lee, the man who spent his entire Phoenix residency exhibiting his personality through his own very personal arrangement of rocks and cement. He dared to strike a blow at tradition, to knock the "dent" in "residential." Regrettably, he passed away as this book was being written. I'm honored to have been a guest at his unique home and to have witnessed his matchless creativity firsthand. To him, I dedicate this chapter.

Louis Lee's Rock Garden

Your typical rock garden consists of a few scattered stones, maybe a bed or two of gravel, and a few well-placed plants, all fairly level and unassuming. But this—and you know where we're headed here—isn't your typical rock garden. At the Lee homestead in Paradise Valley, a rock garden means lots of rocks, fortified by lots more rocks, all spanning, arching, and towering to their limits.

Louis Lee, the attraction's gardener, spent literally half a lifetime cultivating the display. He began in 1958, following the completion of an ordinary retaining wall intended simply to level out the front yard. Once that was complete, he set about erecting a series of decorative partitions that grew ever taller and more complex as the years passed. There was no plan. He just improvised. Whatever didn't work, he'd raze and redo, no problem. "I enjoy doing this," he said, shrugging. "I put some up, and if it didn't look too good to me, I'd tear it down and build it again."

We can only guess at the number, but let's say gazillions of rocks, most no bigger than a golf ball, comprise the stupefying maze. For certain projects, Louis might pick up the occasional sack of rock from the hardware store, but most of it he collected from the surrounding landscape. Adding a few bricks and a handful of stepping stones to the mix, he slowly formed a network of arches, ledges, and pathways that would likely require an experienced cartographer to comprehend.

What's more, you'd probably have to hire an archaeologist just to inventory all the knickknacks, gimcracks, and bric-a-brac embedded throughout the structure. Bottles, license plates, toys, trophies, and even the occasional toilet seat protrude from every direction; a lot of this came from visitors looking to recycle their unwanted odds and ends. It's sort of like an everlasting yard sale.

And, oh, the Buddhas! Bald ceramic men everywhere. How many? "I don't know," Louis said. "So many. Little ones, big ones. Yeah, all over." Esther, Louis's ever-patient wife, said, "He'll still go buy them. We've got Buddhas all over, but when we go to San Francisco, he'll still want to go buy some more." Teasingly, she added, "I told him we've got Buddhas to SELL!"

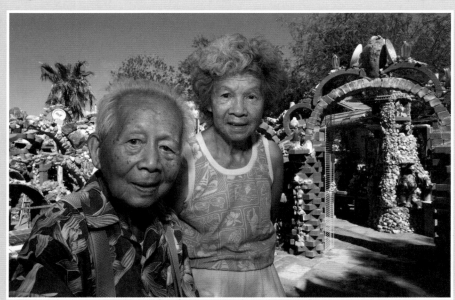

The whole assembly looks as though it's delicately balanced, like a stack of Jenga blocks thirty moves into a game. Even the smallest among us can feel like a bull in the proverbial china shop while navigating the garden's one-third acre. Narrow gravel towers and rows of carefully positioned figurines border the path. "Watch your head" is a frequently voiced caveat here. But everything is soundly cemented together. Mr. Lee said he'd never had

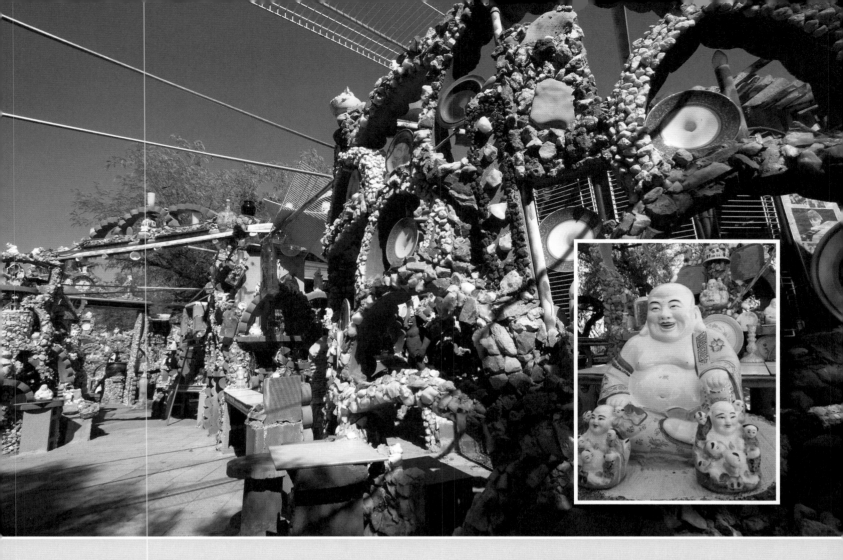

a major collapse, only the occasional pieces coming free, usually due to weather. The last few years, he concentrated mostly on upkeep. "I do a lot of repair work, you know?"

He and his family purchased their home, near the corner of East McDonald Drive and Fortieth Street, for a reported $40,000, in an area where houses today can go for several million dollars. Yet no residence can compare in value to the imaginative masonry achieved by Louis Lee, which has become a priceless work of folk art and a point of pride for Arizona. It was always hard

to convince Mr. Lee of that, though. Even as he hosted a steady stream of reporters, television crews, and visitors from around the world, he was continually surprised that people found his personal indulgence so fascinating. It pleased him, though, that his creation made people smile.

Sadly, Louis Lee passed away July 18, 2006, at the age of ninety-two. He worked on his rock garden up to the last, sweeping leaves and watering plants. In an interview following his death, his oldest son, Errol, credited the unconventional labor of love for his father's long life. "He had a reason to get up every day," he said.

Garden of Gethsemane

In the shadow of "A" Mountain, at the corner of West Congress Street and North Bonita Avenue in Tucson, lies the Garden of Gethsemane, a sculpture park and retreat for the world-weary. Here people come to meditate, to read, or if they're so inclined, to lunch with Jesus.

The park preserves what remain of the sculptures created by the late Felix Lucero, a self-made artist who once lived in a plywood-and-cardboard shack beneath the nearby Congress Street bridge. The pieces were a fulfillment of a promise Lucero made to God while lying injured on a World War I battlefield. He told God that if he survived, he would dedicate his life to creating the statues.

The homeless artist began sculpting his monuments along the bank of the Santa Cruz River from sand and other debris. When a flood washed them away, he started again, higher up the bank. He also began to use concrete. What resulted from Lucero's tireless work was a collection of tableaux depicting Jesus at his various watershed moments: after birth, at his final meal, on the cross, and in his tomb. A diorama portrays his judgment before Pontius Pilate in the all-too-infrequently utilized medium of action figures.

Though his work was generally admired by the locals, they say Lucero was ridiculed at least once for his efforts. According to legend, a drunken man on a horse approached the artist and taunted him, insulting his statues and encouraging his horse to trample part of the sculpture. When the man rode away, God had the last laugh by spooking his horse with a snake. The man was thrown to the ground and died instantly from a broken neck.

Lucero himself passed away in 1951 and left his garden behind to face the ravages of urban progress. The whitewashed Jesuses have been relocated at least twice, once when Congress Street was widened in the early 1970s and again in 1982 when the river was lined with concrete. As Jesus did in the original Gethsemane, the statues suffered persistent torment, but in the form of reckless vandalism, being repeatedly spray-painted and having their heads smashed in.

The statues were restored, and the site is now protected by high stucco walls and a gate, open to the public only during specified hours or by appointment for weddings and parties. For many, it has become a shrine for those who wish to pray or leave a candle. It's also an occasional hangout for a few of Tucson's homeless. One can only assume they too are studying to be artists.

Camelback Castle

Orthodontist Mort Copenhaver taught himself the art of stonecutting for a single purpose: He wanted to build himself a castle. As a child, he had seen one in a movie, and it became his lifelong dream to live in something similarly fabulous. It took about ten years of hard labor, but by the end of the 1970s, he was living in the highest and most impregnable home in Phoenix.

Blasting rock from the nearly vertical parcel of land he purchased on the side of Camelback Mountain, Copenhaver moved each stone into place by hand. He used no machinery but simply cut everything down to a size he could lift, then stuck it all together with 50,000 bags of cement. He got a little help here and there, employing workers from south of the border and exchanging construction projects for dental services, but he spent so much of his own time on the endeavor, he reportedly lost a wife and two girlfriends before he was finished.

The completed structure comprises eight levels of eighteen-inch-thick granite walls. The floor plan, which is reported to be between 7,000 and 8,500 square feet, boasts five bedrooms, seven and a half bathrooms, ten balconies, and servants' quarters. Amenities include four fireplaces, a seventeen-foot waterfall, and a dungeon with a bar. In the living room, guests will find a sauna, a twenty-person whirlpool spa, and a rollback roof. Plus, it's all connected with secret passageways.

Unfortunately for Dr. Copenhaver, hard times forced him to put the castle on the market after living there only a few years. In 1985, he listed it for $7 million. A buyer offered $5.8 million, which Copenhaver refused, only to watch the selling price drop to $2.5 million months later. In the end, he lost the castle due to bankruptcy. It finally sold in 1989 for the rock-bottom price of $985,000.

It's still referred to as Copenhaver Castle by some, but today it's owned by Texan Jerry Mitchell, a real estate developer who specializes in dude ranches and western resorts. Since the bank that formerly owned the property stripped out all the medieval furniture and fixtures, Mitchell redecorated in his own style, adding turn-of-the-century antiques, western artwork, Indian rugs, and firearms.

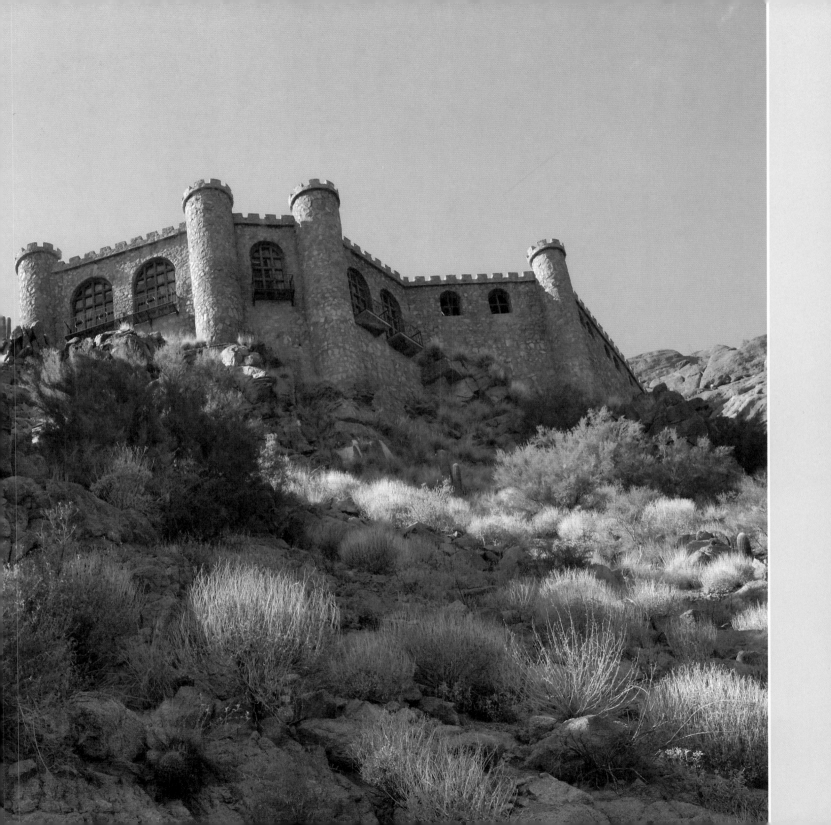

Mystery Castle

In 1945, Mary Lou Gulley received word from a lawyer in Arizona that her father had just passed away. The news was entirely unexpected, as neither she nor her mother had heard from him since he disappeared from their home in Seattle, Washington, more than fifteen years before. They had assumed he was long dead, not alive and well and living in the Southwest.

They were even more surprised to find out they had inherited a large estate south of Phoenix, an eight-thousand-square-foot home surrounded by almost eight acres of land. This whole time, Boyce Luther Gulley had been toiling away in Arizona, and the fruits of his labor were his gift to his family.

In the weeks and months that followed, Mary Lou would learn her father's story. While still living in Seattle, Boyce Gulley discovered that he had contracted tuberculosis. Without telling anyone of his ailment, he disappeared. "That was kind of cruel on my mother, in a way," says Mary

Lou, now entering her eighties. "But she figured it was for the best. . . . See, he couldn't be around little children. He had to be put in a sanitarium, and he didn't want to go into one." So he ran away and eventually ended up in Phoenix, where he staked a mining claim in the foothills of South Mountain and began building a home.

As the teenage Mary Lou learned the details of her father's undertaking, she recalled a memory from a time before her father ran away. She had played with him on a beach as a child, spending hours building sand castles, which would inevitably wash away with the incoming tide. As one afternoon's effort fell to pieces, she pleaded, "Please, Daddy, build me a big and strong castle someday that I can live in." Mary Lou realized this secret house was it. This was her castle. Though he had left his daughter behind, Boyce Gulley had spent the rest of his life fulfilling his promise.

Gulley had labored in the desert, collecting natural stone and river rock to form the walls that would make up the castle. He was an inveterate recycler, incorporating old railroad ties, unused telegraph poles, and discarded metal into his design. He used natural copper ore to create a fireplace mantel. Glass trays and parts of an old car formed portholes. He rescued siding from a boxcar, along with railings, windowpanes, and furniture from derelict buildings.

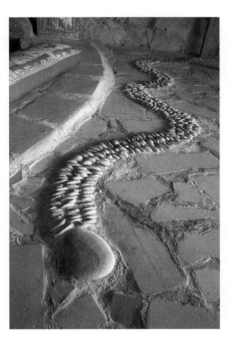

In many ways, the self-made architect was ahead of his time. Among Mary Lou's favorites are the blackened and distorted bricks he used as accents. "These were the rejects in the kiln," she explains. "In my father's day, they were called clinkers. The late Frank Lloyd Wright started using them, and now they're called expensive." Boyce Gulley made ingenious use of space as well, incorporating fold-up tables and what was likely one of the earliest hideaway beds.

Before his death, Gulley completed eighteen rooms. Among them can be found a caretaker's quarters, a bar, a chapel, thirteen fireplaces, and a wishing well. Had he been able to continue, there also would have been a swimming pool.

When they found out about the castle, Mary Lou and her mother moved in almost immediately. Gulley had stipulated in his will that if they stayed there at least three years, they would also be allowed to access a trapdoor, under which they would discover a surprise. That surprise turned out to be two $500 bills, gold nuggets, and a Valentine's Day card Mary Lou had made for him as a child. After that, Mary Lou fell totally in love with her castle. She lives there still today, offering tours during Arizona's cooler months. The home is just as Boyce Gulley built it, complete with its oddly integrated turrets and parapets, a lasting version of the castles he and Mary Lou once built together.

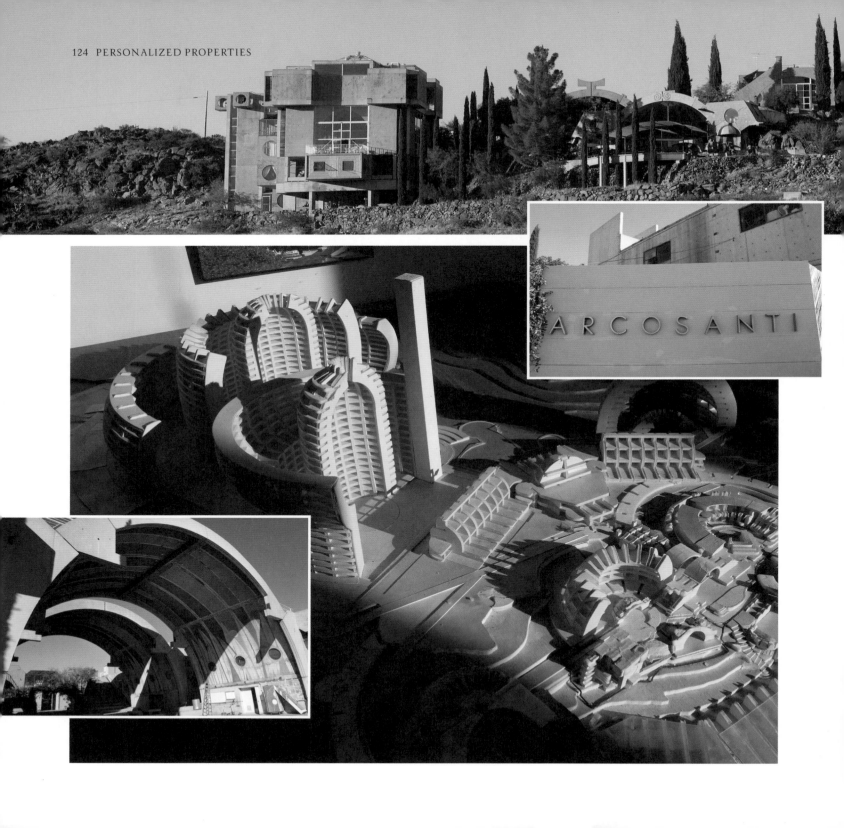

Arcosanti

Arcosanti is what you might call an urban laboratory, an experimental city based on the philosophy of merging architecture with the environment, all wrapped up in a sort of dated space-age package. *The New York Times* probably summarized it best as "a lab for future cities, part commune, part Flash Gordon."

It lies on more than four thousand acres of undisturbed land northwest of Cordes Junction, about sixty miles up Interstate 17 from Phoenix. You reach it by driving a long dirt road out to its multistory visitors center, where you can take a virtual tour of the complex and learn about how its innovative design just might save the world from urban sprawl.

In essence, that's the motivation behind its construction: to develop architectural systems that coexist with Mother Earth rather than take advantage of her, a model termed arcology by the city's originator, Paolo Soleri. (The expression is an amalgam of the words "architecture" and "ecology.") His vision, intended to house five thousand people when complete, incorporates techniques like passive solar construction and integrated water collection that are intended one day to be the model for future metropolitan growth.

Alas, the city of tomorrow wasn't built yesterday. Arcosanti has been under construction for nearly forty years and isn't anywhere near completion. The current population varies between only seventy and one hundred and twenty, made up of the interns and workshop attendees who are helping build the place. And what's standing has already begun to show its age. The concrete is weathered, and rust stains run from the windowsills. Critics say that, at its current rate, it could take hundreds of years to complete and that the so-called "green" building practices currently making it into mainstream structural planning have already advanced beyond what Arcosanti can teach us.

Not that it's a bad idea. It just comes off as more of a quixotic commune than anything else, where the inhabitants have been forced to produce merchandise to sell to the community's fifty thousand annual visitors just to sustain their society. Particularly popular here are handmade bronze Soleri Windbells, for which Arcosanti seems to have become a factory. They're on display by the hundreds in the visitors center, where you can also pick up packets of dried herbs, certain variations of which we suspect to be one of the greater influences behind this place.

But who knows? Perhaps when the rest of us are wiped out in World War III, Arcosanti will still be going strong, its hopeful tenants repopulating the earth in a new *Logan's Run* utopia.

Biosphere 2

It looks like a 1960s encyclopedia illustration depicting a colony on Mars in 1985. And, in part, that's what it was. Built to demonstrate the viability of an isolated, self-sustaining ecosystem, one of its original goals was to help in developing interplanetary outposts. What it turned out to be was more like a soap opera under glass, sitting in the desert about twenty minutes north of Tucson.

The experiment was named Biosphere 2 in recognition of the "original" biosphere, Earth. It was conceived by John Allen, a dominant member of a New Mexico commune who had ideas of developing an autonomous refuge from impending global doom. Allen envisioned a glass-enclosed habitat in which plants and animals would live in symbiosis, completely sealed off from their environment, providing for all the needs of their human caretakers. In essence, a giant people terrarium.

The focal point of the project would be a 7.2-million-cubic-foot, glass and space-frame laboratory made up of crew quarters, an enormous vegetable garden, and five distinct biomes: a desert, a rain forest, a savannah, a marsh, and a 900,000-gallon ocean with an artificial reef. It would all be quarantined from the outside world by individually sealing every one of its 6,500 three-layer windowpanes with double applications of caulk. The desert-bound ark, literally more airtight than the space shuttle, would then be stocked with 3,800 species of plants and animals. A highly intricate, computer-controlled infrastructure would regulate and monitor all environmental functions like air pressure and precipitation. It would be a gleaming-white cathedral of ecology.

Largely bankrolled by Texas billionaire Edward Bass, construction on the facility began in 1987 at a cost of $200 million. It was managed by Space Biospheres Ventures, a subsidiary of the Institute of Ecotechnics, companies whose names bring to mind subversive mining corporations in an under budget space odyssey. And when Biosphere 2 was finished, it looked like the sort of place they would be headquartered—a shining, futuristic, autonomous compound in the middle of the desert. Actually, it's surprising that the place was never used as a den of villainy in some James Bond movie.

Following completion, Biosphere 2 launched its first mission. On September 26, 1991, four men and four women, dressed something like interstellar rent-a-cops, voluntarily entered the sphere to begin two years of self-supporting isolation. As crowds cheered and cameras flashed, uniformed Wells Fargo guards sealed the eight volunteers inside. A Crow Indian chanted, and a Tibetan monk blessed the crew. There was a catered party with lasers and fireworks.

Over the next twenty-four months, the eight Biospherians were watched like pets in a human Habitrail. As they lived and worked inside their glass house, tourists peered curiously through the windows — interested, of course, less in the science of the thing than in what kind of sexcapades were going on inside. Unfortunately, what was happening on the other side of the glass wasn't nearly that pleasant.

Problems surfaced quickly. Fish, too many in number, began to die off, reportedly clogging the ocean's filtration system. Rapidly growing morning-glory vines threatened to choke the rain forest. Condensation was overly watering the desert. Plus, greenhouse-variety "crazy ants" infested everything. There were cockroaches too.

In addition, El Niño brought unusually cloudy weather, inhibiting plant growth and, subsequently, food production. Some Biospherians allegedly began hoarding and stealing food. Then, on top of starvation came asphyxiation. Halfway through the experiment, oxygen levels in the sphere's air had dropped from a normal twenty-one percent mixture down to fourteen percent. Simple chores were leaving the Biospherians out of breath. As they would later discover, the overly rich soil used in the project caused an explosion of oxygen-depleting bacteria. Eventually, project managers were forced to pump in oxygen from the outside.

By the end, Arizona's little Sim City was a virtual disaster. When the crew emerged, they had lost, on average, fifteen percent of their body weight. The ocean had become acidic, the air polluted. Temperature control was a mess. As for the animals, nineteen of the twenty-five vertebrate species had gone extinct.

Then came the rumors. It was said that, while inside, the Biospherians quickly split into two rival factions. Working together had become impossible. Allegedly, they still won't talk to each other. It was supposedly due in large part to cultism. Apparently, the whole project had been set up as part of a following led by founder John Allen, who — mentioned for the sole reason that it's funny — wrote books under the pen name Johnny Dolphin. The cultists called themselves "synergists" and built Biosphere 2 as a "synergia."

Less than six months after the end of the first mission, management made a second attempt to man the facility. This time, it would be five men and two women (one of whom had answered an anonymous want ad announcing a position for a greenhouse gardener). Crew members would be replaced at varying intervals, performing research continuously for the next one hundred years. Emphasis would be on science rather than survival.

But that's when things really started to shake up. Financier Edward Bass ousted the project's management team less than a month into the new mission. In retaliation, two former Biospherians attempted to sabotage the project by opening the habitat's doors and breaking several windows. The mission was terminated just a few months later after new management reevaluated Biosphere 2's purpose; they decided to convert it to an open research facility.

From there, things went fairly smoothly until the compound mysteriously accumulated dangerous levels of nitrous oxide — that's right, kids: laughing gas — and

management decided to, in their words, hit the RESET button. In 1995, they cycled out all the air and replaced the soil and water. The facility was then leased out to Columbia University for student education and legitimate research. Tourism became a major focus as well, especially in 2000, when the biomes were finally opened to the public. (The airtight seal was no longer a concern, which was good, because ants had burrowed through the caulking long ago.)

Things were looking up for Biosphere 2. It was finally becoming a respected research facility, as well as a popular tourist attraction. That is, until Columbia backed out of its lease in 2003 and cut off all funding. Research came to a halt. Tours continued, but not enough to pay for the upkeep. Finally Ed Bass was forced to put the place up for sale.

In February 2006, someone agreed to buy the property. Bass had hoped to draw scientific interests, but it looks as though the whole deal will go to a housing developer. As this book is being written, it seems Biosphere 2 will become a closer reflection of Earth's environmental processes than originally intended, as it may be torn down in favor of an upscale housing community.

Dry-Docked at the Quartzsite Yacht Club By Mark Moran

Sometimes a property that would seem perfectly ordinary in one location can be totally weird when found in another. Take for example a yacht club. While no one would give it a second thought if it were found on the shores of Long Island Sound, it is the last sort of establishment you expect to come across in the middle of the burning Arizona desert. It was late June 2006. My *Weird U.S.* partner Mark Sceurman and I were on a road trip that had taken us from Las Vegas, through the deserts of southern California, en route to Phoenix. We were on the final leg of our journey and had traveled several hours since our last stop, at the Salton Sea in California. Oh, yeah, and it was HOT — I'm talking 114 degrees hot. We were still about 125 miles west of Phoenix on Route 10 when we decided to take a break from the dry, dusty highway and spend the night in the city of Quartzsite.

For those folks who have never been to Quartzsite, it is often described as a mecca for rock hounds and snowbirds. This is because about a million and a half gem and mineral enthusiasts descend upon the town for a couple months each winter. That's when Quartzsite's seventy RV and trailer parks are filled to capacity and two thousand vendors cater to all your rock specimen needs at a variety of swap meets. For Quartzsite, which has a year-round population of about 3,500 people, this is a very big time, to say the least.

But Mark and I were not there in the winter; we were there in June, when the city of Quartzsite looks very different indeed. The flat, sprawling, parched community seems like a veritable desert ghost town for most of the calendar year. Almost all of the businesses that are there to service the millions of rock hunters are closed in the long off-season; the restaurants, shops, and bars are all empty.

So finding a place to spend the night was going to be a little more of a challenge than Mark and I had anticipated. We stopped at a gas station–convenience store to ask for directions to someplace where we might find some dinner, drinks to wet our extremely parched whistles, and a couple of rooms for the night. The guy behind the counter (who seemed pretty bored and lonely himself) told us the only place in town that was open was the Quartzsite Yacht Club, which was right down the road.

The Quartzsite Yacht Club? We were a bit perplexed by this recommendation, being that we were presently in the middle of the sandy Arizona desert, miles away from any navigable body of water. But if the place had food, beer, and was open — well, you know what they say, any port in a storm.

When we pulled into the empty parking lot of the Quartzsite Yacht Club, we noticed the usual decoration you'd expect to find hanging on the walls of any nautical-themed dining establishment: crossed oars, a ship's wheel, hemp rope, etc. But out back, instead of a marina full of luxury sailing vessels, there were trailers docked in full hook-up slips. Beside the door to the bar was a sign that you'd most likely not see at any other yacht club in the world urging patrons to please not bring their firearms inside. Since neither Mark nor I were packing heat at the time, we were happy to oblige and proceeded to enter.

We took a couple of seats at the bar and asked the bartender for menus. Inside, the yacht club seemed pretty much like any other bar — some pool tables, a jukebox in the corner, a few drunken customers scattered about. But the nautical accents of the decor continued to confound us. Were all of these seafaring overtones just part of some sort of elaborate desert joke? we wondered.

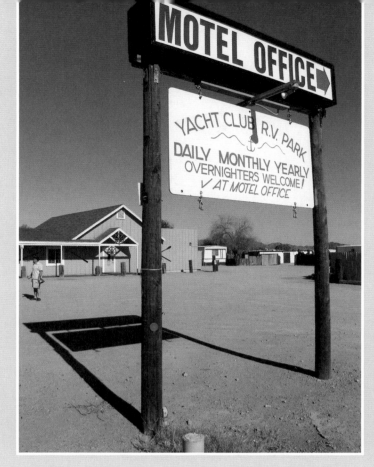

Al had always been gifted with humor, wit and an active imagination. He decided to have some fun and changed the name to "The Yacht Club" with the motto "Welcome aboard—long time, no sea!" To get the ball rolling, Al sold memberships in the Yacht Club to any qualified visitors (in those days you needed $10.00 to qualify), and lo and behold, he became an instant Commodore. . . .

Before long the number of memberships started to grow and grow. There are members from every state in the U.S. and from countries all over the world. We now boast of a membership total of over 4,600. Some members have even used their wallet cards to be admitted to exclusive yacht clubs that have reciprocity! . . .

The Commodore's legacy is still very much alive [although Al himself is not]. . . . Who knows—if an earthquake ever sends California into the ocean one day, the Yacht Club could end up as beach front property!!

As it turns out, the answer is yes—and no! You see, as the bartender informed us, while there is an element of humor involved, the Quartzsite Yacht Club actually is a legitimate, fully chartered yacht club. Our helpful host handed us a pamphlet that explained the origins of this strange landlocked desert enigma. It read:

Al Madden, who had an investment company in California, worked on a gold mine venture for clients in Quartzsite, Arizona during the late 1970's. Although this business venture was not successful, Al spent a lot of time in Quartzsite and had noticed that the local beer bar, "The JIGSAW", was for sale. . . . Al must have seen some potential that others had missed and he bought it anyway with the help of his sons and family.

As Mark and I finished reading the pamphlet, we were joined at the bar by another patron, who must have noticed our curiosity about the establishment. He was an extremely large man, perhaps six-feet-three inches tall, and weighed somewhere in the neighborhood of three hundred pounds. He took our hands in his monstrously large mitt, shook them, and introduced himself as Bill. Fortunately for us, Bill seemed like a pretty friendly sort. But then, out of nowhere, this total stranger began to try to convince Mark and me that we must become members of the club.

"Us, become members of the Quartzite Yacht Club? Why would we do that?" we asked. "We don't sail where we live, and we live two thousand miles from Quartzsite!"

By the time Mark and I were ready to pay our tab for the night, we'd decided that we might just be yacht club material after all. And if our crewmate Bill, a gigantic drug smuggling ex-con trucker, was willing to sponsor our membership, then we were prepared to come aboard!

"Where do we enlist?" we asked the bartender, who proceeded to give us a form to fill out. After the paperwork was done and the $25 membership fee for each of us had been paid, Mark and I became Quartzsite Yacht Club Charter Members numbers 6,800 and 6,801, respectively. Along with all of the rights and privileges associated with membership, we were also each given a T-shirt bearing the club's official logo, a sailboat plying through the cactus-strewn sands of the Arizona desert, a burgee (a three-cornered pennant) embroidered with the initials QYC, and an official laminated membership card

"That's okay," Bill assured us. "We have more members than just about any other yacht club in the world, 6,799, and they live all over the country and even around the world! And the best part of becoming a member is that you gain access to any other yacht club in the world that has a policy of reciprocity!" Over the course of a few beers, Bill filled us in on the details of his life story and how he had come to live in Quartzsite. As it turns out, our new friend Bill was not a gem enthusiast but did have some experience with crystals—crystal meth, that is. He was a retired trucker who had just recently been released from a five-year stint in the joint for running drugs cross-country in his rig. After his time in the slammer, Bill settled down in a trailer in Quartzsite because it was affordable and . . . well, he'd gotten used to living in a tiny, hot, and confined space.

and certificate suitable for framing.

I don't know if Mark and I will ever make it back to Quartzsite to belly up to the bar once more with our yacht club brothers. But I can't wait to see what happens when I proudly pull that membership card out of my wallet, invoking the sacred laws of reciprocity, and demand a drink at the clubhouse of some exclusive yacht club elsewhere—perhaps one that actually caters to a seagoing clientele. Something tells me I might just be left standing high and dry.

Barrett's Village By Mark Moran

The Quartzsite Yacht Club is not the only oddly personalized property to be found in this lonely desert outpost town. There is actually an entire stone village here, including houses, a general store, churches, windmills, a lighthouse, and even an English castle—all built completely by the hands of just one man. And believe it or not, the entire village fits onto a narrow strip of sand bordering the back parking lot of the Quartzsite Historical Museum at the Tyson's Well Old Stage Station. That's because the largest of these intricately constructed concrete and mineral-stone edifices is no more than a few feet tall. The architect of the diminutive dwellings was a man named Walter Barrett; he began the construction of this Lilliputian paradise on his own property when he first moved to Quartzsite in 1970. So how did this strange scaled-down town end up in the dusty museum parking lot? Well, the story is probably best told by the weathered plexiglass-covered plaque that is posted at the site, which reads:

Walter Barrett and his wife Edith came to Quartzsite from Ferndale, Washington around 1970. Like many other Quartzsiters he was a "Rock Hound," so it was natural for him to find a use for the rocks in addition to the jewelry that he made. He also had built their Quartzsite home out of stone.

There were many birds in their yard, so his first project was a birdbath. After that he built the Miniature Village. The lighthouse and the fishing village were inspired by his summers of fishing in Washington. Nostalgia inspired him to construct his birthplace in Farmville, North Carolina, which is complete down to the summer kitchen. After that he built a replica of his sister's summer home in North Carolina. . . .

Mr. Barrett's daughter, Diane Ercolin, and her brother Walter donated the Village to the Quartzsite Historical Society as a memorial to their father. The Village was moved to the Historical Society Museum in March of 1991.

Kravetz's Medical Museum

Stamps are fine for some people. Others collect coins or Pez dispensers. A number of people (probably more than we care to know) enjoy porcelain cows. Dr. Robert Kravetz, on the other hand, takes pleasure in the more distinctive topic of medical whatsits. In fact, he has decorated the north wing of the Phoenix Baptist Hospital with them. Though retired, Dr. Kravetz still keeps an office there and maintains about twenty glass cases full of medical antiques scattered on each floor. Trepanation, bloodletting, phrenology—you name the obscure, sometimes shady, medical practice, and he's got an implement to carry it out.

To be fair, it's not all about quackery. Dr. Kravetz has legitimate paraphernalia too, like old-fashioned catheters and amputation kits. One of his favorite items is a portable medicine chest from the 1700s with bottles still half full. Some things, though, are borderline, like the formaldehyde room sanitizer or the medical whiskey flask. The cupping bowls, for example, were suctioned to the body to create great big hickeys in the name of "circulation." They sort of worked, but not really. He owns at least two sets.

Still, the more interesting pieces tend to be the oddball items like the leech jars and opium pots, or the somewhat disconcerting electromagnetic

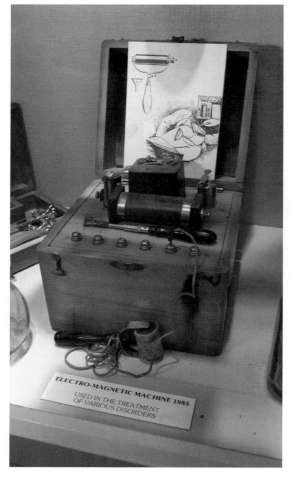

ELECTRO-MAGNETIC MACHINE 1885
USED IN THE TREATMENT
OF VARIOUS DISORDERS

generator and its little roller attachment for use in the treatment of "various disorders." You can even see a genuine ear trumpet in the collection—Eh? What's that you say, sonny?

From an educational perspective, the display focuses mainly on medical history as it pertains to Arizona in the late 1800s and early 1900s, which is Dr. Kravetz's area of expertise. He's written books on the subject and assembled pertinent artifacts for the past thirty-plus years. Really, anything you might want to know about the state's turn-of-the-century influx of health seekers, he can tell you. Yet he's full of great generalized trivia too. Do you know the difference between a smooth antique medicine bottle and a ribbed one? The ribbed ones contained poison. You know, in case you grabbed one in the dark.

The good doctor doesn't consider himself particularly weird, despite his multilevel display of antiquated apparatus. And he's right—Dr. Kravetz is a friendly, down-to-earth professional with a healthy interest in the history of his vocation. But even so, how many places of work do you know of that are adorned with a mint-condition set of vintage rectal dilators?

BREAST ASPIRATION SET

...hogony case containing
...up with characteristi...
...glass resev...

CUPPING INSTRUMENT SET (CA. 1860)

A more sophisticated but equally ancient method of blood letting was
that of cupping. The object of the practice was to draw blood to the surface
of the skin.

Dry cupping was that practised when the skin was unbroken, and wet
cupping after the skin had been scarified (cut).

The cups before being applied to the skin were warmed, creating a partial
vacuum. Earlier ones were warmed over a flame but during the Nineteenth
Century valved cupping glasses appeared for use with a pump to withdraw
the air.

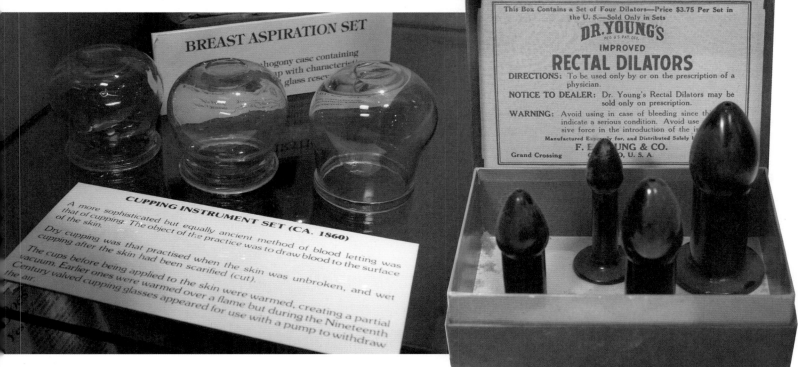

This Box Contains a Set of Four Dilators—Price $3.75 Per Set in
the U. S.—Sold Only in Sets

DR. YOUNG'S
REG. U.S. PAT. OFF.

IMPROVED

RECTAL DILATORS

DIRECTIONS: To be used only by or on the prescription of a
physician.

NOTICE TO DEALER: Dr. Young's Rectal Dilators may be
sold only on prescription.

WARNING: Avoid using in case of bleeding since th...
indicate a serious condition. Avoid use...
sive force in the introduction of the i...

Manufactured Expressly for, and Distributed Solely b...

F. E. YOUNG & CO.

Grand Crossing   C...GO, U. S. A.

Roadside Oddities

Four and a half million people visit the Grand Canyon each year, astounded by the size of Arizona's most popular attraction. But how many have walked through the state's roadside rattlesnake, marveled at its towering Kokopelli, or tried to score a hole in one at a vintage outhouse?

While odd sights like these are fading away in much of the country, they appear to thrive in Arizona. Together with oddball museums, trees that sprout arrows, and wigwams for every purpose, such Copper State weirdness seems to have no end. Since the interstate highway system bypassed so many small-town throughways, many of these alternative attractions have become mere blurs in motorists' peripheral vision. These days, they're acknowledged mostly with an excited "What was that? Pull over! Pull over!" originating from the car's aft section, too often ignored by those up front.

This chapter, we hope, will pay tribute to these lonelier roadside wonders and perhaps encourage future adventurers to give in to those back-seat pleas. After all, the Grand Canyon can wait. It isn't getting any smaller.

Goodyear Giants

If you haven't taken Interstate 10 eastbound toward Phoenix before, get ready to do a double take as you pass through Goodyear. Just before reaching Cotton Lane, a startling vision will appear in your periphery from a field just off the highway: a giant, two-story baby playing with farm implements as though they were die-cast toys.

The infant's regular-sized mother, frying pan in hand, looks on in stern disapproval as her child plays Old MacDonald with a couple of very frightened farmers. One is frozen in disbelief from the seat of his tractor-cum-plaything as the other flees in terror. At a distance, the scene is astoundingly lifelike even though it lacks a third dimension, since the whole thing is made of plywood cutouts like some enormous pop-up book.

The display, erected in 1998, has been puzzling drivers for years. It looks kind of like an ad, but what is it advertising? Is it a warning to the locals concerning some kind of gene-altering nuclear radiation emitted from nearby Luke Air Force Base?

Actually, it has more to do with what's in the soil. Arnott and Kathleen Duncan, the vegetable barons of Duncan Family Farms, had the titanic toddler put there as a sort of promotion for their educational farm. In fact, they installed giant families all over the area. The couple admits, however, that the plywood people weren't put up so much for advertisement as amusement. In reference to the big baby, Arnott Duncan told a reporter, "It's not a billboard. It's just for fun."

The photorealistic cutouts are the work of West Coast artist John Cerney, whose unusual compositions adorn roadsides all over Monterey County, California. The Duncans, after seeing Cerney's work out west, asked him to create similar pieces for their business. The whimsical

creations were a perfect addition to the couple's petting zoo and pick-it-yourself farm, which thousands of kids visit each year.

Unfortunately, things lately seem to have taken a turn for the worse. The twenty-two-foot baby has escaped harm, but his life-size pals have suffered the loss of two heads, a leg, and, in Mom's case, an entire body. Plus, due to conflicts with Luke AFB (it turns out the Duncans' educational farmyard was in an "accident potential zone"), the farm had to be closed, so it's uncertain whether the damage to Cerney's characters will be repaired.

You have to admit, though, with a colossal mutant baby wielding his might over all the freshly mutilated bodies, the scene has adopted a far more interesting premise.

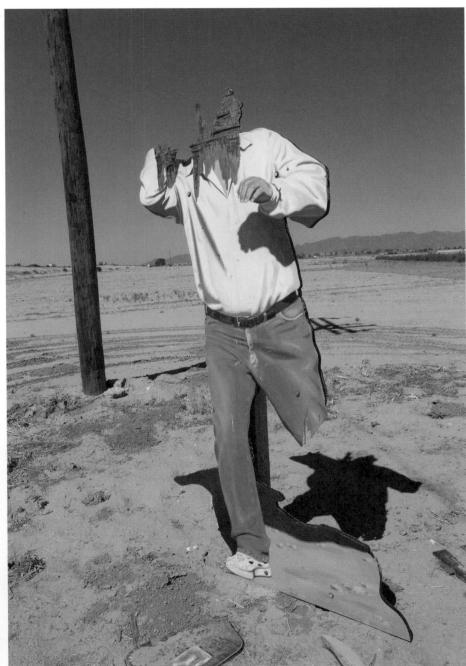

Hobo Joe

The biggest bum you could ever meet lives in Buckeye, just a few miles west of Phoenix. He hangs around in front of a fifty-year-old meat-packing plant where East Monroe Avenue joins North Apache Road, a quiet little corner that sees few visitors who aren't looking specifically for the drifter they've heard so much about. Drifter might not be the most appropriate word, however, seeing as he never drifts any farther than the concrete platform to which he's bolted.

Once characterized as a World Traveler, Philosopher, and Connoisseur of Good Food, Hobo Joe was the huckster for a chain of regional coffee shops that formerly bore his name. All the eateries are gone now, save for a re-creation in Cottonwood, so these days Joe is a derelict in both image and occupation. Just exactly how he got to Buckeye is a bit complicated.

The Hobo Joe's restaurants were a chain of popular diners that opened in the 1960s, each of which featured a statue of Hobo Joe. Most of the figures were only about five feet tall, though for three locations, larger versions towering about twenty-five feet were commissioned. Each location shared the same decor and served the same menu, which included items like the Hoboburger. Overall, it was a fun family dining experience. At least on the surface.

Underneath, Hobo Joe's was, in part, a scheme to filch money from a sizable bank loan. The lowdown tale is told in Michael Wendland's *The Arizona Project*, which details the investigations following the infamous 1976 car-bomb murder of *Arizona Republic* reporter Don Bolles. Seems the chain's owners brought an investment firm into the Hobo Joe's business, making the firm a partner in the company in exchange for its guaranteeing a $3 million bank loan. The loan was supposed to be paid off using restaurant profits, but at least one of the partners embezzled the money instead, leaving the investment firm stuck with the debt while the swindler built himself a pricey Phoenix home, as well as a posh duplex in Mesa intended for Mafia sex parties.

In the ensuing financial trouble, at least one of the aforementioned giant Joes was never paid for, and therefore never installed, before the chain went out of business. So, Marvin Ransdell, fiberglass expert and the man chosen to fabricate the larger statues, kept that Joe for himself and installed the big man atop his swimming-pool business. When he died, he left the big bum to his friends Ramon and Helen Gillum, who had stored the figure for him when Ransdell ran into his own financial problems. As a tribute to Joe's engineer, Ramon reassembled the giant vagabond on his property in Buckeye and installed a plaque at his feet:

> HOBO JOE
> built by and
> stands in memory of
> MARVIN RANSDELL
> (1928-1988)
> by
> his good friend
> RAMON GILLUM
> JULY, 1989

World's Largest Kokopelli

Who's the horn-blowin' cat with the rockin' mohawk? He's Kokopelli, and he's here to seed your tribe!

Despite the hunched back and the fact that he plays a flute instead of a guitar, Kokopelli is, at least in many Native American cultures, the guy who gets all the chicks. Or rather, he's the one who gets to decide when they're preggers.

Kokopelli is a fertility god who, like most fertility gods, umpires reproduction. The most impressive evidence of this deity dances high above exit 287 in Camp Verde. This is five and a half tons of steel god with a hairdo that tops him out at thirty-two feet.

The giant statue was built for the Krazy Kokopelli Trading Post, but the big man apparently did a better job of blowing his own horn than that of his proprietor, as the business no longer exists. It's been replaced with a string of storefronts capped by a Starbucks, whose sign now dwarfs the lemon-yellow spirit in the parking lot. Of course, if Starbucks is smart, they'll adopt him as their own spokesmodel and replace his flute with a grande Grande Macchiato.

Carefree Sundial

The controversy over what constitutes the World's Largest Sundial has, over the years, inspired heated debates and an unnecessary amount of mudslinging between the various pro-sundial factions. By what attributes should it be determined? The area of the face? The length of the gnomon? The height of the gnomon above the surface of the face? (*Gnomon*, incidentally, is Latin for "the pointy bit.")

When K. T. Palmer sought to create a fresh townscape north of Phoenix in the 1950s called Carefree, he couldn't have imagined the clash of trivia in which his new burg would become entangled. He simply wanted to erect an eye-catching centerpiece that would grab the attention of potential residents and entrepreneurs. His plan: Build the largest sundial ever seen by man.

John Yellot was commissioned to make the idea a reality and quickly learned that India was home to a sundial almost one hundred and fifty feet long, much larger than Carefree had the means to construct. Nevertheless, the decision was made to forge ahead.

Completed in 1959, the attraction was launched as the World's Second Largest Sundial at sixty-two feet long and thirty-five feet high, with a base ninety feet in diameter. Perhaps to make up for its number two status, it was enhanced with a special energy-conserving feature: A building across the street made use of the dial's copper skin and radiation-absorbing paint to heat water. Unfortunately for the status seekers, the concept was found to be inefficient and was later abandoned.

Following its initial defeat in seizing the rank of World's Largest, the dial continued to suffer from a relentless series of titular qualifiers. As the debate over sundial supremacy carried on, Carefree's instrument soon dropped down the list to become the Largest Sundial in the Western Hemisphere. Then others entered the fray: Florida, Canada, and Sweden each built its own enormous dial. Carefree's was redesignated the Largest Sundial of Its Kind in the Western Hemisphere or, sometimes, the Largest Horizontal Sundial.

These days, not even Carefree can decide what it's got. The town's official Web site calls it the Second Largest Sundial in North America. The chamber of commerce site uses the long-winded designation Third Largest Working Sundial in the Western Hemisphere.

So where does that leave Carefree? It's hard to say. Many argue, somewhat predictably, that size doesn't matter—only the instrument's accuracy makes a difference. But nobody takes a picture of the family standing next to an attraction because it's easy to set your watch by.

For now, we'll just go by what the plaque says: CAREFREE SUNDIAL.

Biting Bridge of Tucson

There is a truly unique structure near downtown Tucson that has a fierce glare and a mean bite—Rattlesnake Bridge. It's a pedestrian bridge that spans across Broadway, which is the street leading to downtown. Its red eyes light up, and its tail rattles when you exit through its rear. It also lights up at night. It was built in 2002 and managed to win an award from the Federal Highway Administration for excellence in design that same year. I have been to the snake once with my dad, and it really is impressive!—*Peter Baskerville*

Diamondback Bridge

Across the treacherous, six-lane span of East Broadway in Tucson slithers the world's lengthiest snake. He's a western diamondback rattler measuring 280 feet, and he's got to be the coolest pedestrian bridge in America. Like a big tattoo on the arm of the city, he's burly and intimidating. And at the same time, comical. Watching a Spandex-clad cyclist roll into his mouth is hilarious. Seeing him come out the other end is even funnier.

The diamondback hangs seventeen feet in the air and measures eleven feet high by fourteen feet wide. He's got a twenty-eight-foot-tall, 34,000-pound head adorned with bulletproof-polymer eyes that glow red in the night. His tail reaches twenty feet high and is topped by a 300-pound fiberglass rattle. The sidewalk leading from his mouth forms the shape of a forked tongue. A motion sensor at his south end detects passersby and, when it's working, emits an aggressive rattling sound. From below, however, all his fearsomeness

Pedestrians exiting the snake's south end are greeted by his twenty-foot-tall tail.

has been lost by badly planned landscaping that now obscures all but his midsection.

Still, he measures seventy times the size of his real-life brethren. That means, all things being equal, his poison glands would store six to seven fluid ounces of venom. And while half a beer can doesn't sound like much, that's enough to kill more than four hundred full-grown men. That is, if the eleven-foot fang bite doesn't do the job first.

For some time, even before its completion, Diamondback Bridge was ridiculed as a "bridge to nowhere." Though the overpass makes it infinitely safer to cross Broadway, pedestrians end up trapped between two more roads on the other side. The plan, however, is to build six more bridges to complete a contiguous bike trail. Unfortunately, they won't all be rattlesnakes.

Next on the list? The Basket Bridge. No kidding.

HERE IT IS!

Most trading posts try to bait drivers off the highway with phrases like Sand Paintings—Buy Direct, or Indian Jewelry—Stop and See! Then one day your windshield frames a more unusual invitation: RIDE THE RABBIT.

It's a proposal you probably never considered before. Should you decline, you at least have to know what it means. The only way to find out is to pull off Interstate 40 at exit 269, then just swing over to an old ribbon of Route 66, and look for the sign that says, HERE IT IS! It's a rabbit, all right. And yes, he's wearing a saddle. Welcome to the Jack Rabbit Trading Post!

It's a gimmick that's worked for nearly sixty years now. The outpost was opened in 1949 by James Taylor—an entrepreneur, not the singer-songwriter of bittersweet folk rock—during the heyday of Route 66 (also known as the Mother Road). Taylor bought out a snake farm in Joseph City, remodeled the building, and, much to the locals' distress, let all the snakes loose. (Another source says it was simply a Santa Fe Railroad building, but the snake story is more interesting.)

To pull in shoppers, Taylor put up signs for miles along the highway. The signs said very little, but featured an intriguing, though small, iconic hare. As drivers closed in on the trading post, the hare grew larger, eventually reaching the size of a full billboard. Then that climactic phrase HERE IT IS!

When drivers stopped, they discovered a mechanical version of a jack rabbit similar to the creature on the billboards. It was just big enough to sit on, so visitors adopted the practice of photographing each other while riding it. Eventually, they wore him out, and he had to be replaced in the mid-'80s with the version seen today.

The big sign across the road, however, remains the same. Although most of Taylor's roadside billboards are long gone, the two-sided HERE IT IS! stands as it has since 1949. It has to be repainted every few years, but almost all of it is original. Today, it's arguably the most recognizable Route 66 sign in existence. In fact, the trading post sells more souvenirs sporting images of the sign than it does of the Jack Rab.

Longhorn Grill—Steer on Over

The largest bovine skull in the world measures about fifteen feet tall, with horns that spread an estimated forty-five feet tip to tip. It serves as the entrance to a restaurant in Amado, about thirty-five miles south of Tucson. Patrons enter through the longhorn's nasal cavity.

It dates back to the early 1970s, possibly late '60s, but no one in Amado seems to know who built it. Other sources report it's the work of an artist named Michael Kautza, the same man, they say, who built the thirty-five-foot-tall wine bottle at the Boondocks Lounge in Tucson, as well as the giant cowboy boot at the now defunct Tack Room restaurant, once located on Sabino Canyon Road, a half mile north of Tanque Verde Road.

The building, just west of Interstate 19 at exit 48, has reportedly served, among other things, as a bar, a produce stand, a tackle shop, a graphic-design studio, and a boat rental with man-made ponds. It's also served as a movie set, making appearances in *Alice Doesn't Live Here Anymore* and *Boys on the Side*. Today, it's the Longhorn Grill, perhaps the only place on earth where you can eat a steer while sitting inside one.

Geronimo's Castle

We caught up with the family that ran the Corner Store in Bowie just as they were hanging out the CLOSED sign for the last time. The store was going out of business. It was a familiar sight in these parts. As the proprietor put it, "When the freeway went around, well, nothing comes into Bowie anymore."

Oh, sure, Bowie still gets visitors, but they don't stay long enough to have a meal or buy much. They just pause to take a picture of the giant teepee and move on. And that's why the giant teepee is closed too.

When asked about the teepee, the most the Corner Store owner could say was, "It's been here forever" and "It was a bar," though the bar part was pretty evident from the big, block-letter BEER signs that flanked the front door in earlier photographs. A little more research into the matter, however, revealed that the big wigwam, or "bigwam" if you will, was built back in the early to mid-1940s. It stands about thirty feet tall and is likely one of very few tents in history to have both a second floor and a basement. It was originally called Geronimo's Castle and served as a filling station, a restaurant, a bar, and a curio shop, as well as the local Greyhound bus depot. Its postcards, now rare, welcomed recipients to "Stop in for a bottle of beer!"

For some time, the castle's claim to fame was the fact that it was alleged to have been built on the very site where Apache renegade Geronimo surrendered to the U.S. Army. This, of course, was a complete fabrication, as Geronimo surrendered a good sixty miles away in a canyon near the New Mexico border. Apparently, in those days, a hook was more important than historical accuracy. In more recent years, Geronimo's Castle has been known simply as the Teepee Cafe and Bar.

The establishment has changed ownership a few times in the course of its life, going out of business sporadically, as it did around 2004. Sadly, the teepee remains closed as of this writing, and its owner fears it may be a while before it opens again, if it ever does. In the meantime, one of the Buddhists from nearby Diamond Mountain is using it as a workshop.

Wigwam Village No. 6

Being an avid roadside enthusiast, which we assume you are, you're probably used to staying in the usual highway hostels night after night, all virtually identical, with the same little soaps and the same hideous bedspreads. Those places are all right if you're just looking for a place to snooze and shower, but why should you have to put the road trip on hold just because you need to sleep?

Ask yourself, "Have you slept in a wigwam lately?" No? Then stop at the Wigwam Motel in Holbrook and check yourself into a teepee!

This distinctive inn, decades old, is one of only three of its kind still standing. Originating in Kentucky, Wigwam Village was conceived and patented in the mid-'30s by Frank Redford, an entrepreneur who built two of his motor courts before lending the design to others across the country. Seven were built in all.

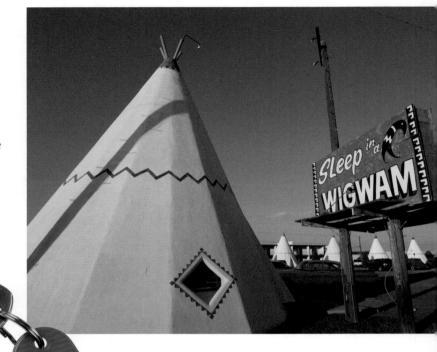

The Holbrook location, number six, was opened in 1950 by a man named Chester Lewis, who agreed to pay Mr. Redford all the dimes from each of the fifteen teepees' coin-operated radios in exchange for use of his design. Chester's son John, whose job it was as a kid to collect the dimes, and daughter Elinor, run the establishment today. Though it was closed in 1974 after Interstate 40 bypassed Holbrook, it remained in the Lewis family and was reopened in 1988.

Like the other Wigwam Villages, Lewis's originally featured a much larger, central teepee as its office. Unfortunately, pressure from Texaco forced him to tear it down years ago, as the franchise station he appended out front wasn't selling enough gas to make the suits happy. The problem was, in order to take pictures of the big building, drivers always stopped on the OTHER side of the road. So in 1957, Lewis reluctantly replaced that teepee with the ordinary office seen today, after which sales surprisingly boomed. Other than that, the motor court appears as it has for nearly sixty years, right down to the original hickory furniture.

The teepee fills up nearly every night, and John says people come in all the time and share their memories of the place from as long as fifty years ago. One of his best stories came from a woman who visited in 1952 when she was only four. She was asleep in the back seat of her parents' car when they stopped at the Wigwam Village. When she woke up and saw the teepees all around her, she thought her family had been captured by Indians.

Clifton's Cliff Jail

Clifton was the first of three towns, the others being Morenci and Metcalf, to develop in the same general spot after copper was discovered in the area in the 1860s. As mining intensified, Morenci and Metcalf were swallowed up, almost literally, by the expanding open-pit mine. A new Morenci has since emerged, but the only thing remaining of the original development is Clifton. Sadly, after both a labor strike and a severe flood in the 1980s, even Clifton has become practically a ghost town, although oddly enough, it's still the county seat.

Yet it does have at least one attraction of note: its jail. A late-nineteenth-century town filled with rough and rowdy diggers, Clifton quickly found the need to construct some sort of detention facility. So, the Lesinsky brothers, who owned the mines, hired Margarito Verala to build one.

As the town's name suggests, there's an abundance of vertical terrain in Clifton. Even the local cemetery is situated on a precipitous slope. So it only made sense to take advantage of the topography whenever possible. Doing just that, Verala bored directly into the side of a cliff, carving out two cells sharing one grated door and one narrow grated window. It was not much more than a hollow drilled into solid rock, and legend has it that no one ever escaped.

We don't know everyone who was locked up in the Cliff Jail, but it's pretty clear who christened it. As the

story goes, a local man had recently completed work on an arduous contract job. Having received payment for his hard work, he decided to hit the dance hall and get juiced. Well, the laborer let his celebration get just a touch out of hand and started shooting up the place. He was promptly arrested, dragged to the rock face, and tossed into the newly finished clink. Margarito Verala, the man who had built the jail, was the first to be locked inside it.

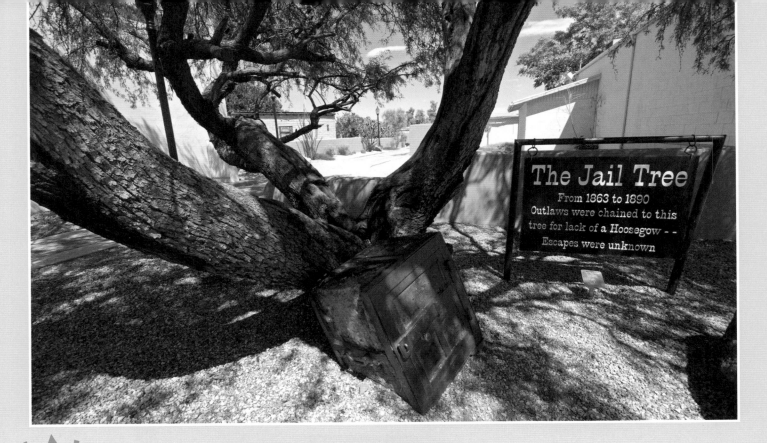

The Jail Tree

From 1863 to 1890
Outlaws were chained to this
tree for lack of a Hoosegow --
Escapes were unknown

Wickenburg's Jail Tree

If you head, as the brochures pithily recommend, "Out Wickenburg Way," you'll find a nice photo opportunity in the town's much advertised Jail Tree. It's a two-hundred-year-old mesquite, tucked absentmindedly behind a Circle K near the corner of Tegner Street and Wickenburg Way.

According to legend, and the tree's metal sign, the ancient mesquite served as Wickenburg's "hoosegow" from 1863 up until 1890, when the town finally got itself a real jailhouse. Myth has it that convicts were sentenced to the tree and chained there until they either died from exposure or, if lucky, they completed their stretch. But, in truth, the tree was simply a holding facility. Offenders were shackled or tied to the tree only until a Phoenix lawman could make it up that way to retrieve them. Still, according to Wickenburg's chamber of commerce, this could be anywhere from two to five days. At least they had some shade.

An e-mail from a woman who claims to have been a resident of Wickenburg in the early 1930s, however, insists that it's all just a tall tale told to the kids. (Likely followed by "and if you don't start doing what you're told, we'll walk right over to that tree. . . .") She added that the shackles were introduced in more recent years to legitimize it as a tourist attraction.

Yet the history books suggest that the legend is true and that whatever shackles were added later were probably new ones to replace the long-gone originals. Either way, the new set appears to be gone too, replaced by an antique strongbox, placed there for mystifying reasons after it was donated to the city.

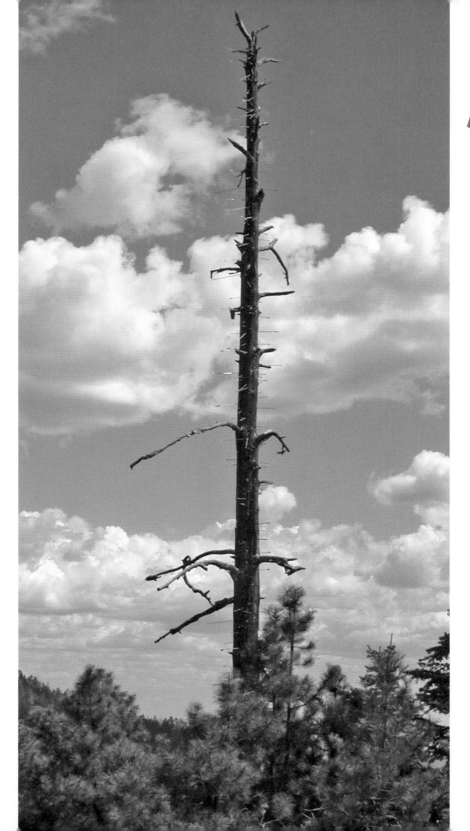

Alpine's Arrow Tree

Just off the Coronado Trail, south of Alpine, there's a tall dead tree that's become a real sticking point for archers. The tree is filled, at least along one side, with dozens and dozens of arrows. One count places the total at around two hundred and fifty.

Nobody seems sure of the point, so to speak, but there are a few theories. Some believe the tree is a sort of good-luck charm, whereby hunters land one in the trunk before a hunt. Others think it's just the result of a drunken round of "Who can stick it the highest?" Similarly, the tree may have been the target of Boy Scouts participating in a game supposedly played by Native Americans, the goal being to knock others' arrows off the tree with your own. From the evidence, the Scouts weren't very good at it.

Of course, with no way to ask the original marksmen, the answer is left to the imagination. Perhaps a wounded hunter was trying to gain the attention of rescuers with the two gross of arrows he just happened to be lugging around. Or could the tree have been alive when it all started, slain by some lost, delirious huntsman driven to dendrophobia—the fear of trees? Or maybe, just maybe, the Arrow Tree is just that—a rare and magical arrow tree.

Track it down and come up with your own hypothesis. You can find it along U.S. 191 near mile marker 223, a couple of miles south of the Blue Vista Overlook.

Titan Missile Museum, Sahuarita

For twenty-four years, an arsenal of eighteen Titan II ICBMs sandwiched the city of Tucson, nine to the north and nine to the south, each awaiting its order to launch. Had the cold war ever come to a head and the missiles been sent to their targets, the Old Pueblo sky would have lit up like a terrifying Fourth of July celebration.

As the world well knows, those orders never came. So the whole lot, including the other thirty-six in Kansas and Arkansas, were thankfully deactivated by June of 1987, ending the threat of nuclear annihilation—unless you count America's stockpile of nearly ten thousand warheads and the five hundred Minuteman bunkers currently deployed in the north.

However, to commemorate Arizona's role in mutually assured destruction, a single Titan II silo was allowed to escape demolition. While other sites were gutted, backfilled, and sealed, site 571-7 in Sahuarita was adopted as part of the Pima Air and Space Museum and opened to the public as the only museum of its kind in the world.

Located off exit 69, just twenty miles down Interstate 19 from Tucson, the Titan Missile Museum allows visitors

For twenty-four years, an arsenal of eighteen Titan II ICBMs sandwiched the city of Tucson . . . , each awaiting its order to launch.

to tour an area which, twenty years ago, they would've been shot on sight for entering. Volunteer guides lead tours three stories underground through an access hatch, then past six-thousand-pound blast doors to the control center, where four-man crews once worked around the clock for more than two decades. There, you get to play witness to the chilling procedure no crew member ever completed, in which authentication codes are retrieved from the red emergency war order safe, launch orders are confirmed, and the two launch keys are inserted and turned simultaneously, just like they do in the opening scene of *WarGames*. If you're lucky, you may even get to be one of the guys who turn the keys.

On the surface, or "topside" as they say here, you can stare down the barrel of the big gun, which houses an actual Titan II delivery vehicle. This particular missile was used only as part of a training facility and never carried a real payload.

The Titan II carried the most powerful nuclear weapon ever deployed. The warhead that topped each of the rockets had a yield of nine megatons, about thirty times the destructive energy of the deadliest warhead in service today. To put that into perspective, if a nuclear explosion on the order of only one megaton—a fraction

of Titan II's capability—were to occur above Tucson's city hall, it would produce a crater one thousand feet in diameter, obliterate nearly everything in a circle reaching from Grant Road to 29th Street, and whisk away any residential buildings for another mile beyond that. Plus, given the right wind conditions, radiation would kill everyone from Tucson to Nogales within two weeks.

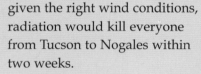

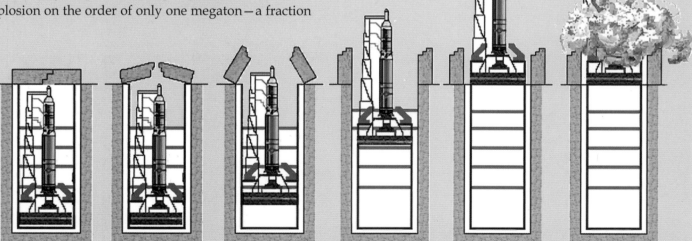

Finger Rock

The southwestern environment is often severe, cruel, and unforgiving. But does it have to be vulgar too? I mean, we all receive enough obscene gestures on the road without getting them from the landscape. But that's exactly what drivers have reported seeing as they drive east out of Laughlin.

Up Union Pass along Arizona 68, an unmistakably digital formation rises into view, as if flipping an enormous bird to all Kingman-bound traffic. Perhaps it's earth's response to the increasing number of cars stinking up the air or the urban development metastasizing across some of the most magnificent terrain in the country—a one-finger salute to the golf courses and swimming pools climbing up every butte.

Many of the locals have admitted they can't help but snicker at the giant *digitus impudicus* every time they see it. They've even started calling it Finger Rock. Considering what else it could resemble, though, that's probably the least offensive name they could give it.

Rocky the Frog

Directly in front of you, as you head up Highway 89 out of Congress, you may catch a rather stone-faced amphibian in your field of view. He sits perched atop a hill, waiting patiently for the occasional fly or, perhaps, Volkswagen Beetle.

Bright green and spotted, the enormous frog has sat there since the 1920s, when there wasn't much more to do in the area than there is today. It was the inspiration of Sara Perkins, a legislator's wife, and her two boys, who were the original artists to clamber up the hill and decorate the sixty-ton rock.

At the time, Highway 89, which passes within tongue's reach of the big guy, was the major route between Phoenix and Prescott. The enormous greenback proved to be a popular roadside diversion in an otherwise desolate area—much to the benefit of the Perkins family, who owned a nearby service station and tourist attraction they called the Arrowhead.

Years later the lovable amphibian still crouches above 89, as bright as ever. He's become a sort of community project and local mascot. After all the Perkinses had either, er, croaked or moved away, custodial duties were assumed by a succession of locals daring enough to perform touch-ups. The most recent was Rose Mary Goodson, an artist who, even at seventy-six, would schlep an extension ladder and three gallons of paint up the craggy incline. Hey, it ain't easy being green.

The Arrowhead still exists as well, although now it's a bar and steakhouse. The staff, who continue to field questions about the frog, sort of half agree his name is Rocky and will sell you a frog-adorned T-shirt if you ask. If you're interested, the place is just a hop, skip, and jump across the highway. Careful crossing over, though, lest you be squashed, frogger-style.

Skull Rock

At its best, Date Creek Road, which connects Congress with the ghost town of Hillside, is an experience in vehicular convulsion. Devil trucks barrel down the road, with no hesitation about running you and your pristine paint job off into the thorny brush. But should you find reason to brave the drive up this way, you may come across what might be the world's largest phrenology bust. It's a huge skull-shaped boulder, whitewashed and detailed with eye sockets and a ghastly grin.

Information on the behemoth braincase is virtually nonexistent, but what little history there is suggests that it was painted somewhere around 1900. It's reportedly the work of a railroad crew whose job it was to maintain the signposts down this stretch of track. Along the way, they thought it would be funny to scare the heebies out of Santa Fe passengers coming round the bend.

The passenger lines no longer roll this way, but the big noggin remains after more than a century. Though menacing as ever, Skull Rock is a practical joke that has lost all practicality.

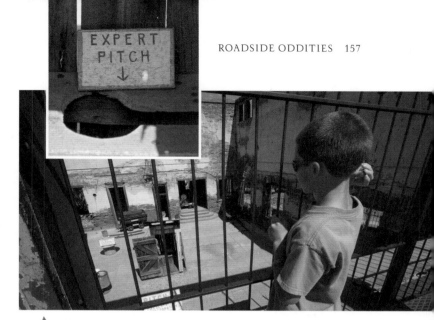

Wishing Outhouse

As with any other tourist trap on a busy day, the town of Jerome typically sees a row of tourists all lined up, anxious to hit the toilet. Except here, they all try to hit it at once and from yards away.

They're aiming for a vintage outhouse, which sits at basement level on the site of the old Bartlett Hotel. Visitors toss coins, mostly pennies, trying their best to hit a hole in one.

The Bartlett is now just a shell, most of its materials having been sold for scrap, after it and several other buildings became unstable in the 1930s and started sliding downhill. But that's the reason for the coin commode. The Jerome Historical Society collects all the pitched pennies for restoration efforts—a former copper-mining town digging for copper the modern way.

Some tourists toss not just pennies, but nickels and dimes. Most go for accuracy, flinging one at a time, but some play the odds and hurl entire handfuls. A few high rollers even chuck in dollar bills, either folded into paper airplanes or, sometimes, tied to rocks. By the end of each month, Jerome collects about $1,000, all money down the toilet.

Flintstones Bedrock City

Arizona is an amateur archaeologist's dream, rife with ancient cliff dwellings and petroglyphs left here by some of America's earliest clans. For the avid prehistorian, this is the place to spend your summer. But if your interests lie with less archaic American history, Arizona still has the ruins of a more modern Stone Age family in Flintstones Bedrock City.

Located about half an hour south of the Grand Canyon, where Highway 180 meets 64 in Valle, this often lonely attraction is a wonderland for those of us who grew up in the '60s and '70s, especially those who adore a nice cheesy roadside stop. In two pathetically punful words: It rocks.

Take a tram ride through a forty-foot volcano or crawl through the dark belly of a giant prehistoric snake. Have a Bronto Burger at Fred's Diner, then witness some of your hosts' cartoon misadventures at the Bedrock Theater. Of course, don't forget to slide down the tail of Slate Rock and Gravel's big, green brontosaurus and belt out a hearty "Yabba-dabba-doo!"

Mostly, you'll have a gay old time exploring Bedrock's faux-stone buildings. There are the Flintstones' and Rubbles' houses, of course, as well as a post office, beauty parlor, gas station, and police station with jail, among others. All the details are there: saber-toothed tiger–hide bedspreads, a pterodactyl record player, and pet dinosaurs. At the general store, you can pick up some dinosaur ribs and comically large watermelon slices for dinner. Outside see if you can kick-start one of the scattered foot-powered vehicles.

Bedrock City has been around since Francis Speckels, son of an investor in a similar park in South Dakota, built the place with his family in 1972. And, although the park recently replaced its somewhat homely statues of the show's main characters with glossy new fiberglass versions, tourists report that the place is starting to show its age, suffering from entropy and a touch of graffiti. Evidently, the statues' prerecorded voices no longer work, dust covers every-

thing, and building corners are starting to crumble. But most seem to agree that the subtle hints of disintegration add to the park's fantastic weirdness.

Me, I'm waiting for somebody to open Jetsons Orbit City.

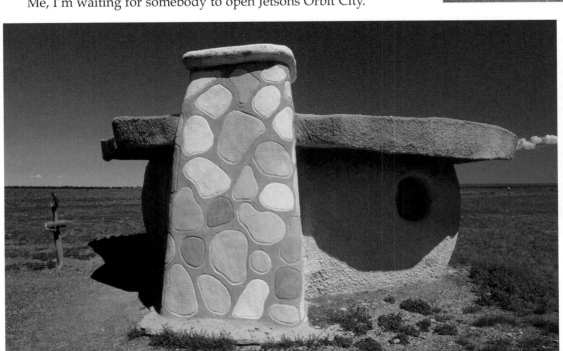

This often lonely attraction is a wonderland for those of us who grew up in the '60s and '70s, especially those who adore a nice cheesy roadside stop.

Dinosaurs of Holbrook

If your inner child still digs the dinosaurs, plan a Saturday to hit Holbrook. These big lizards have taken over the town like they took over that island in the second *Jurassic Park* movie. To find them, just toss your copy of *Weird Arizona* in your navigator's lap and follow along.

Your first stop is the Rainbow Rock Shop at 101 North Navajo Boulevard. The yard out front contains one of the most impressive and most recognized collections of roadside dinosaurs on Route 66. More than a dozen in all, they tower up to twenty-nine feet in height. The smallest,

Petrified Rock Garden dinosaur

three little brontosaurs about four feet long, huddle in the shade under Mama's belly.

They were all handmade by the shop's owner, Adam Luna. He formed his first steel-and-concrete dinosaur in 1987, continuing to add to the family for, by his estimation, the next eight years. He ended up with mostly nonthreatening herbivores, but a couple of fierce meat eaters made it into the menagerie, as well.

For the sake of the kids, Luna tried to make them all friendly. "I don't like for them to be mean, you know what I mean?" he says. There are already enough things, he adds, that aren't positive for children. That's why most of them have smiles. Except for the *T. rex*. "The *T. rex* has a lizard in his mouth," he explains. "You know, he's ready to eat him. But he doesn't look mean, you know?" Not unless you're a lizard.

Just one block north, at Hopi Drive, a more lonesome, and more ferocious, dinosaur snarls at cars passing his home at Living West Park. His irritable demeanor remains unexplained but could stem from his origins in New York. That's where the Lundeen family purchased him for their house in Fountain Hills, where they intended to hook him up to a water pipe and use him as a poolside shower.

Unfortunately, his five tons turned out to be too much to lift into the backyard, so they donated him to the city of Holbrook. The city has given no formal name to the bronze beast, so we'll give him one now: the Lundeenodon. It's official now.

Denizens of the
Rainbow Rock Shop

Damsel in distress at Stewart's Petrified Wood

Next on your safari is the Petrified Rock Garden, another rock shop, just up the road where Navajo Boulevard meets California Street. Two reptiles guard what appears to be a former gas station, as well as all the geodes and petrified wood it now contains.

One, some breed of velociraptor, bares his teeth to potential trespassers, hoping they won't notice the embarrassing trailer he's fastened to, or its flat tire. The other, more primitive, looks like an early model of Godzilla doing the pee-pee dance. Though both do their best to look menacing, they have trouble scaring even the birds, which have made nests in the creatures' mouths.

Next, head east along Interstate 40 to exit 292, where you'll discover the real meat of the collection. Along the way, just off the highway you may spot a few ferocious creatures, which are all part of this stop, the combination Museum of the Americas, International Petrified Forest, and Marion Hatch Dinosaur Park.

It's the realization of a boyhood dream for Terrence Reidhead and Marvin Hatch, longtime friends and avid collectors of antiquity. They've assembled a large collection of fossils and Native American artifacts, which they put on display here at their museum.

Plus, out back they've opened six thousand acres to the public, where you can drive a 3.5-mile tour to see live buffalo, petrified wood, and, of course, some fourteen life-size dinosaur statues. You can see them all from your car or get out and view them up close. Rumor is that more are on the way.

The most bizarre beasties, though, are a bit farther east at exit 303. Charles and Gazell Stewart run Stewart's Petrified Wood, which draws inquisitive visitors with their ads for free hunks of petrified wood and, of course, their array of comical dinosaurs. These guys are possibly the most attention-getting in the entire tour, what with their cartoonlike composition and crayon-palette

Many of the life-size terrors at Marion Hatch Dinosaur Park, like the giant T-rex protecting his pea-green kill are viewable from I-40.

skin. The whole layout is like a 3-D interpretation of something a six-year-old would draw—except, of course, for the bevy of half-naked mannequins looking on as their sisters get eaten.

Though they might technically count as dinosaurs only because they couldn't be classified as anything else, the Stewarts' reptiles are just so strange that, out of all the dinos in Holbrook, theirs would have to win the Weird Award. If only one existed.

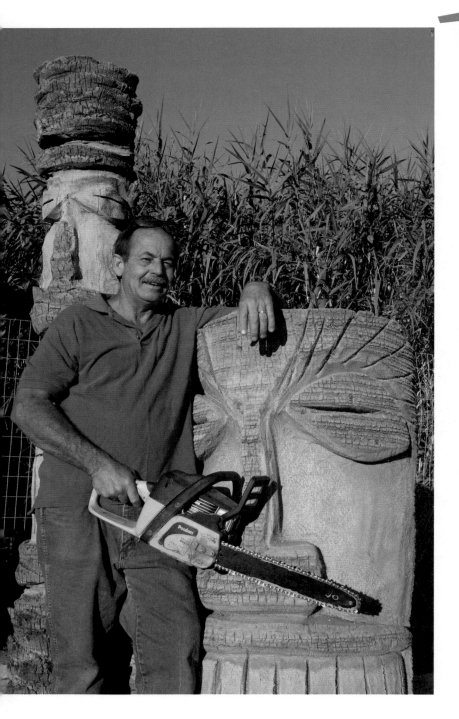

Tiki Gods of Wickenburg

America's zeal for Polynesian pop may have faded with the passing of the 1960s, when sobering swingers traded in their bamboo torches and backyard huts for lava lamps and bubble chairs, but one man is determined to reignite the mai tai culture in the twenty-first century. His role in the resurgence? Repopulate the desert with that amusingly gruesome idol of the South Seas, the tiki.

His headquarters, of all places, lies at the side of U.S. 60 in front of a Wickenburg trailer court, two and one-half miles south of the Hassayampa River. That's where Richard Cleghorn, working exclusively with a chain saw, feverishly carves out as many island statues as people will carry away. And they move pretty fast. Arizonans on their way to and from Las Vegas spot his operation alongside the highway and are hit with tiki fever. They can't help but buy one or two and toss them into the back of their SUVs before moving on.

In the beginning, his merchandise was mostly animal carvings. "The first year, I sold more pink flamingos than I did anything," Richard recalls. He still makes those too, but the tikis have become his signature item. Those menacing grins have charmed the drive-by public like a basket of free puppies.

The cab driver turned artist developed his gift with the help of his nephew, an accomplished woodworker from West Virginia, who briefly set up shop in nearby Wittman.

"When my nephew came, it was like a godsend," Richard says. He was worn out from the daily grind and trying to keep his ranch from falling into the bank's hands. The tikis provided the way out. He and his wife, Kay, gave everything up and started over, establishing R&K Chainsaw Carvins. It was a

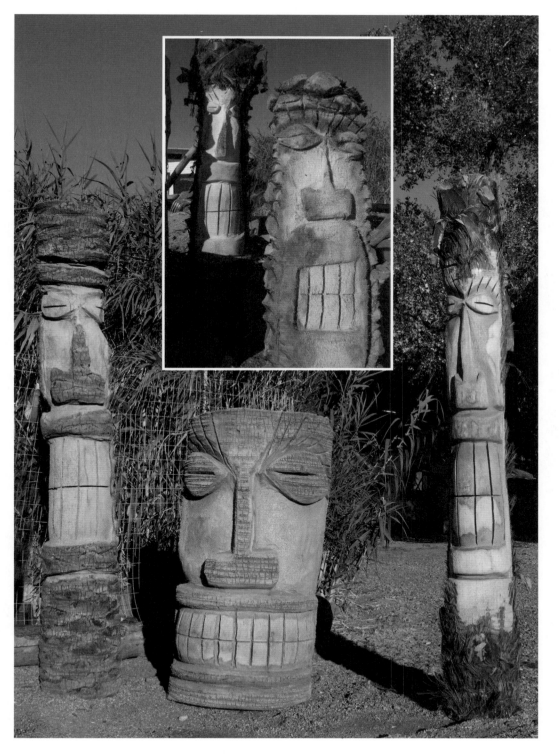

challenge at first, Richard admits, "My first coyote looked like an alien." But, he and Kay, who does all the painting, were soon making a living at it. Richard actually hoped the new vocation would allow him to take it easy for a while and recoup from the rat race, but the tikis had other plans. The business became a bigger success than anticipated. "People have tried to get me to go on the Internet," he says, "but it took me a year and a half [just] to get a phone again. You know what I mean? I drove a cab in Phoenix. That was nuts!" His creative outlet has since revived him, and now he's decorating high-dollar resorts and crafting custom poolside motifs with tikis squirting water out their mouths. People just can't seem to get enough of these palm-wood deities carved in the Arizona sun.

Fort Yellowhorse

When you head west along Interstate 40 into Arizona, Juan Yellowhorse's place is the first one you come to. It's hard to miss with its huge wooden fort and towering yellow letters. Of course, that's the whole idea, to catch your attention. Fort Yellowhorse was built to sell you stuff, and for decades, Juan was a master at doing just that.

He began trading in these parts when he was merely a child. It was in his blood. Juan's grandfather, William Beasley, made a living selling furs and supplying local zoos with horse meat. His son Arthur ran moonshine until Prohibition ended, then hit the jackpot selling petrified wood to tourists.

Arthur later built his own trading post, called Wonderview, which he ran with the help of his four sons, including Juan.

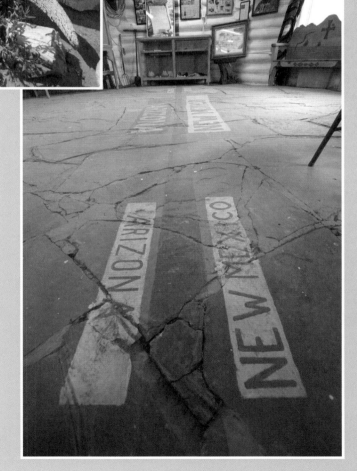

Juan, whom everyone simply called "the Chief," took over Wonderview after his father died. Then, in 1965, he had an opportunity to buy the Cave of the Seven Devils, an enormous cliff-side hollow. The Chief purchased the site, took his mother's Navajo name, and redubbed the cave Fort Yellowhorse.

The establishment, set against a striking backdrop decorated with colorful teepees and plywood buffalo cutouts, was a tourist magnet. Visitors couldn't help but pull off Route 66 into the Chief's parking lot to see what he had to offer. CHIEF YELLOWHORSE LOVES YOU his billboards said. WE TAKE-UM MASTERCARD. Kids scrambled to see the live buffalo that lived inside the cave and convinced their parents, with the Chief's help, to buy a few genuine Indian souvenirs before setting back off down the road.

One of the Chief's favorite additions was a fat red stripe he painted right down the wall of his trading post and across the floor, allegedly marking the Arizona-New Mexico state line. When a visitor would point out a sign down the road and imply that the border ran in another direction, the Chief would pause and reply, "It makes a little jog right here."

Chief Yellowhorse passed away in 1999, but left long-lasting memories with those who met him. According to his sons, who now run the place in his stead, people still come by and ask, "So, where's the Chief?"

Roads Less Traveled

For most of us, piling into a car with friends and taking off for some deserted road with a bad reputation is a rite of passage—or at least a good way to kill a Saturday night. Rumors of things like a demon-possessed bus terrorizing motorists or a man-eating vapor lurking along some dusty byway have enticed adventuresome drivers since we first put our pedals to the metal.

In our minds, we know the stories are probably just fabrications inspired by someone's overactive imagination. Yet something draws us to Arizona's foreboding roadways again and again. Is it a genuine desire to find out if there may be some truth to these legends? Or is it just a good way to get your terrified girlfriend to cuddle closer? It's hard to say, but it's probably a good idea to lock the doors and roll up the windows, anyway. Just in case.

Route 666: The Highway to Hell

You would think our nation's highway planners would know enough to avoid naming any road Route 666, the sign of the Antichrist. You would think wrong. There used to be a Route 666, the sixth branch of the long-gone Route 66, which once ran through four states in the west. It was 605 miles at its longest and zigzagged its way from Utah down through Colorado and New Mexico, hellbound to its southernmost terminus in Douglas, Arizona. In recent years, the triple-6 designation has sadly been eliminated, although nefarious happenings still occur along what locals have dubbed the Devil's Highway.

One enduring legend of Route 666 speaks of a young girl in a white dress who wanders along the desolate dark road in the middle of the night. Since there is nothing around for miles, most motorists who see the girl attempt to stop and offer help. Invariably, when they do, she disappears into the thin air of the night.

More malevolent spirits of the road will go so far as to climb into your car with you. It's said that Native American shape-shifters, known as skinwalkers, terrorize motorists along Route 666. They first appear as various animals in front of moving vehicles, hoping to cause drivers to swerve and crash. If this does not work, they appear in the back seat of the car, attempting to steal passengers' souls.

Linda Dunning, author of *Specters in Doorways: The History and Hauntings of Utah,* tells of an experience her husband had on this treacherous road. He was driving alone on Route 666 one night when suddenly "he saw a truck that looked like it was on fire heading straight for him, right down the middle of the highway. The truck was going so fast that sparks were flying up off the wheels and flames were coming from the smokestack." He estimated that the vehicle was traveling 130 mph.

He pulled off the road and fled into the desert until the imposing, flaming apparition passed him by.

According to Linda, the mad trucker is not the only thing one should be wary of while traversing this cursed ribbon of asphalt. She says, "Packs of demon dogs have been seen on this highway as well. They attack at night with yellow eyes and sharp teeth, shredding the tires of those silly enough to stop along this highway at night. There are many other tales of people who either disappear along this route or suddenly appear out of nowhere. There are even tales of the same person, disappearing at one point along the highway and then reappearing at another location miles away, without having any recollection of where they have been or what they have been doing."

After much public pressure, all branches of U.S. 666 have been rechristened with different numerical designations. In their petition to federal officials, the states included the following justifications for changing the road's name:

WHEREAS, people living near the road already live under the cloud of opprobrium created by having a road that many believe is cursed running near their homes and through their homeland; and

WHEREAS, the number "666" carries the stigma of being the mark of the beast, the mark of the devil, which was described in the book of Revelations in the Bible; and

WHEREAS, there are people who refuse to travel the road, not because of the issue of safety, but because of the fear that the devil controls events along United States route 666; and

WHEREAS, the economy in the area is greatly depressed when compared with many parts of the United States, and the infamy brought by the inopportune naming of the road will only make development in the area more difficult.

In 1992, Arizona's segment was the first to go, becoming an extension to U.S. 191. The remaining three states followed suit in 2003, renaming their segments U.S. 491. The new designations haven't stopped the strange incidents from happening on the road, however, nor have they stopped people from telling stories about it.

"Drive Route 666 at night, and you drive at your own risk," warns Linda Dunning. "Even in the daytime some of the long, deserted stretches are enough to frighten drivers, or at least put them to sleep, which is just as dangerous as seeing anything. Take a lot of people with you and don't leave any space for unwanted passengers who just might decide to appear in your backseat. Pull off the road if a huge diesel truck comes bearing down on you from either direction. Don't be curious to see if there is a driver in that single car passing you in the night. Don't look for lights floating in the sky. Hope you don't see any young girls in white dresses. Never stop if you spot something peculiar and don't pick up hitchhikers. Lastly, if demon dogs approach you in the night, just keep driving."

Ghosts of London Bridge

One of Arizona's oddest, and oldest, tourist attractions stands along the western border in Lake Havasu City. Shipped across the pond, as they say, it's none other than England's London Bridge, the very one immortalized in the nursery rhyme in which it's falling down, falling down, falling down.

The bridge was purchased from the Brits in the late 1960s by city planner and theme-park designer C. V. Wood Jr. and town founder Robert P. McCulloch, the team who also brought us the 560-foot-tall water jet in Fountain Hills. Rebuilt along Lake Havasu, the bridge proved for many years to be a popular tourist draw, though today the authentic English village at its eastern end is a virtual ghost town.

The deck of London Bridge, however, remains quite active, with vehicular traffic crossing Bridgewater Channel, as well as a number of foot passengers, some of whom are evidently unaware of what country or even what dimension they're traveling through. Expatriates of both the U.K. and of their own bodies, it seems, have been witnessed treading the span's walkways.

In one report, a woman present at the bridge's 1971 dedication in Lake Havasu City saw four people dressed in period clothing ambling a short distance away. She assumed they were just a part of the ceremony, hired as ye olde street atmosphere, but just as a number of other attendees began to notice them, the group vanished. Since then, visitors to the bridge have witnessed other apparitions on various occasions. The figures are typically clothed as though they're from another era, and they will evaporate if anyone gets too close.

Such hauntings are no surprise, given the centuries of violence that occurred at London Bridge. For example, an early, wooden version of the bridge served as the execution site for those accused of witchcraft. More death

followed with the completion of the first stone version in 1209, though this time it was the result of the structure's very design. The archways beneath the span were so narrow that they caused violent rapids that resulted in the drowning of boatmen who tried to pass beneath it. To add to the deadly history, homes and shops stacked as high as seven stories along the bridge created crowded conditions that resulted in tragedy when both ends caught fire simultaneously in 1212, trapping and killing a reported three thousand people.

Undoubtedly one of the greatest sources of restless spirits was the countless disembodied heads on display at the structure's gates. As many as thirty noggins at a time were stuck atop pikes and propped up for the viewing public like candied apples at a state fair. Criminals and enemies of the king, such as Sir Thomas More and Guy Fawkes, suffered the bloody fate, as did many others for well over three hundred years, all exhibited at the venerable London Bridge.

The overpass that now resides in Lake Havasu City, only one incarnation of the bridge, was built in 1831. But it inhabited the same stretch above the River Thames as did the earlier spans and served as part of the overall lineage of the famous London Bridge. As such, it must have harbored much of the great structure's history, and being the only one in the line not to be demolished, carried that history with it to Arizona. Within its granite blocks are memories of its past—memories that, should you cross the bridge some quiet night, you may witness yourself.

Sad Spirit Roams Saguaro Boulevard

At first glance, Saguaro Boulevard in Fountain Hills seems a quiet residential street nestled in a peaceful desert suburb. Generously spaced adobe houses, landscaped by cacti and rock, line the curving road. It seems a pleasant, if isolated, neighborhood. But there are those who say that on Saguaro Boulevard an unnatural secret lurks in the dark.

As the story goes, a young girl was kidnapped in the early 1980s, and her fate was a horrible one. They say that she was murdered and dismembered, her body parts found in one of the houses on this otherwise normal street.

As twilight descends, there have been those who claim to have seen the girl's sorrowful spirit lingering by the house where her life was stolen and her body desecrated. Sometimes the wraithful vision is accompanied by the awful sounds of sobbing and screams. She often appears to be in a state of terror as she tries to flee her inevitable fate.

Those who stop to help her say she disappears completely in a blink of the eye as they try to figure out what is appearing before them. It is always the same: The phantom girl replays her horrible fate in front of those unlucky enough to catch a glimpse and then vanishes before the startled viewer can make sense of what he has seen.

So if you are ever driving along Saguaro Boulevard as the sun dips down behind the Arizona mountains, keep your eyes and ears well open, for you too may see the specter of the tragic murder victim who is said to haunt this road still, and possibly will for all eternity.–*Heather Shade*

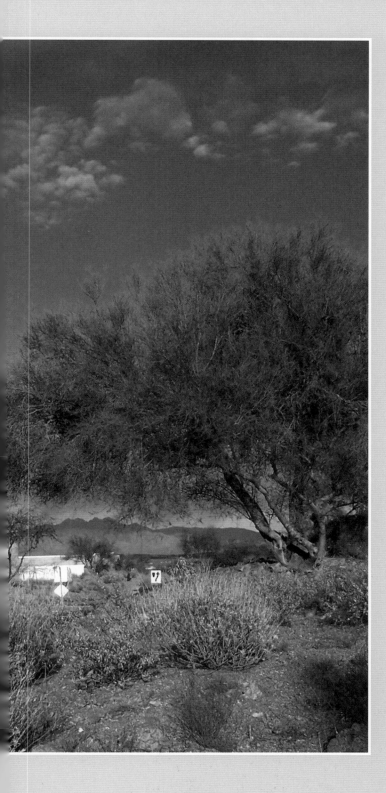

Crater Range Honeymoon Crash

A drive up Highway 85 toward Gila Bend will take you into the Barry M. Goldwater Air Force Range and through the eastern end of a stretch known as Crater Range, a scenic area filled with saguaro cactus and jagged, rock-strewn peaks. It's a spot that can make for a nice, leisurely detour, particularly at sunset. If you happen to find yourself there after dark, however, keep an eye out for hitchhikers in outdated formal wear.

A couple of Arizonans, it seems, have been spotted there flagging down motorists on numerous occasions and have been doing that for the last five decades. According to the story, the pair are newlyweds, or were newlyweds, married sometime in the 1950s in Ajo, located just to the south. They planned to take their honeymoon at Lake Tahoe in Nevada and hoped to hit the road early in the evening, but their nuptial celebration ran long. Rather than stay the night in Ajo and arrive late for their reservation, the couple decided to cover what distance they could that night.

Sadly, their decision to drive through the darkness ended in tragedy. They made it only about twenty-five miles before veering their car off the road sometime around midnight and running head-on into a large rock. The cause of the accident is unknown, but speed is believed to be a major factor, as they were both killed on impact.

Ever since, drivers passing through Crater Range have caught a glimpse of the couple's shattered car not too far from a spot known as Deadman Gap. The sightings occur just after midnight and often include the newlyweds themselves: a young, distraught couple in wedding attire trying to thumb a ride from the side of the road. As yet, no Samaritan has successfully rendered aid, since man and wife recede into the darkness whenever anyone stops.

The Anthem Hitchhiker

Driving down sections of highway through Arizona can sometimes be a lonely experience, with nothing but empty, uninhabited desert and wide-open sky as far as the eye can see. It's possible to drive for hours without glimpsing another living soul, and as the sun begins to sink below the mountains on the horizon, darkness descends like a shroud across the land. Of course, seeing the occasional hitchhiker is not unheard of, even in the most isolated stretches of road.

But in Anthem, just north of Phoenix, there is one hitcher in particular who is anything but the usual. They call him the Anthem Hitchhiker, and he differs from your normal hitcher in one very serious way—this shadowy figure, seen holding out a lantern, waiting for a ride, is said to have been dead for many, many years.

They say this unfortunate soul was struck and run over by a car on the highway as he tried to hitchhike his way to Phoenix. The legend claims that at certain times of the year he can be seen—a dim, mournful silhouette standing alongside the highway, his lantern held aloft, eternally waiting for the ride that will never come. Some may try to pull over and offer a lift to this "hitcher," only to witness him vanish. Others have said that the sight of him chilled them so completely that they feared to stop, only daring a look in the rearview mirror as they passed him by—again, to see that he has faded away into the night.

So, if you are ever out on Interstate 17 as twilight settles over the desert, keep an eye out for the murky figure with his lantern glowing in the gloom. You just may spot the Anthem Hitchhiker.

—Heather Shade

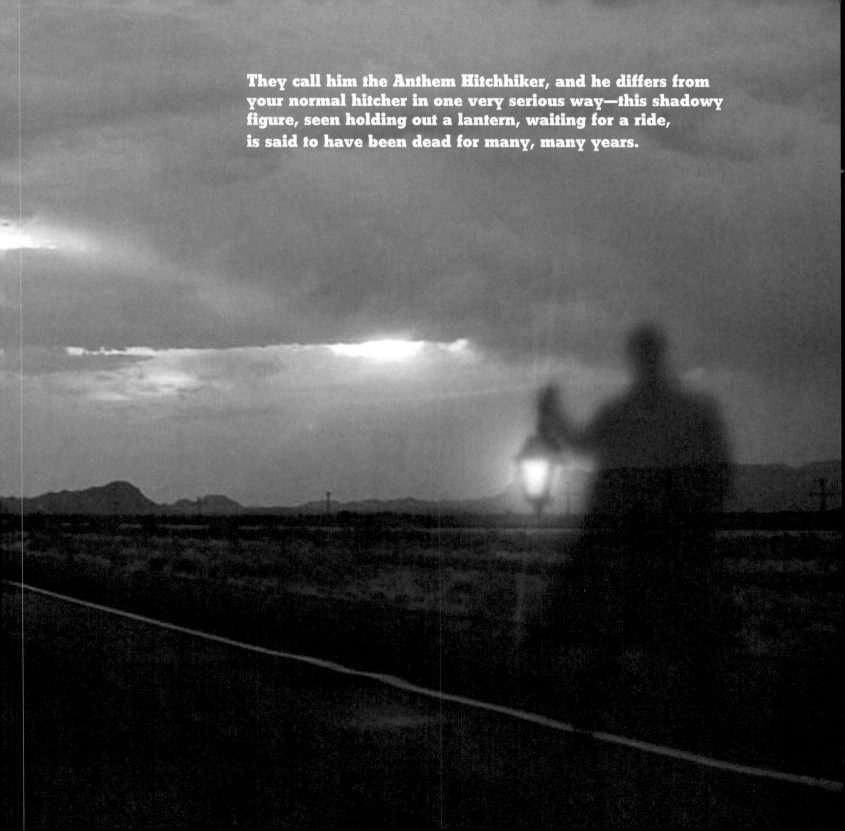

They call him the Anthem Hitchhiker, and he differs from your normal hitcher in one very serious way—this shadowy figure, seen holding out a lantern, waiting for a ride, is said to have been dead for many, many years.

Ghost Bus Prowls Highway 93

Some people call it the Ghost Bus of U.S. 93. Others call it the Ghost Bus of Union Pass. Its name depends on where the silent motorcoach overtakes the unwary traveler, and scares the starch right out of his clothes. Comedians who haven't actually seen the ghost bus call it the Grim Weeper, mocking reports that its headlights weep tears of molten chromium. Don't scoff until you've seen the coach in your own rearview mirror.

The story starts with Bus 777, which vanished thirteen years ago while it was carrying 48 feverish gamblers to Laughlin, Nevada. Each passenger expected to make a killing in the casino that day, but perhaps "killing" is an unfortunate choice of words. No one knows what happened to the passengers. Only the driver, a man named Joe, was found. He was wandering on the shoulder of Arizona Highway 68, looking for his bus. He was incoherent, and suffering from a bad case of brain dandruff. He said he last saw his bus in Union Pass, which is on Highway 68 northwest of Kingman.

But others have seen it, or its specter. Most sightings of the ghost bus have been along U.S. 93 between Wickenburg and Wikieup, where the trouble began. The following story was related to me by a dispatcher at the bus company that Joe worked for and who was in radio contact with the driver as the strange events unfolded.

Highways 93 and 68, plus a stretch of Interstate 40, make up the route of "turnaround" buses from the Phoenix area to the casinos of Nevada—buses that go up in the morning and come back at night. In the morning, the buses are filled with gamblers eager to get to Nevada before the slot machines stop accepting money. When the buses return late at night, most of the passengers have been subdued by fatigue and disappointment.

Joe's turnaround bus made its last pickup in Sun City on a very warm July morning. Bus 777 was black with trim of red and aqua and yellow, plus the usual amount of chrome. The bus was painted to get attention, not to win design awards. Early on, number 777 stopped at a fast-food place in Wickenburg so the passengers could have coffee and doughnuts, then hurried on, urged by riders who would rather gamble than eat. North of Wickenburg on U.S. 93, the air-conditioning began to fail. The interior of the bus heated up quickly under the summer sun. After a few miles, the driver pulled over, explained the problem, and asked if the passengers wanted to turn around and go back to Phoenix. "No!" they yelled in chorus.

Joe sighed and continued driving. He needed the money, but it was going to be a long day.

Going through the hills between Burro Creek and the Big Sandy River, Joe noticed that the bus seemed a little short of power, and it was trailing blue smoke. Around 10 a.m., he pulled over into a parking lot in Wikieup and told the passengers the bus was losing power. He could turn around and go back to Phoenix, he said, or he could send for another bus. This one was as hot as an oven, he pointed out.

"No," the passengers cried again. "We'll push the bus if we have to! Our slot machines are waiting for us!"

Joe pushed on, with considerable misgivings. He argued with himself: He was the captain of bus 777, was he not? Should he be risking the lives of his passengers just because they demanded it? On the other hand, the casino was paying to have Joe bring a busload of pigeons. And secretly, Joe kind of liked slot machines, so the bus growled on, getting hotter and hotter. It groaned onto I-40, rolled through Kingman, and found its way to Arizona 68, going west toward Laughlin. This was the homestretch. The casinos were only 30 minutes away.

As the bus climbed the grade toward Union Pass,

it really began losing power. Once through the pass, Arizona 68 swoops down to the Colorado River and the bridge to Laughlin. Joe was having a hard time coaxing the bus the last few hundred yards to the summit of Union Pass. Finally, he pulled onto the shoulder and told the passengers, "This is it, folks. The bus won't go anymore."

The passengers mutinied. Joe remembers one of them advancing on him, a malevolent look on his face. He recalls that the man's eyes were slits of hot coals, and his pointed ears had turned red. The next thing he knew, he was standing dazed beside the road as the passengers pushed bus 777 over Union Pass and clambered aboard as it started down the west side, out of his view. Someone had taken his shoes.

A tourist from Iowa, driving up toward Union Pass from the river, said he saw the bus speeding down the grade toward him. It went around a curve where a small hill hid it from view—and it never emerged. When he got to the place where he should have met the bus, there was nothing—no bus, no skid marks, no debris, nothing. That was the last sighting of bus 777 in this world. Lawmen combed the arroyos along Arizona 68 for days, but not so much as a skid mark or piece of chrome was ever found.

Joe retired from driving and began delivering newspapers to apartment houses on foot.

It was about three years before the ghost of bus 777 started to appear—sometimes in Union Pass, sometimes down around Morristown, but most often on U.S. 93 between Wickenburg and Wikieup. Here's the way most of the sightings go: You're traveling the highway late at night, alone, about the time the tangible turnarounds are returning from Laughlin. Suddenly, a bus comes up rapidly in your rearview mirror. You detect more than its headlights and clearance lights; it has just the suggestion of a silver glow to its dark profile. You think the bus is going to rear-end you. It's about that time that you see its headlights are dripping chromium tears.

All of this happens in a heartbeat. There is no time to react. The bus passes swiftly over your car, enveloping it, and moving on. Your car doesn't falter, but there's a buzzing in your head, tingling in your limbs, terror in your gut. As its rear bumper clears your grille, the bus melts and becomes a pool of chrome on the asphalt. You don't even have time to blink before the pool of chrome is gone, and it's only you, your headlights, and the asphalt ahead.

Wait . . . you are no longer alone. Every seat in your vehicle seems to be filled with a grim, quiet passenger who was not there before. If you are really lucky—if you don't panic and flip your car—you stop on the shoulder and turn to ask, "Who the hell are you?"

There's no one there.

You say you're thinking of going to Laughlin for a little gambling? The trip might just turn out to be more of a thrill than you're betting on!–*Jim Cook*

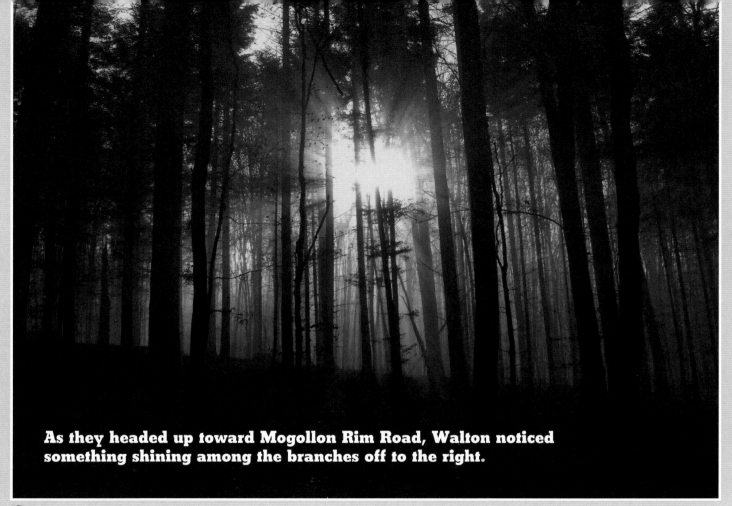

As they headed up toward Mogollon Rim Road, Walton noticed something shining among the branches off to the right.

Alien Abduction in Turkey Springs

It was just past six o'clock as Travis Walton and his six fellow log cutters finished off a long day of thinning undergrowth in the Apache-Sitgreaves National Forests. The sun had set and darkness was falling quickly, as it tends to do among the tall pines along the Mogollon Rim. With it, an increasing November chill was coming over the men, and they anxiously piled into their truck to head for home.

It would be at least an hour before they reached Heber to the north, so the men settled into their seats as best they could for the jarring drive up the forest's uneven dirt roads. The smokers in the group hastily lit the first cigarettes they'd had in hours. Walton, one of the only two nonsmokers on the crew, sat up front in the passenger's seat, enjoying the fresh, cool air and watching the pines pass by.

As they headed up toward Mogollon Rim Road, Walton noticed something shining among the branches off to the right. The others saw it too, and the chatter from the back seat fell quiet. The spaces between the trees flashed by too quickly to make out what the object was, but a clearing up ahead revealed a yellowish glow that washed across the road in front of them.

When they reached the clearing, the men were

astonished by what they saw. Less than a hundred feet from the edge of the road, a glowing disk hung in the air, floating motionless between the trees, only fifteen feet off the ground. The truck slammed to a halt, and Walton opened his door to get a better look. There was no sound, save for a startled cry from one of the cutters: "My God! It's a flying saucer!"

As he recounts in his book *Fire in the Sky*, Travis Walton then stepped out of the cab and walked toward the object. The others begged him to come back, but he felt compelled to get a close-up look. Coming within six feet of the craft, Walton stopped and stared up at its glowing underside.

Suddenly, the silence along that dark, isolated road gave way to what Walton would later describe as the thunderous swell of a turbine engine. That's when a narrow beam of light fired from the bottom of the disk and struck Walton in the chest. It lifted him up, then knocked him to the ground like a thunderbolt. In a panic, the rest of the crew sped away toward the main road, terrified.

When the men regained their senses, they returned to the clearing to rescue their friend. Unfortunately, the craft was gone and so was Walton. Despite a thorough search of the area, they could find no trace of him and were forced to drive home, one crew member short. When they reported what happened, the authorities discounted the men's tale as a ridiculous attempt to cover up a murder and launched an extensive search for Walton's body. They searched for several days and found nothing. Walton reappeared outside Heber five days later and corroborated their story, with the addition of what happened aboard the spacecraft.

Walton's story of what was considered the best documented, or at least the most publicized, close encounter ever recorded, details the bizarre events that took place following his abduction on November 5, 1975, including a frightening brush with large-eyed, pale-skinned creatures and his attempted escape inside the alien spacecraft. It's a story that's debated even today, despite the unusual number of eyewitnesses to the initial events and the fact that those witnesses have never strayed from their accounts in more than thirty years.

The precise location of the abduction is known to very few, but details from *Fire in the Sky* lead to a fairly accurate position. South of Heber, the crew followed Mogollon Rim Road about a mile east of Forest Road 87, where they turned north to an area known as Turkey Springs. It was somewhere along this road that the crew allegedly encountered the UFO.

It's Going to Be a Bumpy Ride

There is a curious display in the visitors center at Yuma Crossing State Historic Park. It's an old Model T sitting on top of a section of what looks like boardwalk, and it's the wood that is actually the most interesting draw of the exhibit. It's one of the few remaining portions of the Plank Road, which helped drivers traverse some serious sand dunes in the days before interstate highways.

Except in the case of dune buggies, sand and automobiles are natural enemies. And sand is something the deserts of the American Southwest have in abundance. With the presence of paved roads being somewhat inconsistent in the early days of the automobile, the massive sand dunes of the Imperial Valley presented something of an issue to those jonesing for efficient automobile transportation between Yuma and points west, including San Diego, CA. Therein lies the building of the Plank Road.

In early 1915, workers used oak planks to create a six-and-one-half-mile-long wooden highway consisting of two tracks running parallel to each other. The resulting roadway was successful and quickly became an official road linking Arizona and California.

The Plank Road's popularity, along with the frequent maintenance required to scrape shifting sands off the surface, took its toll on the wooden planks. The road was completely replaced in 1916 by a single-lane wooden road, which presented its own problems.

Imagine being a driver on this wooden roadway through the desert. You're cruising along at a top speed of ten miles an hour. The planks have been beaten by wind, sand, maintenance, and previous traffic, creating a ride so bumpy you can see why the route was nicknamed Old Shaky. Add to that having to stop to allow other cars right-of-way, which often involved backing your car up to the nearest pull-off. Sometimes convenience is awfully inconvenient!

Drivers contended with the Plank Road until 1926, when its replacement, Interstate 8, was opened. Bumped, bruised, and harried drivers quickly abandoned wood for pavement, and the Plank Road began to disappear bit by bit, reappearing alternately as museum displays or as especially seasoned campfire wood. Today, in addition to the section of the Plank Road that remains in Yuma, there's at least one other portion that plank aficionados can see in its natural state, over the border in California. The state's Bureau of Land Management Web site says it's at the west end of Grays Well Road.

Route 66: Arizona's Lost (and Found) Highway

"Flagstaff, Arizona, don't forget Winona, Kingman, Barstow, San Bernardino. . . . Get your kicks on Route 66."

Who could forget those immortal lyrics penned by Bobby Troup way back in 1946? A decade before Jack Kerouac was credited with sending a generation of beatniks on cross-country road trips with his book *On the Road*, Troup's song "Route 66" inspired throngs of postwar thrill seekers to motor west in search of adventure on the quintessential American highway. Once one of the nation's most traveled roads, Route 66 spent most of the latter half of the twentieth century as a road less traveled due to new interstate highways, which bypassed much of its original route.

Historical Kicks

Before Route 66 was a cultural icon, it was . . . a highway. A highway created by an act of Congress in 1925 and thereafter patched together Frankenstein-like from an already existing network of formerly unpaved roads and main streets in eight states. It started in downtown Chicago and traveled through the Midwest and Southwest, ending in Los Angeles, and wasn't fully paved until 1938.

In that time, however, Route 66 became more than just a soulless highway. At first, it was a passage west for millions who were looking for work or for the good life on the golden California coast. But with the end of World War II, this road of roads would morph into an American icon. As postwar Americans fell in love with their cars, they took to driving them everywhere, including on Route 66. With the influx of tourists came industries catering to them: places to sleep, eat, fuel up, and be entertained. And like the loudest carnival barker, the louder the Route 66 attraction, the more likely it was to draw in families. The highway became known for its eye candy of unique roadside architecture and tourist traps, all competing for tourist dollars.

The same post–World War II lifestyle that fueled the car vacation would also generate the interstate highway system, which was the beginning of the end for Route 66. As Americans realized they could get to major destinations faster (and safer) on the burgeoning interstate system, they started to bypass Route 66. As a result, vast stretches of that highway, and the towns it once brought life to, lay abandoned and wasting away, especially in the Arizona desert. The federal government decommissioned Route 66 in 1985.

It wasn't the end of the road for Route 66, however. With a resurgence of interest in American roadside culture and the work of various preservation societies, many of the old stretches of 66, once left for dead, are now enjoying a rebirth of sorts. Signs have been posted along them declaring them HISTORIC ROUTE 66. Still, much of the original "Mother Road," as John Steinbeck described it in *The Grapes of Wrath,* remains desolate and deserted today.

The glory days of Route 66 have long since passed, but there are still adventures to be had on this legendary byway. These days they're just a little bit weirder, especially on the abandoned fragments of it. We sent *Weird Arizona* photo correspondent Troy Paiva down this famed road to see if he could still find a kick or two there.

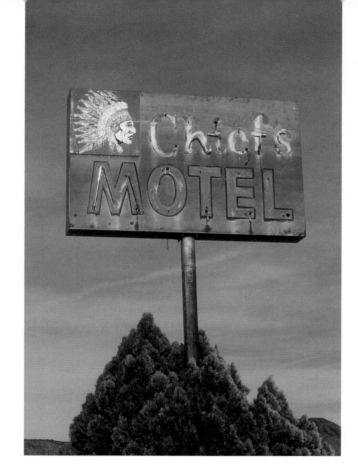

Still Getting Kicks on Old Route 66

Is there another highway name that conjures more feelings and emotions in Americans, and even elsewhere in the world, than Route 66? The Mother Road has been depicted in countless classic books and movies. Even the song "Route 66" has been covered over two hundred times by artists from Rosemary Clooney to the Cramps. Its legendary status in pop culture is well justified: America's soul is laid out in a line, straight across the Southwest for everyone to see.

The Arizona stretch contains the most still functioning miles of Route 66. These old Miracle Mile towns are steeped in the history of twentieth-century western expansion. But these are not Wild West towns. They are road towns. Instead of old mines, saloons, and whorehouses, they are made up of car culture relics: gas stations, motels, and cafés. These towns once all sported multiple drive-in theaters, almost all of which are gone without a trace. The long-closed Tonto

Drive-In on the western fringe of Winslow is still standing, but squatters populate the snack bar. As I slipped through the fence to take pictures, shady characters drifted from the cinderblock building and over the back fence, their sleeping bags and piles of dirty clothes left behind in the dusty corners. I'm sure they slipped back in right after I left.

Some sections of 66 now serve as nothing more than frontage roads for Interstate 40. One night at Chambers in eastern Arizona, I was shooting an abandoned Chevron station. It was a '30s building with '50s gas pumps, all decrepit and worn out. The night was cold, and storm clouds were speeding by almost as fast as the highballing semis on Interstate 40, just a few feet away. While I was shooting, I began to hear dogs barking, getting closer. Then the shadow of a man appeared out of the darkness. It was an American Indian guy in his twenties, a rifle casually cradled in his arms. He was clearly drawn out of his warm house by my colored strobe flashes. A man of few words, once he understood I wasn't a vandal, he left me alone.

Kingman is home to one of the West's countless World War II training airfields. Much of this airport is still just like it was in the '40s. The Kingman airport is legendary as one of the main aircraft reclamation facilities after the war. Tens of thousands of bombers and fighters were shredded and recycled there. Even today there is still aircraft reclamation done at Kingman, but on a smaller scale. On the south side of the airport is a huge section of fifty-year-old concrete hardstand used to store '70s airliners before they can be chopped up and melted down. Sneaking over the fence to take pictures at night can be a real thrill; you have to be careful to avoid the authorities as well as the grazing cows under the planes' wings. Any urban explorer looking for abandoned culture could do a lot worse than to spend a week slowly cruising Route 66 through Arizona. There truly is something for everyone.—*Troy Paiva*

Ghosts of Arizona

There are many things in this world that defy explanation—mysteries that remain just beyond the reach of rationality. Stories of the unexplained fill our lives; they are depicted in feature films and whispered in school lunchrooms. They saturate our culture. Heck, this book is full of them.

Of course, many of these mysterious phenomena are dismissed as simple folklore. But ghosts are different. Even the most fearless among us will freeze at a creaking door in a dark, old house, wondering what hides in the shadows. Perhaps there lies within us some instinctive connection with the spiritual realm that drives this instinct, something innate in our natures that looks for proof of an afterlife.

On the other hand, it may be just about letting our imaginations run wild. But whether we believe in ghosts or not is immaterial. Either way, part of us, whether we admit it or not, hopes we do encounter something behind the creaking door—a chance to touch the Other Side.

Thankfully, Arizona is full of opportunities to do so. With almost every town boasting at least one phantom resident, an entire book could be dedicated to the state's ghosts. Unfortunately, we had room for only one chapter. We hope the phantoms that were left out don't get too upset.

Museum Club

When Dean Eldredge opened his roadside novelty gallery in 1931, he sought to add to his unusual assemblage of oddities by placing the following ad: "Wanted: freaks, antique guns and prehistoric Indian curios." An avid collector of stuffed creatures and other curiosities, Eldredge was interested in expanding the collection he had gathered together in a distinctive pine lodge outside Flagstaff. It was an uncanny assortment that included such rarities as one-eyed, six-legged, and two-headed farm animals.

Unfortunately, the bulk of Eldredge's collection is now long gone. Luckily, his unique building is still there, and the freaks have been replaced with other, more intriguing oddities—namely, poltergeists.

After Eldredge passed away, the place reopened under the name the Museum Club as a post-Prohibition roadhouse that served some of the county's first legal booze in nearly fourteen years. After several fairly successful years and a string of new owners, a man named Don Scott bought the building in 1963 and turned it into a highly popular honky-tonk, drawing some of the biggest names in country music.

In 1973, however, the good times came to a tragic end when Don's wife, Thorna, fell down the stairway that leads to the club's upstairs apartment, fatally breaking her neck. Depression subsequently overtook Don, and he ended his own life in 1975 by putting a gun to his head in front of the club's fireplace.

The Museum Club soon reopened under new management and continues to serve customers in Don and Thorna Scott's absence, although many people may disagree with the accuracy of that statement. An increasing number of disturbances, mostly benign, have taken place within the establishment, leading some to believe the Scotts haven't really left.

The most innocuous of the incidents are the occasional creaking and footsteps heard emanating from the second floor. More disturbing are the times a manager will hear

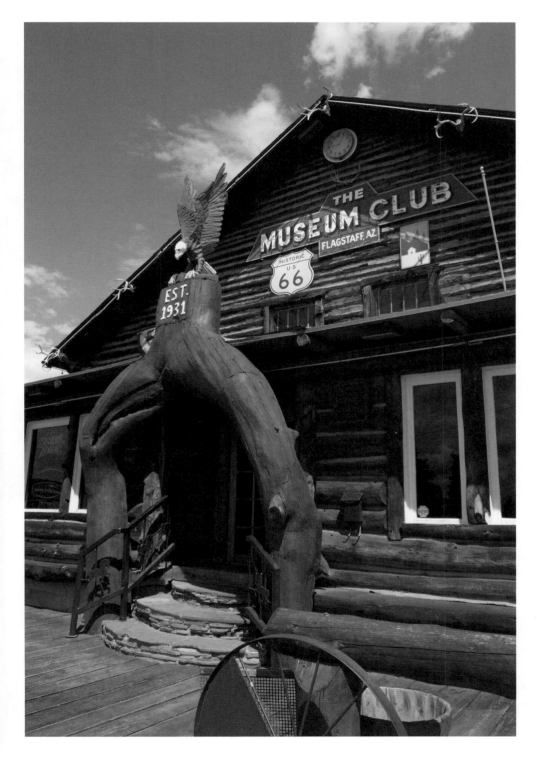

voices coming from outside his office well after closing time or, in one instance, spot the TV remote flying through the door. At the bar, employees often see a row of liquor bottles clink together one after the other as though someone were running a hand along the tops. At least once a bartender has come in to open up and discovered the bar in total disarray, bottles scattered and knocked over, even though everything had been cleaned up before closing time the night before.

Some people have seen the image of a woman in the building when no one else was around. She sometimes walks across the dance floor but is more likely to hang around the back staircase. Customers have attempted to buy drinks for the woman after spotting her sitting alone in a booth, only to have her vanish before the waitress can deliver the order.

The most disturbing incident occurred in 1984 when Richard Bentley, the staff handyman, experienced a too close encounter with the mysterious woman. Bentley, who was living in the upstairs apartment, was roused from his sleep late one night by a woman sitting on his chest and pinning his arms to the bed. She told him he shouldn't be afraid because "only the living" could hurt him. Bentley struggled his way free and jumped out the upstairs window. After calling the club's owner from a motel to explain what happened, he quit his job and left Flagstaff.

Bird Cage Theatre

After surviving two devastating fires, the flooding of its mines, and near ghost-town abandonment, Tombstone has come to bill itself as the Town Too Tough to Die. Despite repeated hardships, it continues to thrive after more than 120 years.

Since Tombstone's resurrection as a historic tourist stop, however, the motto has taken on a different meaning. The town's former population, it seems, just won't leave. Countless men and women, many of whom suffered sudden and brutal deaths during Tombstone's early decades, refuse to give up their connection to the place they seem to have loved. Phantoms haunt the street corners where cowboys once lived and died, and practically every building in the historic district boasts at least one otherworldly presence.

Perhaps the single most haunted spot in Tombstone is the Bird Cage Theatre. Built in 1881 on the corner of Allen and Sixth, the Bird Cage quickly became one of Tombstone's hottest businesses, serving as a one-stop saloon, opera house, gambling hall, and brothel. You could say it was the town's convenience store of iniquity,

drawing names like Wyatt Earp, Johnny Ringo, and Curly Bill Brocius. Doc Holliday himself dealt faro at a card table that still sits in a corner of the saloon.

According to the site supervisor, Teresa Benjamin, the opera house was supposed to be a place of neutral ground. Regardless, an astounding 140 bullet holes perforate the walls, floors, and ceiling as a result of the numerous confrontations that took place here. Slugs more than a century old remain embedded in the walls, and just recently a stiletto blade was uncovered that's been connected to the jealousy-fueled murder of one of the establishment's prostitutes. In all, twenty-six people have

graphs seems to be the poster of Fatima the belly dancer. "Ninety-nine percent of the time," says Teresa, "you take a picture of Fatima, and you will get something." A woman once had her picture taken beneath the poster and discovered in the camera's preview screen another woman standing right beside her. When the visitor moved over to the mystery woman's spot and had the picture retaken, the apparition traded positions, as well.

lost their lives under this one historic roof.

As a result, it's not surprising to have at least one ghostly experience a day. Most, according to Teresa, are photographic. "Ninety-five percent of our sightings in this building come from the camera," she says. "They love having their picture taken." For example, a mirror in one of the more expensive bordello rooms downstairs often produces the image of a lady in white. The cheaper rooms overlooking the gambling room result in their fair share of spirit images, as well. Teresa herself has caught a floozy or two up there.

One particularly active spot for phantasmal photo-

Not only do the spirits show up for still photos, but they've also appeared on video. A family of tourists once marched into the gift shop and complained that they hadn't seen any ghosts, calling the place nothing more than a tourist trap. When they got home, though, they called Teresa to apologize. On their videotape, they discovered two frightening specters staring straight into the camera. The family kept Teresa on the phone for half an hour while they described the images. One was of a man sitting up inside an antique hearse that was on display. The other was

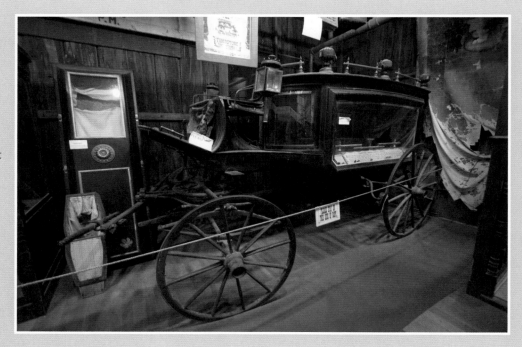

of a woman in one of the bordello rooms, clearly upset at their presence. "They said it was strange," Teresa recalled, "because they could actually see the expression on her face go from shock to rage instantly."

What's really unusual about the events taking place here is that they vary so widely in nature. A manager who has since left always felt somebody shoving him out of the way whenever he walked around the card table. He also once had something buckle his legs out from under him on the stairs. During one particular week, women kept getting pinched. Teresa insists this sort of thing is uncommon, since the ghosts are typically friendly, but it does happen.

Sounds and smells fill the air as well. Girls giggle upstairs, and the echoes of men's chatter frequently emanate from the main hall just as audibly as if actual people were having a conversation. The scent of lavender perfume drifts by, as does the odor of stale cigar smoke, sometimes so strong it will make your eyes water. A

woman once had a severe allergic reaction while visiting the museum, complaining that someone blew smoke right into her face, though she could never see who it was. "Then there's times," Teresa says, "where the smell of death is so strong . . . that you actually have to leave the building for at least a couple seconds to get some fresh air. It is so nauseating and so overwhelming."

Why so much activity at the Bird Cage? Well, despite the passage of time, the opera house stands basically as it did a century ago. The original lights, draperies, stage curtains, wallpaper, and furniture are still in place. It's so well preserved that when the building was reopened in the 1930s, original whiskey barrels were discovered full of liquor. Perhaps these unaltered surroundings, which stand in contrast to the many renovated and brightly painted buildings up the street, are a major reason why the deceased find the Bird Cage so welcoming. It seems as if they've never left. And maybe they haven't.

Haunts of Fort Huachuca

Its slogan, From Sabers to Satellites, speaks of Fort Huachuca's important role in U.S. history. It was established during the Indian wars of the late 1800s, played a role in the campaigns against Geronimo and Pancho Villa, and was home to four regiments of Buffalo Soldiers, the African American army units of the late 1800s and early 1900s. In 1954, it became the site for advanced testing of electronics and communications equipment, and today it is the Army Intelligence Center and School and its Information Systems Command

Carleton House is the oldest building on the base. It was originally constructed as the post hospital back in 1880, and in following years was used as housing for officers, a café, and a schoolhouse. More recently it has been the residence of the hospital commander or other officers assigned to the base. Many of the families who have lived there have reported ghostly happenings, including the rare sighting of a female ghost.

One of the first sightings of the ghost occurred when the Koenig family was in residence. A neighborhood boy came to deliver a message, and went up the front steps and knocked. He later told his parents that Margaret Koenig walked right down the hall toward him but ignored his knocking.

Bothered by this, the boy's mother later telephoned Mrs. Koenig, who in turn insisted that she and her family had just arrived home and that no one had been in the house at the time of the boy's visit!

After the Koenigs left Carleton House, the family of Colonel Roy Strom—the deputy commander of the U.S. Army Intelligence Center from 1980 to 1982—moved in. Even today Colonel Strom calls the house haunted. His wife, Joan, would eventually name the ghost Charlotte.

The day they moved in, the house's ghostly side was quickly made evident to the family when one of the moving crew became jittery and refused to go inside. "I'm not going in there," he said. "That house is haunted." That same day the Stroms piled boxes in what had been the hospital's morgue. Later that night they discovered the boxes had been pulled open and the contents strewn about.

A few days later the doorbell began to ring over and over again. Each time, the family would check to see who the visitor was, only to find no one there. Colonel Strom guessed it to be kids pulling a prank, and the next time it rang, he ran around the side of the house to catch the culprits. But no one was there. He eventually disconnected the wiring to the bell.

The family also experienced lights turning on and off, erratic electrical problems, and wall hangings that refused to stay straight. In one corner of the living room, the air was drastically colder than the rest of the house and the overhead light above the area refused to work properly. Joan dubbed this Charlotte's Corner.

She also got a rare glimpse of what she believes is Charlotte's ghost. One morning she thought she saw her teenage daughter Amy walk down an adjacent hallway from the kitchen. Joan called out a greeting to her, but Amy never stopped or returned it. Thinking this was unusual behavior, Joan went to Amy's room to check on her, only to find the girl sound asleep. When she checked her other daughters' rooms, she found they were also asleep and had not been in the hallway.

Joan believed Charlotte was the ghost of a woman who had died in the fort's hospital during the early 1880s. She searched fort records and a cemetery trying to find evidence of Charlotte's life or death but was never successful. Charlotte's identity may never be confirmed, and one wonders if her spirit will eternally remain to chill her corner of the living room in Carleton House.

—Troy Taylor

Brunckow's Cabin

As Frederick Brunckow slapped together the adobe walls that would form his new home, he had no idea he was erecting what would become known as the bloodiest cabin in Arizona history. In the years that would follow, the dirt beneath his feet would turn red time and again as at least twenty lives, including his, would be violently claimed.

Brunckow, a German immigrant and employee of a regional mining company, established a claim in the late 1850s just a few miles southwest of what would later become Tombstone. Joining him were a chemist by the name of Morse, camp cook David Brontrager, and fellow miners James and William Williams. Assisted by a team of Mexican laborers, the crew built a supply store, along with living quarters, and by the summer of 1860, they were well on their way to drilling for ore.

Progress, however, would not continue for long. On July 26, William Williams arrived back at camp after purchasing sacks of flour at nearby Fort Buchanan. He had left on Monday, three days earlier, but had trouble obtaining a wagon to haul back his load, so he was unable to return until late Thursday night. When he arrived home, Williams discovered a gruesome scene.

By the light of a flame, Williams found the supply store in shambles. The camp's provisions had been knocked from their shelves and strewn across the floor, much of them missing. An overwhelming stench choked his airway from the moment he arrived in camp, though he could not immediately determine its source. Then, as he surveyed the damage, he saw it. Among the supplies scattered at his feet lay the body of his cousin James, long dead and reeking of decay. Williams panicked and bolted out the door. Searching for the rest of the crew would have been futile; their fates were conveyed by the unnatural stillness in the air. Williams scrambled back

aboard his wagon and tore out across the desert.

When soldiers from Fort Buchanan returned with Williams to investigate, they discovered two more bodies. Morse, the chemist, lay in the dust outside, obviously dead and ravaged by wild animals. Brunckow was found near a mine shaft, reportedly impaled with a rock drill. Bolstered by whiskey and armed with camphor to fight the stench, the soldiers buried what was left of the men.

Brontrager, the cook, turned up on Friday after allegedly spending four days walking across the desert. He said the Mexican laborers working at the mine attacked them only hours after Williams left for Fort Buchanan. They hijacked a shipment of goods that had just arrived, stole money and horses, and fled. Brontrager said they spared his life because they believed him to be a good Catholic. The Mexicans were never found.

Several years passed before anyone dared make use of Brunckow's cabin again. The memory of such violent deaths and the fact that three bodies were buried nearby made for a less than welcoming atmosphere. The stigma grew even stronger when the Arizona Territory's first U.S. marshal, Major Milton B. Duffield, moved in and was promptly murdered. Then the cabin seemed downright cursed, sublet by Death himself.

In 1881, Prescott's *Arizona Democrat,* as quoted in Judy Martin's book *Arizona Walls,* confirmed the cabin's history of "uninterrupted . . . violence and murder." The article affirmed that, in just over twenty years since the slaughter of Brunckow and his companions, an additional seventeen men met their fates on the property. The report also attested to the site's reputation for supernatural phenomena. "The graves lie thick around the old adobe house," it read. "Prospectors and miners avoid the spot as they would the plague, and many of them will tell you that the unquiet spirits of the departed

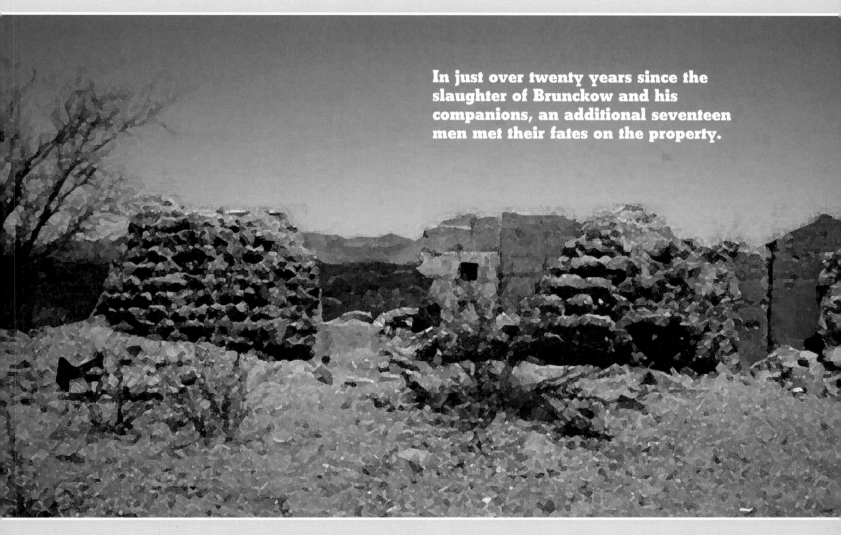

In just over twenty years since the slaughter of Brunckow and his companions, an additional seventeen men met their fates on the property.

are wont to revisit . . . and wander about the scene."

Such reports of ghostly activity continue even today. Those who visit the cabin's ruins often insist the site is haunted. Many in years past who've braved sundown and camped nearby have reported terrifying disturbances and even visions of spirits. It isn't a welcome place to be, they say, and is worth a visit only if you're bent on either meeting or joining the dead.

What remains of the cabin lies about eight miles southwest of Tombstone, near the intersection of Charleston Road and Brunckow Road. It can be seen past the first set of ruins, down the trail toward the San Pedro River. Unfortunately, not much is left these days. Erosion, and likely vandalism, are quickly delivering the walls of adobe to the bodies buried below.

Solitary Spirits at Yuma Territorial Prison

Many old prisons are haunted: California's Alcatraz, the Ohio State Reformatory, and Eastern State Penitentiary in Philadelphia are perhaps the best known. All are full of deceased prisoners who refuse to leave their cells and are plagued with bloodcurdling screams, ghostly voices, and the sounds of rattling chains. Another prison to add to this haunted list is Arizona's Yuma Territory Prison.

The prison is perched on top of a rocky hill, overlooking the small town that shares its name. From 1876 through 1909, it housed over 3,000 prisoners, including 29 women. Overcrowding essentially closed it and in 1909 all the inmates were shackled together and transported to the prison in Florence, Arizona. After that, it chiefly became a haven for the homeless and their families. Today, it is a museum and part of the State Historic Park system.

But it seems as if some of the prisoners' sentences have extended into their afterlife. Accounts of ghostly activity, both from staff members and visitors, are not uncommon. Especially from the "dark cell."

When a prisoner broke the rules, he was confined in solitary to the "dark cell," a barren cubicle which measured 10 feet by 10 feet. He would be dressed only in his underwear and existed on one meal of bread and water each day. He would sometimes have both legs individually chained to two ringbolts. The only light during the day came from a small ventilation shaft in the ceiling. After the sun went down, the prisoner was in total darkness.

He often shared the space with scorpions

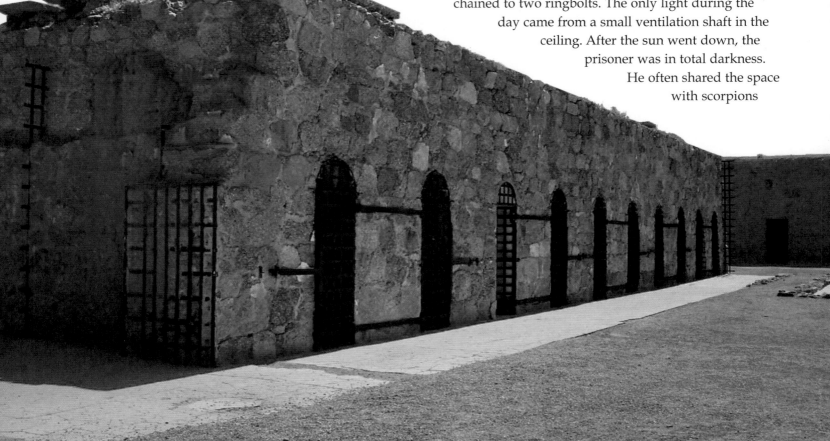

and snakes, and whether these varmints slithered into the dark cell from the outside or sadistic guards dropped them down the ventilation shaft to further torture the inmates, as they claimed, will never be known. After serving their time in the dark cell, some prisoners were sent directly to the insane asylum in Phoenix.

Surprisingly, the most prominent ghost in the dark cell might be that of a small child. This ghostly phantom loves pinching, poking, and touching with icy fingers, but only if you're wearing red clothing. A psychic touring the prison felt the spirit wasn't an angry prisoner but rather that of a little girl. Perhaps her family was one of the many who found themselves homeless and living at the prison until they could get back on their feet.

A staff writer for a regional magazine in Arizona, wanting to experience what the prisoners went through, attempted to spend forty-eight hours in the dark cell. She was shackled to the ringbolt and left with only a jug of water and a loaf of bread. The magazine scribe fell short of her goal by eleven hours, insisting that she felt she wasn't alone in the cell. It probably didn't help that the ventilation shaft was covered, blocking out all rays of light.

The dark cell is only one area where ghostly activity occurs. Assistant Park Manager Jesse Torres says, "At the far end of the corridor is cell 14, which was occupied in the early 1900s by John Ryan. He was not only disliked by the guards but by the prisoners as well. At times, when I pass his old cell, I find myself shivering because of the coldness. John was found guilty of a 'crime against nature,' which meant he committed rape or another crime of sexual deviation. Before he finished his sentence, he committed suicide in his cell."

Other accounts are muffled conversations in vacant rooms, witnesses "seeing" things out of the corners of their eyes, and a woman who sings in the visitors area early in the morning. Johnny, another harmless ghost, doesn't venture out of the gift shop. He's content filching coins from the cash register but always leaves the bills alone.

If you like having the bejesus scared out of you, join the staff on the last Saturday of every October for a ghostly tour. You'll hear all about the killings and suicides that took place behind bars. You'll also learn firsthand from the tour guides about experiences they've had encountering former prisoners who haunt the dark corridors and dreary cells.

The Yuma Territorial Prison State Historic Park is open daily from eight a.m. to five p.m. except for Thanksgiving and Christmas Eve day, when it closes at two p.m. It is closed December 25. For more information go to http://www.pr.state.az.us/Parks/parkhtml/yuma.html or call (928) 783-4771.

—*Ellen Robson*

Oliver House

Bisbee is a unique little town. Looking like a picture-postcard village from an era long, long past, it nestles among towering red mountains. Strange totems and carvings sit, stand, or huddle around and atop nearly every structure: a tree made entirely of metal (including each silvery leaf), crouched gargoyles, squat humanoid figures, and much more. The buildings in Bisbee seem untouched by time— quaint, old-fashioned, and clustered together around twisting narrow streets, many of which do not even bear street signs. But one of its most

interesting-looking structures is probably also one of its most infamous. Perched high atop a concrete "hill," it's the old historic home known as the Oliver House.

You see, the Oliver House is not just an intriguing old place. It's also a bed-and-breakfast with a very violent past and a supposed collection of resident ghosts (at least five, it's said) that rival any spooky legend.

In 1909, Edith Ann Oliver, the wife of mining tycoon Henry Oliver, had the structure built for use as office space and a planning center for the Calumet & Arizona Mining Company. It was also used to house executives from the companies and later served as a boardinghouse for the many miners of the region. Now it is an inn, open to visitors who don't mind sharing their space with the things that go bump in the night.

The handsome red brick house can be seen looking watchfully over the town from nearly anywhere you go. A man-made, water-filled "moat" circles the hill, and the only way to reach the building is by crossing a narrow footbridge that spans the moat, going through an ancient-looking wrought-iron gate, and following a short path that leads you right up to the front porch.

The true number of deaths that have occurred inside the Oliver House is not verifiable, with many of the records lost to time or neglect. There are Bisbee residents who claim that at least twenty-seven unfortunate souls have died inside the house since its construction. But the most famous story of all is an unsolved murder that fascinates people to this day.

On February 22, 1920, a mining company employee named Nathan "Nat" Anderson was found murdered in the hallway at the top of a staircase. According to reports in the *Bisbee Daily Review,* Anderson was shot in the back and in the head during the early morning hours as he prepared to enter room 13. His murderer was never

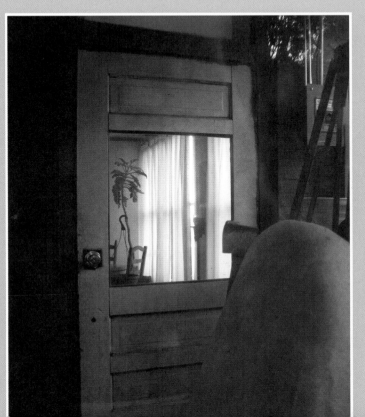

caught, and the crime remains an infamous unsolved mystery. Rumors claim that Anderson was having an illicit affair with a local policeman's wife, and that the enraged policeman killed her, as well as everyone he encountered downstairs in the parlor of the Oliver House, before driving to the edge of town and committing suicide. Though this part of the ghostly tale cannot be verified, it has become an oft-repeated reason for the unexplained killing of Nat Anderson. Much of the anomalous activity reported by guests and staff alike seems to center around room 13. But they say it is not the only room that has a lurking resident spirit.

The Oliver House also has a room called the Grandma Room, where an older lady supposedly died of natural causes. Her ghostly specter has been seen, sometimes sitting in a rocking chair or even dusting the room in the deep dark of the night. People say the rocking chair is sometimes found moved from its usual spot to one in front of the window and sometimes the chair seems to rock on its own. However, the restless spirit in the Grandma Room is felt to be a benevolent one, staying in residence as a sort of protector.

Another member of the undead prefers the Plum Room. Guests there often report feeling watched when no one else is in the room and encountering chilling cold spots. In the Purple Sage Room, people claim they have witnessed the doors and shutters opening and closing all by themselves. They also say that doors in the hallway open and close by unseen hands and that disembodied footsteps can be heard roaming there.

All in all, the Oliver House is a fascinating place with a rich history and many mysterious legends of ghostly phenomena. A stay there would be highly recommended, and most likely unforgettable. That is, if you're the type who doesn't mind rooming with a few restless wraiths.
—Heather Shade

Willcox Haunts

You might say Warren Earp is remembered as one of the "lesser Earps." History has certainly recorded his surname, but it clearly doesn't afford Warren the same recognition it does his brothers Wyatt or Virgil.

Still, Warren did play his part in the Old West, serving as a deputy in Tombstone for a time and later participating in the vengeance killings following the murder of his brother Morgan. But he missed out on that whole eternally celebrated O.K. Corral fracas in between, leaving him well out of the limelight. In the end, his most noteworthy moment appears to have occurred on July 6, 1900: The day he was shot and killed in a Willcox bar.

Warren, a ranch hand at the time, was playing cards in the Headquarters Saloon at the corner of Maley Street and Railroad Avenue. An argument erupted between him and a fellow ranch hand named Johnnie Boyett, which ended when Boyett planted a bullet in Warren's chest. Sad, yes, but when all is said and done, it was a rather lackluster incident as Wild West shootouts go.

Nevertheless, Willcox loosely themes its annual Western Heritage Days celebration around the event, even

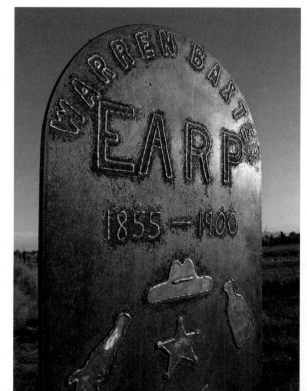

scheduling it during the same month as the killing. But the only real remembrance of what went down that day (aside from Warren) seems to be recorded in the walls of the old saloon, now the Headquarters Western Movie Gallery.

According to the owners, events of that time still play themselves out late at night. About one in the morning, you can go into the back room and hear mumbling. The odor of cigarette and cigar smoke randomly fills the building, as well, along with the strong smell of alcohol. One morning the owners discovered that someone had switched off all the lights and opened the curtains overnight, even though the door was locked tight and the alarm was still turned on.

At a museum dedicated to Rex Allen, volunteers and those who personally knew Allen have experienced what they believe to be his postmortem greetings.

A few doors down from the Headquarters, more inexplicable activity takes place, which has been attributed to another past resident of Willcox. At a different former saloon, which is now a museum dedicated to the cowboy musician and film star Rex Allen, volunteers and those who personally knew Allen have experienced what they believe to be his postmortem greetings.

As a longtime friend of Allen's strolled past the museum one evening, one of the old cowboy's songs spontaneously began playing from the building's outdoor speakers. The museum was closed, and no one was inside. Others have witnessed items being knocked from shelves with nobody near them. Even more surprising was a ghost dressed in cowboy attire that was once spotted casually leaning against a display inside the museum.

There hasn't been any definitive indication that the spirit responsible for the mischief at the museum belongs to Rex Allen, but it wouldn't be out of the question. When the entertainer died in 1999, his ashes were scattered in the park directly across the street.

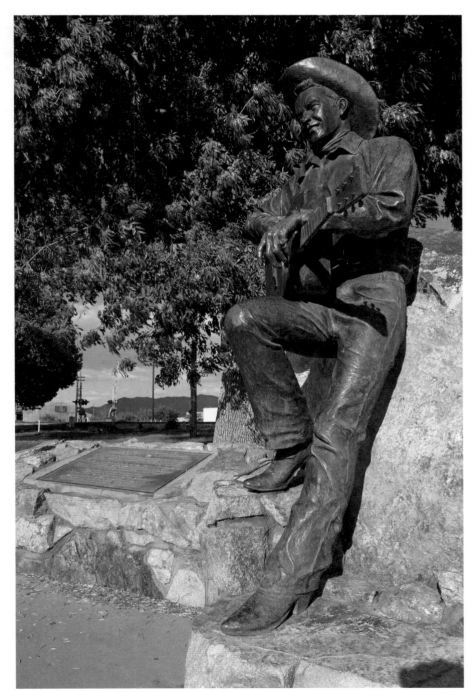

Rex Allen

Acadia Ranch

Just a short drive north of Tucson lies the town of Oracle, which is just as mysterious as its name makes it sound. Oracle was the site of western legend Buffalo Bill Cody's mine and homestead. It's also the location of Acadia Ranch, first established in 1880 and home to at least one ghostly resident.

Originally built by sheep farmers, Acadia Ranch also served as a post office, a guest ranch, a hotel, a boarding house for tuberculosis patients, and a morgue before becoming the museum it is today. It is currently owned and operated by the Oracle Historical Society.

The glory days of the ranch were probably when it was a refuge for tuberculosis patients, who found Oracle's clean air and sunshine beneficial to their health. These "lungers," as they were known, stayed at the ranch until their condition improved . . . or didn't. When patients died, their bodies were stored in a room just beyond the front door of the building until they could be given a proper burial.

When the Oracle Historical Society purchased the ranch in 1978, it began a major restoration effort. About this time, volunteers working on the old house began to experience some strange phenomena involving a ghost they dubbed George. They shared tales of disembodied

footsteps, swinging chandeliers, and flickering lights. George's antics would frequently occur in the evening, often when a volunteer was alone in the building.

The late Agnes Ramsay, who was influential in the activities of the Oracle Historical Society and in the restoration of Acadia Ranch, may have encountered George. Her experience fits his modus operandi: She was alone in the house one day when she was startled by the sound of footsteps. She turned around to see . . . no one there. Was it George?

It's impossible to know George's real identity. So many people have passed through the ranch, and the records kept were less than perfect. Some speculate that he was a hotel guest or perhaps a boarder who suffered from TB. He may have been almost anyone during his lifetime, but he is remembered today as the Ghost of Acadia Ranch.

Visitors to the building find that the wooden floor creaks beneath their feet as they enter, almost as if the house—or something in it—were inviting them to explore further. With its display of western artifacts and historical appliances in rooms that are sometimes murkily lit, it seems that Acadia Ranch would not be complete without a resident ghost. Because of its history, its friendly volunteers, and George, Acadia Ranch is one of the weirdest—and sometimes creepiest—buildings still standing in Arizona.—*Trevor Freeman*

Landmark Restaurant

The grand and elegant building that houses the Landmark Restaurant in Mesa has a history dating all the way back to 1911, when it was a church and a chapel meetinghouse. In the 1950s, it had a reincarnation as an insurance company, and in the '60s it was home to Mesa's first community college. It was converted to a restaurant in 1973 and became the Landmark Restaurant in 1981.

The building's rich and lengthy history may explain some of the ghostly activity that is claimed to continue in the Landmark to the present day. Servers say they have heard their names called out from the front station, only to look and find no one there. The downstairs area seems to be a hotspot for the unexplained; the voices of women have been reported drifting up from downstairs late at night when nobody else is in the building. The track lighting that illuminates the downstairs hallway has blown up. There also seems to be something strange about the stairway's second step up, like a cold spot or an eerie feeling—something that those who claim to have had the experience just cannot put their finger on.

The most well-known Landmark anomaly of all, however, has to be the Lady in the Ladies' Room. She is a painted, life-size, wooden woman standing silent inside the room near the sinks. She's dressed in old-fashioned, finely-frilled Victorian garb, and

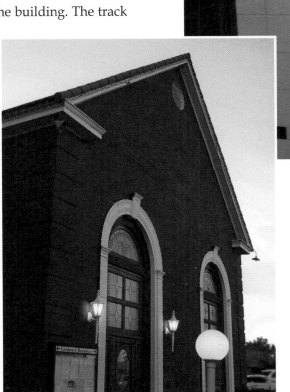

her eyes seem to stare right at you no matter where you stand. There are those who say that when no one is looking, she turns the water faucets on and off. Some have even said they've seen her reflection move in the restroom mirrors. Does this mysterious wooden statue roam the building in the dead of night when no one is there? No one can know for sure, but she has sent chills up many a spine.—*Heather Shade*

Fantasma Colorado

Sightings of this creature began in 1883 when the wives of two ranchers in Greenlee County caught a glimpse of its fiery hide outside their cabin. Only one woman, however, lived to tell the tale. When the survivor heard screams outside her home, she ran to the window in time to see a large, frightening beast trample her companion to death before disappearing into the brush. The monster resembled a horse, but was larger and more grotesque, and was ridden by what the woman believed was the devil himself.

When the women's husbands returned home that evening, they discovered the dead woman's body, crushed and mangled. The surrounding earth bore enormous hoofprints, and coarse reddish hairs were stuck to the nearby willow branches.

Days later a pair of prospectors who were camping several miles away were woken by an animal crashing through their tent. Scrambling outside, they saw the massive beast charging into the darkness. Found in the aftermath were the same large hoofprints and red hairs.

As the two stories came together, locals began referring to the creature as the Red Ghost, or Fantasma Colorado. The beast, many believed, was not of this earth. It was instead a murderous, demonic manifestation, dreadfully hideous and red like the blazes of hell. And it had chosen Greenlee County to mete out its terror.

A few weeks later the story developed a kink. Somewhere near Salt River to the northwest, a man named Cyrus Hamblin spotted the beast once again. This time, however, the demon offered an unobstructed view of itself by wandering into a clearing. From atop a ridge, Hamblin could see the Red Ghost for what it was: a camel.

At the time, camels weren't unheard of in Arizona.

The U.S. Army had imported a number of the animals in the 1850s as part of a transportation experiment. The camel, it was believed, would be ideal for the dry environment of the Arizona Territory and would aid in taming the region. Unfortunately, the animals weren't as submissive as traditional beasts of burden. In the end, the experiment was terminated, and most of the camels were sold off. But several escaped or were set free and roamed the Southwest for decades. The Red Ghost, it seemed, was one such survivor.

Yet, although the tale had found a small foothold in reality, it maintained a firm grasp on the bizarre. From his position, Hamblin could make out a figure straddling the creature's hump. It appeared to be a man. A dead man. His limp corpse was strapped to the camel's back.

Hamblin's story was corroborated several weeks later when the Red Ghost crossed the path of a group of trigger-happy prospectors. Eager for a little target practice, they snuck up on the animal and fired their guns. The men missed, but the noise caused the camel to bolt and dislodge part of its load. The prospectors discovered the item to be a skull, covered with bits of hair and desiccated flesh.

No one could know to whom the corpse belonged, but it was theorized that a stranded and dying man had tied himself to the animal in a futile attempt to find help. The rotting carcass became the already ill-tempered camel's curse, undoubtedly setting off the violence it dealt toward humankind, including the attack on the rancher's wife.

In 1893, a decade after the animal's initial appearance, a man named Mizoo Hastings shot and killed a camel believed to be the Red Ghost. Its headless rider was gone by that time, but the animal still bore rawhide strands secured to its body. Oddly, though, the straps were fastened in such a way that the long-dead

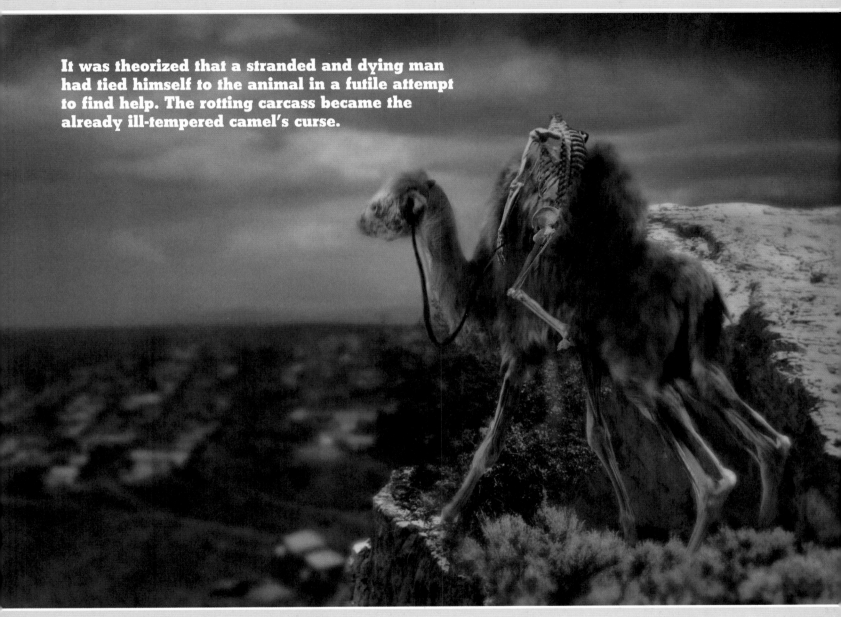

It was theorized that a stranded and dying man had tied himself to the animal in a futile attempt to find help. The rotting carcass became the already ill-tempered camel's curse.

rider could not have tied them himself. Apparently, someone else had lashed the man to the camel's back. Either the unwilling rider had been tied there alive as a merciless means of execution, or as a reporter at the time put it, it was a sick joke by "someone who had a camel and a corpse for which he had no use."

Camel sightings continue to this day. Though the experts will tell you none of the camels that were brought to Arizona, nor their offspring, could have endured all these years, people insist they're still out there. Even the Red Ghost is said to have survived and continues to stir up trouble in and around Greenlee County.

Tom Hess Bill Campbell Young Morley

Cemetery Safari

it's impossible to say how many people lie buried
beneath the Arizona crust. Detailed maps are
freckled with isolated cemeteries and lone, deserted
interments. Many more graveyards lie derelict in hard-
to-reach locations, forsaken when the nearby mines
played out. And some of the places lucky enough to
have been preserved hold more than one lost soul, the
residents' names long blown away in the desert wind.

As for the tombs that have endured intact through
their occupants' postmortem years, a sad number
still go unrecognized, thanks to our death-denying
culture. Modern society tends to push mortality and
the reminders thereof to the back of the mind. Thus
even the most outstanding resting places go unnoticed,
whether they be a burial ground populated by spooks
or a warehouse full of frozen human heads.

To right this wrong, we at *Weird Arizona* have dug
up a number of Arizona's notable shrines to the
passed away. Our goal is to see that these long overlooked, though dead, residents have their moment of
glory at last.

Boothill Graveyard

The most famous cemetery in Arizona, and one of the most notorious in America, is Tombstone's Boothill Graveyard. Established in 1878 with the whirlwind formation of the surrounding boomtown, it provided the city's deceased with a final resting place for only six years before it was replaced by the current cemetery. Yet it acquired upward of three hundred deceased, most of whom suffered an unnatural death in this infamously violent town.

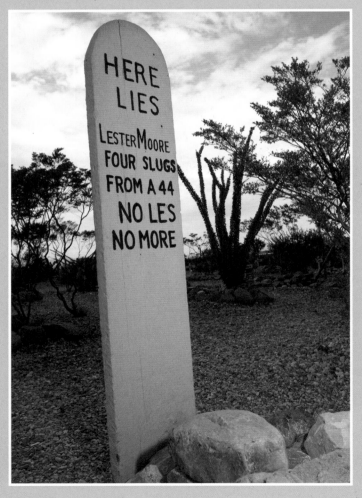

Among the cemetery's more famous dead are Billy Clanton, Tom McLaury, and Frank McLaury (McLowery on the sign in postcard at right), the three men shot to death in the world-renowned gunfight at the O.K. Corral (see "Fabled People and Places"). As it has for decades, their collective headstone states that they were MURDERED ON THE STREETS OF TOMBSTONE, a biased, though not necessarily inaccurate, accusation that their deaths at the hands of Doc Holliday and the Earp family were unjust. Fans of Wild West lore will also recognize the names of others buried here, like Frank Leslie, Dutch Annie, and Billy Claiborne, as well as John Heath, the only man ever lynched in Tombstone (see "Local Heroes and Villains").

Even in a place that stands as a sobering reminder of the city's tendency toward bloodshed, the irreverent wit of the Old West survives: A few men have been made famous in death thanks entirely to their grave markers. George Johnson, for example, was sentenced to hang for possessing a stolen horse, which he insisted he had bought without knowledge of its theft. His defense was eventually corroborated, but not until it was too late. He was buried with the following exoneration:

Here Lies/George Johnson/Hanged by Mistake/1882
He Was Right/We Was Wrong
But We Strung Him Up/And Now He's Gone

Just as memorable is the epitaph of Lester Moore, a Wells Fargo agent shot by a man who was upset over a damaged package:

Here Lies/Lester Moore/Four Slugs From a 44
No Les/No More

Many of those interred here remain unidentified. For years, Boothill lay neglected, its graves eroded by the

elements and its wooden markers faded or stolen. For some time, people actually used the site as a dump. When conscientious citizens began restoring the cemetery in the 1940s, a lack of detailed records resulted in a staggering number of markers labeled UNKNOWN.

Some of those lucky enough to be identified are remembered only by their nicknames—men like the Kansas Kid, Six Shooter Jim, and Red River Tom. Slightly luckier are those whose means of death were recorded, though without explanation: DIED A NATURAL DEATH, KILLED BY INDIANS, DROWNED, STABBED, or SHOT BY A CHINAMAN. Eight committed suicide, eleven were hanged, and twenty-five died of illness. One suffered fatal injuries after falling off a pair of stilts.

So many violent deaths in such a short amount of time has led to Boothill Graveyard's reputation for unusual supernatural activity. It's really no surprise the spirits would be restless, given such mayhem and graveyard neglect. Visitors commonly sense a feeling of uneasiness and experience unusual cold spots even amid the Arizona heat. Some who stand outside the fence at night report seeing strange "spook lights" drifting among the brush.

Tourists' photos reveal a surprising number of anomalies. Most consist of amorphous or vaguely identifiable figures, but on occasion someone will catch something strikingly bizarre. Probably the best example was obtained in recent years by Terry "Ike" Clanton, a relative of men involved in the O.K. Corral shootout. In a photo he took of a friend, another man is clearly seen in the background, wearing a black cowboy hat and apparently holding a knife. Oddly, the unidentified figure can be seen only from the waist up, as the lower half of his body evidently disappears into the ground.

Theories on who the man is vary greatly, but few people disagree that the image is frighteningly strange. So unusual is the clarity of the figure that the photograph has been voted one of the best ghost pictures in history, giving Boothill yet another claim to fame.

John Shaw, Dead Drunk

Sadly, nearly all the grave markers in Canyon Diablo's cemetery, located a couple miles north of Interstate 40's Two Guns exit, have been pilfered by souvenir hunters. Yet, in view of the history of this ghost town and the fact that many of the men killed here were simply buried where they died, the lonely stone wall left from Fred Volz's trading post could rightly be considered one collective headstone.

Of those for whom the wall might stand, few names are remembered. One that is known is John Shaw, a would-be thief who died here in his early twenties. Unlike others from the era, though, Shaw was known not for his fearless exploits but as the butt of a prank so macabre and sophomoric it could only have come out of the Wild West.

The year was 1905, when a man could saunter into a bar and order a round of rotgut without being made fun of for saying "rotgut." The town of Winslow was still growing, and the Wigwam Saloon downtown was a good place for a cowboy to stop and quench his thirst.

That's just what Shaw and his buddy Bill Smith had planned as they entered the Wigwam and ordered up a couple shots of whiskey. But as the pair waited for their refreshment, they turned their attention to the nearby dice game. The rolls at the table were hot, evident from the $600 stack of silver that caught their eyes. Shaw and Smith promptly had a change of plan. Before the two even downed their drinks, they filled their hands with their pistols and their pockets with the players' winnings; then they quickly left the way they had come.

The victims notified County Sheriff Houck and his deputy, who took a westbound train that night in pursuit of the young bandits. By the next evening, they had tracked down the two in Canyon Diablo. When the lawmen spotted the fugitives, a gunfight broke out,

ending with Smith injured and Shaw dead. When the smoke cleared, Shaw was pitched into a pine box and buried on-site.

When the boys back at the Wigwam heard what happened, someone remarked how their muggers never got the drinks they had ordered. In a strange case of cowboy ethics, the group felt it just wasn't right that Shaw would be buried without having a final slug. So, in the middle of the night, bottles in hand, some twenty men hopped a train bound for Canyon Diablo. By dawn, the presumably drunken mob had pulled Shaw from his casket, propped him against a fence, and offered the lifeless thief one last shot of whiskey.

Luckily, someone had the forethought to bring along a camera. Holding Shaw up by the pants, the men posed for snapshots as if they were on spring break. The prints were proudly displayed on a wall at the Wigwam Saloon until it was town down in the 1940s.

Benjamin J. Franklin

This illustrious gentleman, reportedly the great-grandson of founding father Benjamin Franklin, is buried in the Pioneer & Military Memorial Park in Phoenix. He was born in Kentucky, where he began a long career as a respected lawyer, passing the bar at the amazing age of twenty. At twenty-two he was elected to the Kansas senate.

With the outbreak of the Civil War, Franklin served in the Confederate Army, rising to the rank of captain. In 1885, he became a U.S. consul in China. After he returned to the States, President Grover Cleveland appointed him the twelfth territorial governor of Arizona.

And yet, despite all his accomplishments, he will eternally be known as the man whose headstone was spell-checked by a third grader.

Lost Grave of Cochise

Today, the canyon in the southeastern corner of Arizona known as Cochise Stronghold is a naturalist's dream, open to hiking, camping, and climbing. More than a century ago, however, it's doubtful any snowbird in his L. L. Bean trail vest would have made it through here alive.

Throughout the 1860s, the celebrated warrior Cochise and his band of Chiricahua Apache used this area of the Dragoon Mountains as their fortress. Though they had long been at peace with the white man, a poorly handled incident in which Cochise was falsely accused of kidnapping a young boy stirred up old troubles. The accusation resulted in the execution of three of Cochise's relatives, and the Apache leader swore revenge against the U.S. Army and American settlers. For ten years, Cochise and his followers holed up in their granite citadel, hiding among the sheer cliffs, all the while carrying out raids against their enemies.

When Cochise passed away in 1874, his body was interred here, in a secret crevice somewhere in the Dragoon Mountains. Only his people and a man named Tom Jeffords, a white man whom Cochise had befriended, knew the location of the grave. Somewhere among the granite rocks, the bones of one of the most famous Indian warriors in history still lie, but the secret of their whereabouts died with those who buried him.

Nevertheless, some visitors to Cochise Stronghold believe it's still possible to see the famous warrior. A man in Native American dress with long black hair is often seen wandering among the hills. Sometimes campers are startled by an eerie tune echoing among the rocks and look up to witness a man with a flute sitting atop one of the towering peaks. Perhaps Cochise, in spirit, still calls the Dragoons home.

Culling's Well

In the modern age, proof of one's existence is virtually impossible to avoid, what with birth certificates, employment documentation, medical records, and countless other forms and files that track our lives. But just a few decades ago, one might be born, travel the country, raise a family, pass away, and be forgotten entirely within just a few generations. Sometimes the only record a person might leave behind is the name chiseled on the headstone of his final resting place.

Such is the case with Charles C. Culling, caretaker of a remote rest stop northwest of Phoenix. His burial site, once known as Culling's Rancho Way Station, is now remembered simply as Culling's Well, after the lifesaving source of water he tended in the mid- to late 1800s. Mindful citizens have preserved the Culling name with a stenciled white cross and, in recent years, a plaque.

Little information is available on the watering hole, but we do know that during Culling's vigil, it was the only stable water source for miles. Even today it lies in a desolate stretch about three miles north of U.S. 60, some ten or so miles east of Wenden, accessible only in a vehicle with decent ground clearance.

Around the turn of the century, a lamp that hung high atop a pole earned Culling's Well the title Lighthouse of the Desert. The light served as a beacon to those traveling through the desert at night. It was allegedly erected after a young traveler's body was discovered nearby, the man

apparently dead from dehydration within shouting distance of the well. Unlike many Arizona legends, this one is evidently founded on truth, based on an excerpt from an 1894 edition of the *Arizona Republican,* which reports the deaths of two prospectors in the area. One was found only four miles from the well. His colleague, who died about eight miles behind him, held a journal with the entry "I am William Rogers. . . . Goodbye. I am dying of thirst. My partner, Bill McDonald, has left me to go on to Harqua Hala."

Though the aforementioned article says the two men were buried upon discovery, it's uncertain whether any of the handful of graves at Culling's Well are theirs. Railroad ties and unkempt piles of stones mark a short row of plots at the site, but nearly all are unmarked, their residents' names, like so many others, having been lost forever. All except Charles Culling's.

Great Pyramids of Arizona

It seems Arizona has been working to establish its very own ancient necropolis: Several of the state's prominent residents, for reasons yet to be deciphered, have been buried within or beneath pyramids. To date, a few have been identified. With any hope, more will soon be excavated.

Last Camp of Hi Jolly

One of the most bizarre government endeavors in history began in 1856, when a U.S. Navy ship unloaded a delivery from overseas. The project, if successful, would enable the United States to overcome the harsh, arid conditions of its newly acquired western territories and more easily expand its military presence there. The key to the experiment's success, officials hoped, lay in the cargo: camels.

Jefferson Davis, then Secretary of War, believed the camels would solve the U.S. Army's supply problems in the west, as the animals could carry more than mules and would require fewer resources. So he brought several dozen of the animals over from Egypt and Turkey, along with a number of camel drivers.

Among the drivers arriving in the States was a man named Haiji Ali, nicknamed Hi Jolly by those he worked with, either out of jest or simply because they couldn't figure out how to spell or pronounce his name correctly. He and the camels helped in naval officer Lieutenant Edward Beale's effort to establish a reliable wagon route west. Hi Jolly tended to the beasts on the trail and acted as mobile camel expert.

Although the army held high hopes for its so-called Camel Corps, the experiment was ultimately deemed a failure. The camels were hardworking, but they tended to be ill-tempered, and the mere sight of them drove panic into the hearts of other livestock. Eventually, the beasts were done away with. As for their drivers, little is known what happened to most of them, but Hi Jolly stayed in America, adopted Arizona as his home, and ran a few

not-so-profitable businesses, becoming a beloved local character.

In the end, Hi Jolly wound up in Quartzsite, west of Phoenix, where he passed away in 1902. Thirty-three years later, the Arizona Highway Department erected a pyramid-shaped monument over his grave and buried the ashes of the last government dromedary with him. The monument, crowned with a camel, is the most popular attraction in Quartzsite.

Hunt's Tomb

High in the great urban getaway that is Phoenix's Papago Park, a gleaming pyramid shines in the bright Arizona sun. Perched atop one of the park's tallest buttes, it offers an impressive view for its distinguished resident, mustachioed Arizona politico George W. P. Hunt.

When the Arizona Territory gained statehood in 1912, Hunt became its first governor and then was reelected again and again. In all, you might say he served a record seven terms, although that opens up a fairly large can of nits for picking, since at least one of his elections was plagued with some irregularities. But never mind about that.

When Hunt died in 1934, he was entombed in the pyramid among the Papago Buttes, a dazzling sight covered in what appears to be white bathroom tile. Easily accessed by a short trail, the glossy white structure can be so bright under the summer sun it could easily leave any curious visitor with flash burns.

Poston's Folly

Although Hunt's tomb is Arizona's most widely recognized pyramid, it is evidently a copycat. Forty miles to the southeast stands a natural-stone version, the dedication of which Hunt attended as governor in 1925, before apparently pinching the idea. Arizona's oldest-known pyramid, this one holds the venerable Charles Debrille Poston, the man who successfully lobbied to establish the Arizona Territory and consequently earned himself the designation Father of Arizona.

Despite the prominent title, little is generally written about Poston's contributions to the state, which include his service as the first superintendent of Indian affairs and his position as one of the first territorial delegates to Congress. Even less is written, and understandably so, about his one-man effort to unite Arizona in the devotion of sun worship.

During his post-congressional travels to the Far East, Poston became fascinated with Zoroastrianism. He wrote a book titled *The Sun Worshipers of Asia* in 1877 and even apparently became a convert himself. The culmination of Poston's interest in the religion came after his return to Arizona, while serving as land registrar in Florence.

North of town Poston discovered the ruins of a Native American tower atop a three-hundred-foot high butte named Primrose Hill. Believing it to be the remains of a fire temple, Poston decided there must be a connection with ancient Persian sun worshipers, who, he believed, crossed the Bering Strait to North America and brought their religion with them. In reality, the stone tower was probably just an abandoned Indian lookout post built to watch for enemy tribes, but that didn't stop Poston. He restored the tower, spent thousands of dollars on building a road up the hill, and raised on its summit a blue-and-white flag sporting a big red sun.

As his magnum opus, Poston planned to erect a great sun temple on Primrose Hill, which he hoped future converts would visit to participate in ancient Zoroastrian rituals. Unfortunately, he ran out of money before he could build it. Poston wrote to the Shah of Persia in the hopes of obtaining financial support for his undertaking, but none was forthcoming. He was eventually forced to give up the endeavor, and the whole affair became known as Poston's Folly.

Poston was buried in a Phoenix cemetery in 1902. Twenty-three years later, however, sentimentalists decided to honor the former sun worshiper's wishes to be buried on his beloved hilltop and dug him back up. Using the very road Poston had built almost five decades earlier to transport the body, the people of Arizona transferred him to a thirteen-and-one-half-foot-tall pyramid atop what is now known as Poston's Butte. Poston never got his temple, but he was buried facing the rising sun.

The Puzzle of D. Beaver, Grand Canyon

Discovering a lone grave site in a secluded locale can be an exciting experience, full of mystery about the occupant's identity, history, and—though it may be a little morbid—cause of death. It's not so much fun when you find someone freshly buried and in your favorite camping spot.

That's exactly what happened to Georgie White, one of the Grand Canyon's most well-known whitewater river runners. In the summer of 1957, she and the members of the tour group she was hosting stopped at a place called Nankoweap Camp. As they were getting ready to settle in, they were surprised to discover a six-foot-long, recently packed mound of sand along the riverbank. At one end was a marker bearing the inscription HERE LIES D. BEAVER, DIED JUNE 15, 1957.

Georgie knew that one of her colleagues, a fellow rafter named Gaylord Staveley, had led a trip through the area just days before, so she considered the possibility the grave was just some bizarre joke. A quick investigation, though, proved there was nothing comical about it. Georgie dug through the sand just far enough to reveal the dreadful sight and smell of a decaying corpse.

Racing for the nearest phone, Georgie notified the National Park Service that Staveley had lost one of his passengers and that he, D. Beaver, was buried upriver. Astoundingly, Staveley hadn't notified them himself. In fact, this was the first the Park Service had heard about it. When the NPS checked the passenger log Staveley had submitted prior to his trip, they found that not only had he neglected to report the death of Mr. Beaver, he hadn't even listed the man on the itinerary as required.

Things got serious in a hurry. The NPS notified the county sheriff's department, the Arizona Department of Public Safety, and the park rangers at Lake Mead. Staveley was a wanted man. Unfortunately, he and his group had exited the canyon unseen and no one was able to locate him for some time. Naturally, this spawned a host of rumors, including a healthy buzz regarding murder.

When Staveley finally turned up, the park superintendent bestowed a vehement reprimand. But Staveley had a perfectly reasonable explanation. He and his tour group had discovered the body after landing at Nankoweap and covered it merely out of convenience. The stench was overwhelming, and after all, they intended to camp there for the night. Really, he didn't think it would cause so much trouble, and he certainly didn't realize he would have to report it. Even though it was surprisingly large, it was still just a rotten beaver carcass.

The grave marker was his group's idea. The D was short for dead.

Georgie White

Collision in the Canyon

Near the Colorado River's junction with the Little Colorado, rafters floating through the Grand Canyon may notice a curious flash of light coming from high up the canyon walls. Glints of sunlight, which mimic the shimmer of the river's surface, reflect off fragments of aluminum embedded hundreds of feet up the side of Chuar Butte. Like ghostly flickers, these sparks of radiance serve as the sole marker indicating the site of the worst disaster ever to take place in Arizona's largest national park.

On June 30, 1956, Trans World Airlines flight 2, a Lockheed Super Constellation named *Star of the Seine,* lifted off from Los Angeles International Airport carrying sixty-four passengers and six crew members. Beginning a long flight to the East Coast, it would first head northeast toward Daggett, California, before passing over Arizona and making its way toward Colorado. Having been delayed from its scheduled takeoff at 8:30 a.m. Pacific time, the flight left the runway thirty-one minutes late.

United Airlines flight 718, a Douglas DC-7 named *Mainliner Vancouver*, had also been delayed. Originally scheduled for an 8:45 a.m. departure, it left Los Angeles three minutes behind the *Star of the Seine* at 9:04. Its path would take it on a more easterly course to Needles, California, where it would then turn northeast, also toward Colorado. It carried fifty-three passengers and five crew members.

Given their flight times, both planes were expected to cross the Painted Desert line of position—an aeronautical reference point just east of the Grand Canyon—at the same time. This was not to be a problem, however, as air traffic control had assigned the *Star of the Seine* a cruising altitude of 19,000 feet and the *Mainliner Vancouver* an altitude of 21,000 feet, giving the flights 2,000 feet of breathing room.

However, with CAA permission, flights were allowed to deviate from their assigned flight paths somewhat—to give their passengers a better view of the Grand Canyon, for example—provided they remained safely out of each other's way. For this reason, air traffic control denied the *Star of the Seine*'s request to climb to 21,000 feet outside Daggett, because that would eventually have put it in the same air space as the *Vancouver*.

Both the *Star of the Seine* and the *Vancouver* were flying under instrument flight rules, or IFR, meaning their sight lines were obscured or nonexistent and their instruments were guiding them. So the *Seine* amended its request to "one thousand on top," or 1,000 feet above cloud level. For this, they were given the go-ahead. Such a request placed them under VFR, or visual flight rules, and left their altitude at their discretion, since they would presumably be able to see other aircraft above the clouds. Unfortunately, one thousand on top placed the flight at

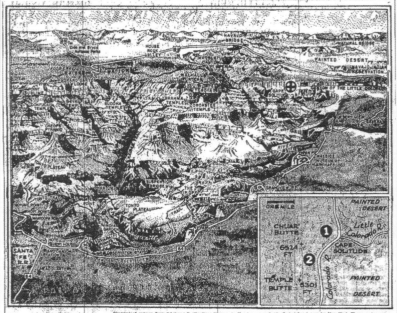

WHERE PLANES CRASHED: The two airliners fell near Cape Solitude (cross). The United Air Lines plane went down on a slope of Chuar Butte (1 on inset) and the T. W. A. craft fell at Temple Butte (2).

21,000 feet, as previously requested.

Few passengers, if any, knew what happened. The resulting collision happened so fast, not even the pilots had time to react. From the angle of impact, it's assumed the crews never even saw each other. At 11:31 Mountain time, radio operators in Salt Lake City, Utah, received the only indication that something had gone wrong, though the words were so garbled it was hard to know what was said. Investigators later deciphered the message, which came from the *Mainliner Vancouver*, as "We are going in!"

Following the collision, both planes fell four miles to earth, crashing on the north bank of the Colorado River. Debris covered the area. Fires melted and charred both planes. Not one of the 128 people aboard survived.

Analysis of the wreckage showed that the *Mainliner Vancouver* had overtaken the slower *Star of the Seine* from above and to the right. The *Vancouver*'s outer left wing severed as it hit, but not before ripping through the *Star*'s fuselage and slicing off its tail. The *Vancouver*, its wing

damaged, flew out of control into the wall of Chuar Butte. The *Star* plunged nose-down onto the northeastern slope of Temple Butte over a mile to the south.

In the days that followed, military helicopters made a reported seventy-six trips to recover the bodies and debris that lay in the Grand Canyon. Investigators could identify only a few of the passenger remains recovered. Most had to be buried in mass graves. Two were established, one in Grand Canyon Cemetery for those onboard the *Mainliner Vancouver* and another in Flagstaff's Citizens Cemetery for those on the *Star of the Seine*. Together they list the names of those who couldn't be identified, ninety-seven in all.

As for the plane wreckage, most of the *Star of the Seine* was cleaned up in the late 1970s. Much of the *Mainliner Vancouver*, however, still remains on the face of Chuar Butte due to its inaccessibility. Bits of fuselage and machinery still hang from the towering cliffs, glinting in the sun, reminding passersby of the tragedy that occurred there more than fifty years ago.

Ernesto Miranda Gets the Right to Remain Silent

A *simple stone* at Block 677, Lot 1, Space 2 in the City of Mesa Cemetery marks the final resting place of a man whose actions had far-reaching effects on our legal process, securing the constitutional rights of anyone ever accused of a crime. Yet he was no politician, judge, or lawyer, but a chronic felon and convicted sexual deviant.

The crime that prompted the criminal's unintentional achievement took place the night of March 2, 1963. An eighteen-year-old girl, who was known by her family to be deeply shy and moderately mentally disabled, had just gotten off work and was walking home. As the girl neared her house, a man grabbed her and forced her into his car. Despite her pleas for freedom, the man tied the girl's wrists and ankles, then drove out to the desert and raped her. He then robbed his victim of the $4 she had in her purse, returned her to her neighborhood, and disappeared.

Ernesto Miranda had been in and out of trouble most of his life. His criminal convictions, which began in the eighth grade, included burglary, auto theft, and minor sex offenses that landed him in reform school and eventually prison. He tried the army, but further transgressions got him thrown into the military stockade before he was dishonorably discharged. After roaming the Southwest and spending time in various detention centers, Miranda returned to his home state of Arizona to start over. Regrettably, his criminal nature got the better of him all over again when he raped the eighteen-year-old girl.

The authorities caught up with him once again. They pulled him into an interrogation room, where a confession came with little difficulty. Miranda owned up to the crime and even identified his victim, affirming, "That's the girl." Police then asked him to write down his confession on paper. The stationery he was given included a disclaimer stating that the suspect recognized that his confession was voluntary and that he understood his rights. Those rights, however, were not listed on the paper, nor were they ever explained to him—a detail that would soon produce ripples reaching well beyond the Phoenix Police Department.

In June 1963, Miranda stood trial before a jury and the aptly named Judge McFate. Miranda's attorney, Alvin Moore, objected to his client's confession being entered into evidence because he believed Miranda should have been informed he had a right to counsel at the time of his arrest, but McFate overruled

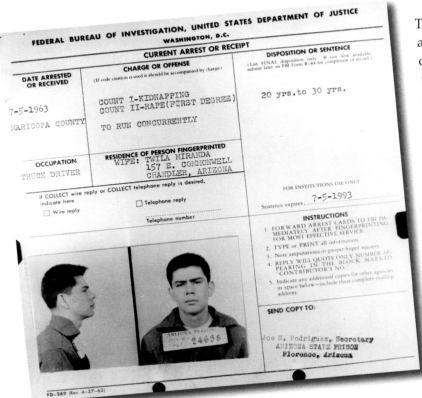

Attorney John Flynn leaves the courtroom with his client Ernesto Miranda.

The Supreme Court agreed, and on June 13, 1966, it ruled that "procedural safeguards" must be utilized to ensure suspects were aware of their rights. This led to the now famous speech heard on every cop show on TV, "You have the right to remain silent. . . ." Known as the Miranda warning, the incantation has embedded Ernesto Miranda's name in the English vernacular, as police are now required to "Mirandize" suspects.

As for Miranda's rape case, it was tried once again without the written confession, and he was still found

the objection. The jury heard the confession, and Miranda was found guilty of rape and kidnapping.

Moore appealed the verdict before the Arizona Supreme Court in 1965, but the original decision was upheld. At this point, the American Civil Liberties Union got into the act. The ACLU had been looking for a case to bring before the U.S. Supreme Court to clarify a suspect's rights. They chose Miranda's.

Attorneys working for the ACLU argued that the suspect's Fifth Amendment right not to incriminate himself had been violated, as well as his Sixth Amendment right to counsel, which should have been invoked from the time of arrest. Furthermore, a man like Miranda, with a limited education, would not be expected to know those rights.

guilty. It turns out that he had also confessed the rape to his common-law wife from prison. And, genius that he was, he told his wife to relay a message to his rape victim: He would marry the girl if she would drop the charges. Of course, this upset Miranda's wife, and she brought his confession to the authorities.

After Miranda gained parole in 1972, he used his notoriety to sell autographed Miranda warning cards for $1.50 each. Name recognition wasn't enough to turn his life around, though, and he continued getting into trouble. Finally, in 1976, he got into a bar fight and was stabbed to death.

When officers captured a suspect in Miranda's killing, they made sure to inform him that anything he said could and would be used against him in a court of law.

Not all of Arizona's graveyards are set aside as a final resting place for human remains. Sometimes the interred deceased were never really alive to begin with, though it can't be said that they didn't go far and fly high in their time.

The Boneyard—Where Old Planes Go to Die

In the Arizona desert is one of the most surreal sights I've ever come across in 25 years of exploring ruins—AMARC, the Aerospace Maintenance and Regeneration Center, also known as the Boneyard. It is next to Davis-Monthan Air Force Base and was created after World War II. It's where old planes go to die. Some are actually just kept in storage until needed, some are converted into pilotless drones to be used for target practice, some are sold to foreign governments, while others are picked clean for parts. But in the end most wind up being sold for scrap to the half dozen or so aircraft salvage yards located around the base.

Right now there are over 4,000 aircraft in the base—that's around $30 billion in tax dollars. I first visited in 1989, and have gone back several times since. When I was first at AMARC there were thousands of F-4 Phantoms that were used in Vietnam and were then being retired from the Air National Guard. Today F-14 Tomcats are showing up more frequently as they're being retired. There are even B-1 bombers, which cost over $300 million each to build.

On one trip I chartered a helicopter for a couple of hundred dollars and with the Air Force Base's permission I was able to fly over AMARC to photograph. A door was taken off the chopper and I was strapped into a harness so I could sort of hang outside with my feet on the skid. The duct tape they put around the latch as a safety precaution didn't actually make me feel safer.

When I first visited in 1989, there were hundreds of B-52s there. Most have since been destroyed as part of the START treaty with the Soviet Union—they used this huge guillotine to chop them into large pieces. The chunks

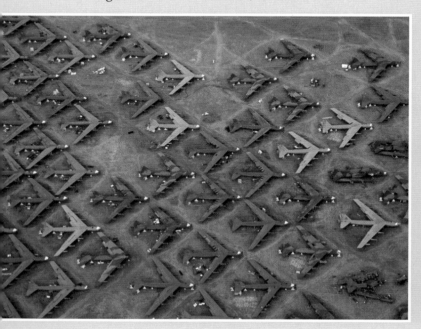

would then be left in place for 90 days to let Soviet satellites verify their destruction before scrapping them.

I climbed into the belly hatch of one of the B-52s and made my way to the cockpit to take some photos with a fisheye lens. For such a big plane the insides are incredibly cramped. I couldn't stand up straight and there were rows of electronic equipment racks lining the aisles. Later, I was warned not to climb into any of the planes, as rattlesnakes like to go inside to stay cool. Getting killed by a snake on a plane that could've killed millions would certainly be an ironic way to go.

A fence keeps you from getting close to the C-123 Providers. That's because the C-123s were used to drop millions of gallons of dioxin-containing Agent Orange during the Vietnam War to defoliate forests to deny cover to the North Vietnamese. During one of my visits I heard that the civilians who work there can't touch them because of OSHA rules (Occupational Safety and Health Administration). So they could still be there in fifty years. Perhaps they should simply be declared a monument to the soldiers and civilians harmed by Agent Orange.

So if you're in Tucson and want to see something truly surreal, drive around AMARC, or, better yet, take the tour offered by Pima Air Museum—www.pimaair.org. If you don't get out that way, I've got more photos of my trips to AMARC on my website—www.modern-ruins.com. There's also a great website about AMARC at www.amarcexperience.com. And you can also have fun at Google Maps—just search "Davis-Monthan Air Force Base" and zoom in and around the planes.—*Phil Buehler*

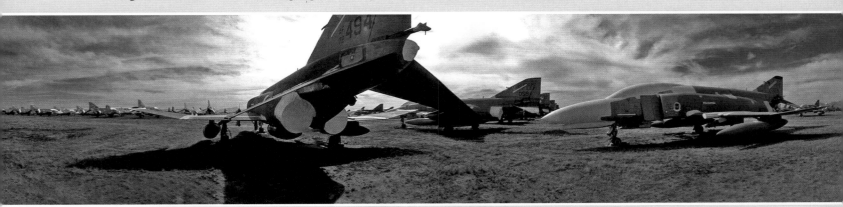

Abandoned in Arizona

Before *I began* Weird Arizona, my interest in derelict structures was mostly superficial. I saw them as good photographic subjects, but that was about it. Fear of venom, tetanus, or worse kept me moving on to less forbidding attractions.

But the more decaying motels and gas stations I encountered on old Route 66, the more my curiosity was piqued. I spotted a chair sitting in the corner of an otherwise empty room, an ashtray with a half-smoked cigarette resting on a windowsill—details of everyday life that were left behind in the final moments before a building's demise. These seemingly trivial elements started me thinking about what had gone on in these places before I arrived. Who had walked through these doors? What made them leave? As I began researching the histories of ghost towns and gutted trading posts, I discovered stories of corruption, misfortune, and murder.

Soon I was pulling off the road at every crumbling edifice I passed, hoping to find evidence of a new, untold story. I endured more scares than I cared for, usually miles from another soul, but these forsaken relics have become my biggest reason to return to Arizona again and again. Of all my investigations across the state, it will be my trepidacious ventures into forgotten history that will remain foremost in my mind.

Two Guns

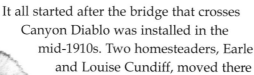

Take any exit along the course of former Route 66 and you're bound to run into something forsaken. The assortment of broken-down buildings found beside Interstate 40 east of Flagstaff is a perfect example. As indicated by the sign at exit 230, they comprise the town of Two Guns—or at least they did. More than once, in fact. Two Guns has been resurrected more times than William Shatner's career, and it's fallen by the wayside every time. It's just one of the reasons the locals insist these acres are cursed.

It all started after the bridge that crosses Canyon Diablo was installed in the mid-1910s. Two homesteaders, Earle and Louise Cundiff, moved there in the 1920s and set up shop along the National Old Trails Highway. The Cundiffs opened a large trading post, a free campground, and cottages for rent. What's left of their original store continues to crumble today at the south end of the bridge.

The name Two Guns came from a somewhat eccentric character named Harry "Indian" Miller, a talented huckster who falsely claimed to be a full-blooded Apache named Chief Crazy Thunder. A partner of sorts with Earle Cundiff, Miller signed a lease to do business on the property and erected a long stone building he dubbed Fort Two Guns. When Cundiff petitioned to open a post office, the name Two Guns was officially rejected in favor of Canyon Lodge, but Two Guns would be the moniker that endured.

Despite being stuck with a rather lackluster name, the town went on to achieve years of popularity as a roadside attraction. And its success was due in large part to the efforts of Indian Miller. For one thing, the extensive complex he called a fort was primarily a wild animal zoo. Held within its stone and chicken wire cages were bobcats, coral snakes, porcupines, and a variety of other creatures.

Miller also exploited the legend of the nearby Apache Death Cave, launching yet another tourist draw. The cave, located just the other side of the canyon, was the site of a mass execution nearly fifty years earlier. A band of some forty Apaches had been discovered hiding in the narrow fissure after committing a series of raids against the Navajo. Trapped inside, the Apaches were burned alive for their crimes. Miller renamed the tomb Mystery Cave and erected a cluster of pueblos and ramps above the entryway. He presented the buildings as ancient cliff dwellings and arranged guided tours, hawking native wares and soft drinks down in the canyon.

Not surprisingly, it was around this time that the legendary curse of Two Guns began to germinate. For reasons unknown, the Cundiffs decided to lease their store to a pair of drifters who subsequently disappeared in the middle of the night with armloads of merchandise. Worse, Cundiff found himself in a dispute over Miller's contract, which prompted Miller to shoot him fatally, in cold blood.

Though Miller was inexplicably acquitted of the murder, he went on to suffer his own misfortune. On two separate occasions, he was clawed nearly to death by a mountain lion and a lynx, both residents of his zoo. And reports indicate he lost his daughter around this time in a car wreck. By 1930, he had packed up and left Two Guns.

Even with the bogus Indian gone, the curse persisted. In 1938, Route 66 was rerouted and moved to the other side of the bridge, on the opposite side of the canyon. Louise Cundiff and her new husband, Phillip Hesch, were compelled to rebuild everything, including the zoo.

Though its large MOUNTAIN LIONS sign was still visible from Interstate 40, the new zoo was shut down soon after it opened, then sold in 1950 along with the rest of the property. Over the years, Two Guns had a series of managers, until the entire complex burned down in 1971, just as I-40 was due to open with an exit specially dedicated to the town.

Further resuscitations have since been attempted, but they've only added to the number of decaying buildings in this ever-expanding ghost town. One simple word, graffitied on the friendly sign near the most recently failed gas station, conveys the message that someone, or something, has been trying to tell us all along: *NOT* WELCOME.

Jerome's Sliding Jail

Jerome, a former mining town, lies at the northern end of Highway 89A, atop Cleopatra Hill. Well, not so much atop as on the side of. The whole town is on a slope. To get from one block to the next involves a climb up a flight of stairs or a walk down a very steep sidewalk. To live there, you have to have the calves of Lance Armstrong.

Houses and businesses began popping up along the peak's steep incline during the late 1800s and early 1900s as nearby mining prospered. As the First World War hit, copper prices soared and Jerome climbed even farther. Its population rose to 15,000, and everyone was building a house with a view, higher and higher on the steep slopes.

The property values wouldn't last, though. As underground mining switched to open-pit excavation, miners employed large-scale blasting to move huge sections of the mountain at once. As a result, the town was repeatedly rocked off its foundation. As the stock market slid in 1929, so did Jerome's residents—downhill—at a rate of about three-eighths of an inch every month. Whole blocks slipped slowly downward. One J. C. Penney store eventually had to build stairs leading from the sidewalk to its front door, which had moved four feet lower than it had been.

The most dramatic shift in location was that of Jerome's jailhouse. A small concrete building, roughly ten feet by twenty feet, it now teeters below a parking area on Hull Avenue. Originally it was on the other side of the street. As a result of the blasting and the subsequent shift in the

underlying fault, Jerome's slammer skated a good 225 feet from where it started.

Strangely, though the town has become a tourist destination in recent years, the Sliding Jail, as it's been named, is practically ignored. You can read about it in plenty of tourism literature, but Jerome doesn't appear to have any signs pointing the way. Instead, you have to ask around for directions. Even then it's hard to spot, as it's almost completely obscured from view by a basketball court, which is nearly level with the jail's roof.

Bars were erected around the jail (to keep people out, ironically), but they've rusted and are starting to collapse. Retaining rods were installed as well, obviously to prevent the structure from collapsing completely, but their effect is diminishing. It's evident the jail is still sliding. In fact, if something isn't done to preserve this local oddity soon, it may end up as an attraction downhill in Clarkdale.

Vulture Mine

Because of changing conditions, countless mining towns in Arizona were abandoned by 1950 and left to fall into ruins. If one looks closely, however, a few gems can still be found among the rocky desert soil. One shining example of a Wild West boomtown is the Vulture Mine, located a few miles south of present-day Wickenburg.

The mine was established in 1863 by Austrian immigrant Henry Wickenburg. As he walked through the desert, according to one legend, a particularly hopeful vulture followed him for days, waiting for the prospector to drop dead. Fed up, Wickenburg picked up a rock and threw it at the bird. He missed, but the rock split open to reveal gold. Vulture Mine and Vulture City were born.

During its peak years between 1880 and 1900, Vulture City had a population of almost 5,000 people. It boasted a post office, school, assay office, machine shop, and housing for the miners and their families. The ore produced was run through an

eighty-stamp mill, which processed approximately 240,000 tons of earth during its heyday.

Although it's slowly deteriorating, the Vulture Mine is perhaps the best preserved ghost town in the state of Arizona. It is located on just over an acre of privately owned land a good twelve miles from town. An estimated $200 million in gold was produced from this mine, and two to three times that much is reported to remain underground.

Today the mine is open to the public for a small entry fee. It is a very authentic attraction for several good reasons. The only tours are self-guided. The buildings have not been reinforced and are believed to be all original. Most are still standing, but a few have collapsed sections. There are no safety nets or fences to prevent visitors from falling down an open mine shaft, and handrails and wheelchair ramps are nonexistent. Vultures

still fly overhead, circling about the sky and gliding on the dry desert air. This is not a place for the weak or the timid.

A walking trail takes visitors in a loop around the town site. It's a little less than a mile, but contains enough attractions to keep anyone busy for several hours. The assay office is the most impressive building, with two stories of original furnishings and lots of surprises. The walls of the office are estimated to contain over $600,000 in gold and silver, since they were built from mine tailings, the waste left behind following ore extraction. One room features an underground safe beneath a sliding hatch in the floor. An old Singer sewing machine, tables, chairs, bottles and cans, and other artifacts remain in place, coated with a thick layer of dust.

Continuing on down the trail, visitors are lured by the sight of a large wooden A-frame jutting up into the sky. It marks the location of the main shaft, which is

elements. No windows or doors remain, and the whole building makes creaking noises when the wind picks up. There's very little machinery left in the mill, save for a large device with some heavy gears attached to it.

As one heads back toward the assay office, large piles of mine tailings are visible. Some have been processed at least twice, and there's probably little gold left in them. Near the assay office is a small pile of crumbling bricks in a rectangular shape. The map identifies the ruins as the site of Henry Wickenburg's original home. On this spot, some eighteen men were hanged from the thick branches of a now very old ironwood tree. The men were accused of stealing ore from the mine. A hand-lettered sign is the only memorial to the miners whose lives ended here over one hundred years ago.

Vulture Mine is a great place for anyone who enjoys a lesson in history as well as danger and adventure. Nowhere else in the state is there a ghost town as well preserved and as authentic as this one.—*Trevor Freeman*

surprisingly accessible. The shaft goes down over 3,000 feet and maintains a perfect thirty-five-degree angle the entire distance. Deep inside, numerous side tunnels were dug about every hundred feet to explore for more ore deposits. The rails from the ore carts are still there; they are visible for about fifty feet before disappearing into the darkness.

Next to the main shaft, the machine shop is easily identifiable by its tin-roof construction. A massive compressor greets visitors who enter the building, and it's quite a sight. Pipes and valves run every which way, somehow connecting to the two large pulleys at the far end of the contraption. The machine looks impressive, as if it still might roar to life one day. The question of how it even got there is a good one.

Beyond the machine shop lies the ball mill, a three-walled structure, with one side completely open to the

Twin Arrows Trading Post

The billboards for this classic highway stop, a few miles east of Winona, have so far survived, but only just. The paint is fading fast, and whole sections of plywood are beginning to fall away. A sign explains why: The NOW OPEN has been stenciled over to read NOW CLOSED.

The demise of Twin Arrows is one of the saddest losses of Americana in recent history, a perfect example of the quirky roadside attraction giving way to progress. The oversized icons, two twenty-five foot arrows, are no longer enough to pique a motorist's interest, so they and the truck stop they once advertised have gone by the wayside. Twin Arrows Trading Post, the "Best Little Stop on I-40," is receding into the timeline.

According to Bob Moore's *Route 66: Spirit of the Mother Road,* it was originally called the Canyon Padre Trading Post, named for the gorge that cuts nearby. The date it came into being, though, is difficult to pin down. It was almost certainly established after 1946, as Jack Rittenhouse made no mention of it in his classic *A Guide Book to Highway 66,* a thorough, stop-by-stop handbook published that year.

Whenever it was established, the waypoint didn't garner real attention until its name was changed to Twin Arrows, a play on the name of neighboring town Two Guns. Combined with the simple addition of slanted utility poles, cleverly trimmed with matching feathers and arrowheads, the change was enough to establish the site as a true roadside attraction.

Unfortunately, as with so many Route 66 businesses, the construction of the interstate through the area in the 1970s spelled impending doom. Despite having exit 219 designated in its name, the gas station/cafe/gift shop soon began to fail. It reportedly changed hands a number of times, reopening for the last time in 1995, before finally closing down for good. When the property was

relinquished to the state, a NO TRESPASSING sign sounded the death knell for Twin Arrows.

Jersey barriers now cordon off the property, blocking truckers who, for a time, used the space to catch some Z's. The station's two gas pricing signs remain, although one has been stripped of its digits. The other, out of reach, is frozen at $1.36 a gallon.

The most disappointing sight is the demise of the arrows themselves. They held out until around the year 2000 when the harsh desert finally defeated them. Since then, they've been decaying piece by piece. In time, unless someone intervenes, they'll be nothing but Twin Chopsticks.

Peak Trading Post

Doing business at the base of Picacho Peak for a reported thirty-plus years, the Peak Trading Post was a successful purveyor of Indian arts and crafts, blankets, jewelry, and other thematic merchandise. Adorned with the usual Native American emblems, it was also an expo of red-skinned stereotype. Wooden caricatures lined the building's façade: a squaw with her hair in braids and headdress-adorned chiefs with their arms crossed stoically. Totem poles, of course, towered above the entryway, despite their being ridiculously out of place so far from the Pacific Northwest.

Most notorious was the twenty-foot-tall, shirtless Indian perched at the shop's corner. Standing sentry over the Peak, the fiberglass brave wore feathers on his head and leather fringe on his pants. With a skyward thrust of his right hand, he greeted approaching customers with a silent "How!" In his other hand, he gripped a hatchet.

Yet, like so many of Arizona's trading posts, most of it is now just a memory. The building vanished suddenly in a fiery blaze years ago. What started the fire is uncertain. A seventy-year-old neighbor, who tried unsuccessfully to extinguish the flames with a garden hose, said she saw a flash of light before it all erupted in a fireball. She had assumed it was lightning, but the sky that night was clear. A former employee, when asked what she thought had been the cause of the fire, responded, "Insurance?"

Today, the Peak looks as it did moments after the smoke cleared. Little remains but ashes and twisted metal. By some miracle, the wooden figures survived, although they're teetering and charred from the flames. The bare-chested warrior, on the other hand, looks as though he exploded. His oversized appendages lie scattered about. Here, an amputated foot; next to it, a leg melted at the knee; over there, two dismembered hands, blackened and fraying. If the big Indian still had a face, a single tear would be rolling down his cheek.

Almost Family Fun World

It was to be known as Family Fun World, but lack of both families and fun prevented this fenced-off collection of oddities from being much more than just a world inside its creator's head. The property, located along Interstate 10 in the town of Eloy, is owned by a man named Richard Songers. Songers reportedly purchased the land in 1995 with the intention of turning it into a combination zoo, racetrack, amusement park, and concert arena, but after years of development, was forced to give up the dream for lack of funds. The COMING SOON sign changed to KEEP OUT.

In 2001, Songers held an auction to offload some of the unusual objets d'art he had assembled for his park that never was. Among the items: unused oil derricks, a set of kiddy carnival rides, antique fire trucks, and rows of enormous tires. Most of it, however, still sits there, the remnants of unrealized amusement. There are numerous, and inexplicable, pink-and-blue gondola cages on stilts, as well as a huge pastel archway and several utility poles buried at unusual angles. Plus, in a far corner rests an Old West town fashioned from semitrailer cargo containers, one side painted like wooden buildings, the other with a badland backdrop, apparently to make visitors feel as if they've been transported away from the modern desert hills that surround them to the desert hills of the Wild West.

Actually, the place looks like it might still serve up a lot of fun. It would be ideal for urban exploration or paintball warfare for the uninvited. Unfortunately, both are out of the question, as the property is patrolled by guard dogs and a shirtless man in a golf cart.

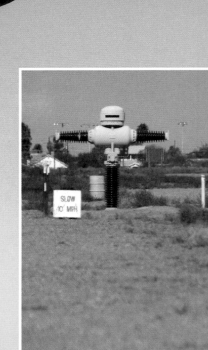

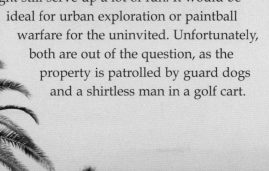

The Luer Rocket

"We have news for you!" Steve LaVigne and his cohorts called out as they hopped down from their vehicle. They had just pulled up in front of Prescott's *Daily Courier* with what they considered a big story.

LaVigne had called a construction company and asked them to help tow a payload to his property in east Prescott. When the company found out his cargo consisted of one thirty-five-foot-long rocket ship, they said they'd do it for free. They just wanted to take it on a joyride.

"We might as well have a little quickie parade downtown. Freak out the people on Whiskey Row," LaVigne recalled with a smile. "So we did just that." Plus, they figured they would drop by the offices of the local newspaper and garner a little publicity while they were at it.

Oddly, the *Courier* wasn't interested. A Jetsons-esque spacecraft rolling through town, and they didn't even bother to take a picture! So, the crew jumped back into their truck and pulled out. When their odd little one-float pageant was over, they tugged the ship up to LaVigne's place and dropped it off. And that's where it's been sitting for more than twenty years.

Now it's just another brick in a wall of oxidizing automobilia. Nose-to-tail with aging school buses and pickup trucks, the rocket sits in a motionless parade of entropy. It has certainly known better days—days when rockets in a variety of designs toured the main streets and supermarkets of an optimistic U.S.A., when kids dreamed

of donning fishbowl space helmets and defending the galaxy with their jumpsuit-wearing television heroes. A time when men like Rocky Jones, Tom Corbett, and Captain Video toured the cosmos to protect the innocent.

It was also an age when brand-name foods bankrolled heroism. Science-fiction serials were big in the '50s and proved to be an effective vehicle for promoting marshmallows and sliced bread. One of the most popular space operas of the time was *Space Patrol,* starring Commander Buzz Corry. Sponsors like Ralston Purina made the most of the show's popularity by finding inventive ways to tie in the program with its line of cereals.

The most creative promotion, involving what is possibly the most exciting giveaway in history, was Ralston's "Name the Planet" contest. Viewers were to submit, along with the correct number of space coins hidden in Ralston cereals, a name for the new planet that had materialized on *Space Patrol.* The viewer who submitted the best name would win a clubhouse in the form of a life-size rocket ship! Billed as Commander Buzz Corry's very own "Terra IV," the grand prize was a thirty-five-foot-long, 10,000-pound, trailer-mounted spaceship, complete with bunk beds, cooking apparatus, and equipment lockers. It even came with a truck to haul it.

The Ralston Rocket, as it was nicknamed, was one of two ships that had toured the country, visiting fairs and strip malls. When Ralston was done driving it from state to state, they stripped out all the space gadgetry, refitted it as an RV, and offered it as their contest's coveted award.

The prize ultimately went to ten-year-old Ricky Walker, but as these things go, Ricky eventually tired of his big toy and the two parted ways. The dream prize desired by millions of cadets was sold to an amusement park in Kansas.

Did it eventually end up with Steve LaVigne? Unfortunately, no. Ricky's rocket landed in the hands of a construction company that—terror of terrors—dismantled it and sold it for scrap in the 1980s.

There was, however, the second Ralston Rocket—the one that was not given away in the contest. Evidence places this twin craft in the hands of Blakely Oil, who used it

to promote its "Rocket Gas" following Ralston's campaign. According to a man named Rodney Welch, Blakely then sold it to the Luer meatpacking company. Welch bought it from Luer to use in a small amusement park he called Welch's Mountain Fantasy. When that operation closed down, Welch donated the rocket to the city of Prescott, which subsequently unloaded it onto a local rehab center. And that's where LaVigne found it. He paid a hundred bucks for it.

This craft differs significantly in appearance from the Ralston Rocket, but there are those who have suggested that Luer remodeled the exterior before using it in their own promotions, which means LaVigne's craft is a reskinned Ralston. Yet there are others who disagree, maintaining that the Luer rocket is one of the copycat ships built to take advantage of the hype initiated by Ralston and that the second Ralston Rocket is wasting away on someone else's property somewhere.

Regardless, LaVigne recognizes that the rocket is a hunk of nostalgia in its own right. He considers it an artifact of better days. "Kids would really get a kick out of simple things back then," he says. "Now that we've got all the computer simulations and everything that we've got, simple just doesn't cut it anymore." He reminisces about the 16-mm projection screen locked inside, possibly used by Luer for some kind of anti-vegetable propaganda film. He also speaks with appreciation of the deteriorating sci-fi control panel and the little motor mounted to the frame that vibrates the floor and makes a rockety *hrrmmmm* sound. "That's why the rocket is a cool thing."

Uranium Mines and Radioactive Hogans

Laid out across the Four Corners region are the ingredients for a grade B science-fiction movie. Derelict uranium mines, vestiges of the vigorous cold war push to develop and stockpile nuclear weapons, pepper much of the state's northeastern territory.

Mostly on Navajo land, these mines were left behind after their deposits were extracted in the 1950s. Arizona proved to have the richest deposits of uranium ore in the country, so the government repeatedly tapped the landscape and hauled out as much of the radioactive element as they could. It's hard to determine exactly how many mines were left behind, but researchers have found well over 1,300.

Piles of uranium tailings also dot the landscape. Two notable piles include the Monument Valley location, a 90-acre site about five miles west of Tes Nez Iah, and the Rare Metals pile five miles east of Tuba City, an impressive mound on a 105-acre former mine and mill that includes ruins of housing and other buildings. The radium contained in these piles emits the radioactive gas radon. Radium, which was once used to make clock dials radiate, does not decay entirely for thousands of years.

In addition to the mines and the tailings piles, radioactive buildings have also been discovered. Locals used tailings dust in the stucco they applied to their buildings, and those who worked in the mines often carried away the easily shaped waste rock for use in constructing houses. Many of the so-called uranium homes have been abandoned, but the total number in existence is unknown.

None of the structures have been found to glow in the dark, but a contaminated hogan located in 2000 did register radon levels forty-four times higher than the Emergency Protection Agency's health standard and emitted penetrating gamma radiation 2,500 percent higher than the level that would normally prompt emergency action. Once discovered, the building was razed. Unfortunately, many like it are still in use.

Arizona's Mysterious Triangles

Exploring abandoned and forbidden property has entered a whole new realm with the advent of bird's-eye mapping tools like Google Earth. Urban explorers are now able to search difficult or unfamiliar terrain via satellite or even to venture into locations that would otherwise be inaccessible.

Of course, panning through aerial photos can never replace the gratification of exploring ruins firsthand. But with a little luck, or a lot of patience, sites that were previously unknown may reveal themselves. Anyone who sees these new finds from such an unusual angle, however, may wind up with more questions than he started out with.

A scan of the desert outside Phoenix, for example, has uncovered an odd little revelation northwest of Surprise. Distinctly geometric, it's hard to miss. But with no markings or supplemental architecture, there's little to indicate its purpose. It appears to be nothing more than a perfectly drafted, two-dimensional isosceles triangle, seemingly molded into the earth's crust like a 4,000-foot manufacturing indicator specifying where the planet's screws go.

Further exploration reveals quite a number of these anomalies spread across Arizona's southwestern region — giant, inscrutable deltas, scattered and abandoned. What are these enormous shapes? Some sort of unearthly communication? Interdimensional portals, maybe? The footprints of alien landing craft? With a bit of research, we soon learned what these puzzling pie pieces really are.

As it turns out, they're not so mysterious after all. Just obsolete runways, left to bake in the sun. Once used for flight training, they're what remain of a large number of airfields built for the army air force during World War II.

Why the peculiar triangular design? Because the airfield comprised three airstrips, each of which allowed

takeoffs and landings from both directions. This effectively resulted in six total runways differentiated by only sixty degrees, which meant that, no matter which way the wind was blowing, pilots in training would never have to fly with a crosswind of more than thirty degrees.

A small number of these landing fields were expanded for the more demanding aircraft of the future, and at least one is still being used for training maneuvers. For the most part, however, these sites sit disused, fading under the dust. And, unfortunately, they closed so long ago that no support facilities remain. So, in this case, there's now less to see from the ground than from a Web browser.

Black Canyon Greyhound Park

Roughly thirty miles north of Phoenix, in a town called Black Canyon, sits a decaying structure once known as Black Canyon Greyhound Park. It's on the north edge of the town, just west of Interstate 17, a large rectangular mass with a dark brown rooftop. The corner has the words Dog Track painted in bright orange, but the T is missing, so the sign reads DOG RACK. Little is known about the track, but it certainly invites visitors to discover more.

A covered entryway leads to a set of large glass doors where employees and customers once entered. Today the only occupants are pigeons and other desert creatures. There are no greyhounds, no employees, no gamblers, and no security.

The facility looks much larger inside than it does from the outside. The absence of walls and the narrow support beams create a feeling of vast openness. Clinging to the high ceiling are rows upon rows of fluorescent lights, yellowed with age. The betting counter runs the entire length of the building, now covered with dust and debris. One can guess that in its heyday the track was capable of handling very large crowds. How large were the crowds really? Was this place a hub of avid gamblers and feverish betting? Or was low attendance a factor in the place's becoming abandoned?

Above the betting counter, a small sign still hangs on the wall. MIN TO POST, it reads, as if it were ready to light up before the next race. The kitchen is right by the front entrance, with an array of equipment still in place. Beside the sink and the grill sits an old soda dispenser, toppled on its side. At the far end of the track there is another small kitchen with a walk-up bar. No longer does it serve burgers and hot dogs and cold drinks.

The seating area is impressive any way you look at it. The chairs are color-coded: yellow seats were seventy-five cents, and red seats were fifty cents. They are hard

plastic, lined in rows on the bare concrete floor. They offer a great view of the track through massive windows, which fill the place with sunlight. Outdoor seats were the cheapest, though they were covered with a shade screen at one point. Was this a year-round track? It is just one of many unanswered questions.

From the rooftop, the outline of the track is clearly visible. The view from here is excellent. One can see the rows of kennels on the north side of the track, where dogs were once boarded. Up close, they reveal another part of the mystery of this place.

Old signs and an office inside the maintenance area indicate that the kennels may have been used as a local mini-storage facility at one time. Inside the main grandstand, signs advertising a weekly swap meet indicate it had another life as well. When was this place

YELLOW SECTION 75¢ RED SEATING

built? Who owned and operated it? Was it ever famous? When and why was it closed?

Inside, there are some clues to the past. An old license plate from 1972 lies on a workbench. Cans of chemicals that were restricted long ago by the EPA are on a homemade shelf in the back. It's timeless, really. The architecture, the design, the conveniences—they could have been built any time within the last thirty years.

The exploration of places like Black Canyon Greyhound Park is a humbling experience. It's about the people who used to work and be entertained there. It's about finding that strange little room or closet that makes you wonder what it could have been used for. It's about being startled by strange noises and nesting birds. But most of all, it's about the totally weird places you'll find if you just keep your eyes and your mind open. –Trevor Freeman

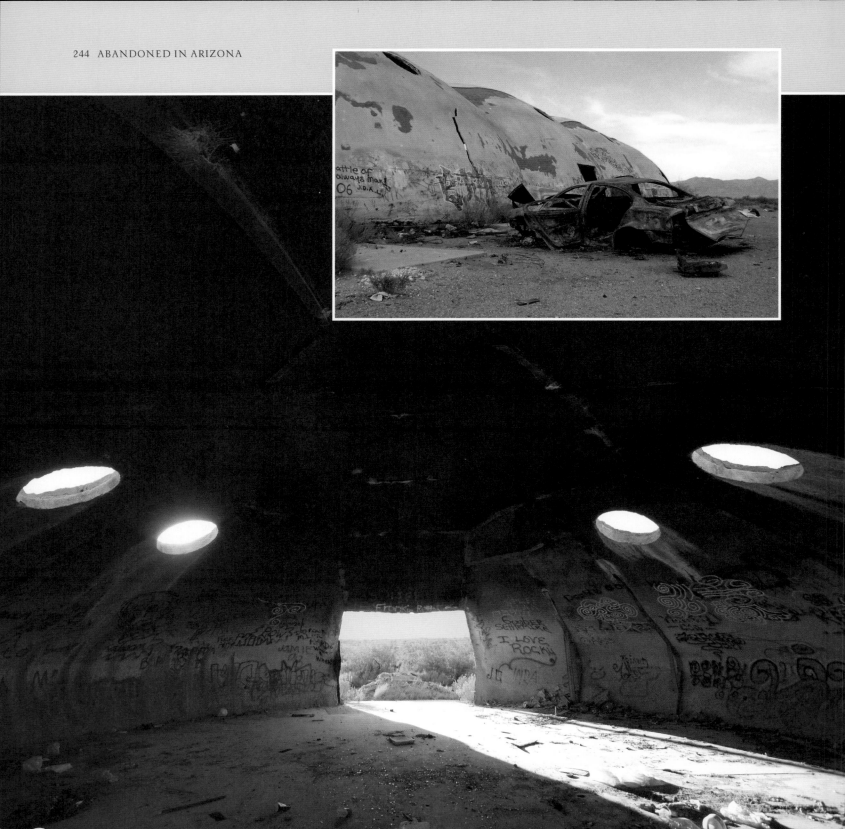

Startled at the Domes

The Domes of Casa Grande is the kind of place that has no real past and not much of a future. It's the kind of place where teenagers go to drink beer and practice their graffiti skills, the kind of place your mother may have told you to avoid.

Trying to describe the scene here is a challenge all its own. Some of the buildings look like giant caterpillars—rounded sections joined together into a long, continuous silhouette. Others are saucer-shaped and look similar to the UFOs in your favorite '50s science-fiction movie.

On the outside, the domed structures are perfectly geometric. The doorways are square, though the doors themselves are nonexistent after years of abandonment and vandalism. The domes are made of concrete and appear to be covered with foam insulation on the outside. There is no supporting rebar in the walls or any other building material present besides concrete. Close by the property are the visible outlines of more foundations. It's likely that more domes were planned, but never built, for reasons unknown.

Inside, the domes are very large and some are quite lengthy. The ceilings are high and are mostly blackened, presumably from smoke. One dome is littered with so much burned trash and melted tires that it's difficult to walk through. Another appears to have been swept clean and is quite spacious inside. Several cars could easily be parked here.

There's a mysterious aura here, though it's hard to describe exactly. Because so little is known about them, one wonders who built these domes, and most importantly, why? What happened here, or what was supposed to happen here, in the desert surrounding Casa Grande?

The other part to the story is equally mysterious. Rumors of a shadowy figure lurking about the domes have earned it a place on numerous lists of haunted sites in Arizona. There have been reports of weird vibrations, tapping noises on cars, and uneasy feelings from visitors.

While we did not encounter any shadowy figures, we were startled several times by strange noises at the site. One turned out to be an empty beer can being pushed along by the wind. Another was discovered to be a plastic bag snagged on a piece of debris. The acoustics inside the domes are impressive, and small sounds are amplified remarkably well. This can be frightening to visitors, especially those who are there alone. The whole place definitely gives off some creepy vibes.—*Trevor Freeman*

The Domes

On my second trip out west in preparation for writing *Weird Arizona,* I found enough courage to drop by a place called The Domes that I'd heard a lot about. I wanted to see if it was as sinister as people had told me. This collection of unusual structures—big concrete domes and other more free-form buildings—is at the southern edge of Casa Grande, just south of Interstate 8 on South Thornton Road. The buildings are tucked away in a rural neighborhood of low-income homes, a short distance after the paved road ends. How they got there and what they were meant for is lost in the mist of time.

Though the structures were certainly unusual, I wouldn't have called them scary. For the most part, they looked like a bizarre dump site. If you were looking for a skinless bedspring, a spare oven knob, or a fresh dose of tetanus, this was the place to be.

As I explored The Domes further, however, my flippant attitude gave way to trepidation. There was an unusual stillness about the place—the kind of tranquillity that makes you feel like you're being watched. As I peered through my camera with one eye, I couldn't help but scan for mutants with the other. The creepy reverberation produced inside the buildings only made things worse, though until sunset the only sounds I heard were those I made myself.

Yet, once the sun disappeared, the whole scene grew absolutely unsettling. I was there long enough before dusk to determine that no one else was around, but in the dark, the noises I heard were no longer just my own. No one could have arrived at this isolated location without my seeing them drive up, yet there was something definitely moving around me and it didn't sound like a small desert creature.

Just as I opened the shutter for my last photo, I heard the sound of a jug being kicked. Not falling over—kicked! It was the longest eight-second exposure of my life. As soon as the shutter closed, I threw everything into my rental car any way it would fit and sped away, tripod legs sticking out of windows and light stands poking me in the back of the head. Of all the sites I visited for *Weird Arizona,* The Domes was probably the most foreboding.

INDEX

Page numbers in **bold** refer to photos and illustrations.

A

abandoned places, 224–247
   Black Canyon Greyhound Park, 240, **240–241**, 242–243, **242–243**
   Domes of Casa Grande, **244**, 245, **245**, 246, **246–247**
   Family Fun World, 234, **234**
   Peak Trading Post, 233, **233**
   Ralston Rockets, 235–236, **235, 236–237**
   Sliding Jail, 228, **228**
   triangles in the dessert, 239, **239**
   Twin Arrows, 232, **232**
   Two Guns, 226–227, **226, 227**
   uranium mines, 238, **238**
   Vulture Mine and Vulture City, 229–231, **229, 230–231**
Acadia Ranch, 202, **202**
Aerospace Maintenance and Regeneration Center, 222–223, **222–223**
Airport Mesa, 74
Ali, Jaiji, 213, **213**
aliens. *See* UFOs and aliens
Allen, A. A., 102
Allen, John, 127
Allen, Rex, 201, **201**
AMARC, 222–223, **222–223**
ancient sites, 26–43. *See also* Native American legends and sites
   Casa Grande, **26–27**, 28, **29**
   Grand Canyon underground chambers, 40–41, **40–41**
   Hole in the Rock, 32–33, **32, 33**
   Meteor Crater, 36, **36–38**, 39, **39**
   Montezuma Castle, 30–31, **30, 31**
   Signal Hill, 42–43, **42, 43**
   Sunset Crater, 34–35, **35**
Anderson, Nathan, 199
Annie, Dutch, 208
Anthem Hitchhiker, 176, **176–177**
Apache Leap, 14, **14**
Arcosanti, **124–125**, 125
Arpaio, Joe, 106–109, **106**

Arrow Tree, 151, **151**
aura photography, 75, **75**

B

Barrett, Walter, 133, **133**
Barringer, Daniel, 39
Bartlett Hotel wishing outhouse, 157, **157**
Bass, Edward, 127, **129**
beasts, bizarre, 78–95
   attacking cactus, 90–91
   burros, 93, **93**
   El Chupacabra, **82**, 83, **83**
   Mogollon Monster, 80–81
   skinwalkers, **86–87**, 87
   small hominids, 84, **84, 85**
   The Thing, 94–95, **95**
   Thunderbird, 88–89, **89**
   white buffalo, 92, **92**
Beaver, D., 216
Bedrock City, 158–159, **158, 159**
Bell Rock, 74
Benjamin, Teresa, 190–192
Berkbigler family poltergeist, 77
Bigfoot, 80–81
Biosphere 2, **126**, 127–129, **127, 129**
Bird Cage Theatre, 190–192, **190–191, 192**
Black Canyon Greyhound Park, 240, **240–241**, 242–243, **242–243**
Boneyard, 222–223, **222–223**
Boothill Graveyard, 208–209, **208, 209**
Boynton Canyon, 74
Branham, William, 76–77
Bravo, Delfina, 17
Brunckow, Frederick, 194–195, **195**
buffalo, white, 92, **92**
buried treasure, 56–58
burros, in Oatman, 93, **93**

C

Cabeza de Vaca, Alvar Nuñez, 46–47
cactus, attacks by, 90–91

Camelback Mountain castle, 120, **120–121**
camels
   Hi Jolly monument and, 213, **213**
   Red Ghost and, 204–205, **205**
Camp Pinal, 14
Cannon, Adolph, 56, **56**
Canyon de Chelly National Monument, 48
Canyon Diablo, 49–51, **49, 51**, 210, **210**
   buried treasure in, 56–57
Carleton House, 193
Casa Grande, **26–27**, 28, **29**
   Domes of, **244**, 245, **245**, 246, **246–247**
Cathedral Rock, 74
caves and tunnels
   Grand Canyon underground chambers, 40–41, **40–41**
   Superstition Mountains, 22, 24–25
cemeteries and tombstones, 206–223
   Beaver's tombstone, 216
   Boothill Graveyard, 208–209, **208, 209**
   Cochise's grave, 211, **211**
   Culling's Well, 212, **212**
   Franklin tombstone, 211, **211**
   Grand Canyon plane crash wreckage, 217–219, **217, 218, 219**
   Hi Jolly monument, 213, **213**
   Hunt tomb, 214, **214**
   lost Opata tomb, 58, **58**
   Miranda tombstone, 220–221, **221**
   plane, 222–223, **222–223**
   Poston's tomb, 215, **215**
   Shaw, photos of, 210, **210**
   of Waltz, 54, 55, **55**
Cerney, John, 138
Cerro Colorado buried treasure, 57
chain gangs, 108, **108**
Chapel of the Holy Cross, 74
cholla cactus, attacks by, 90–91, **91**
Chupacabra, El, **82**, 83, **83**

Claiborne, Billy, 59–60, 208
Clanton, Billy, 59–60, 208
Clanton, Ike, 59–60, **59, 60**
Cleghorn, Richard, 164–165, **164, 165**
cliff dwellings
    Cliff Jail, 149, **149**
    Montezuma Castle, 30–31, **30, 31**
Cliff Jail, 149, **149**
Cochise, grave of, 211, **211**
Copenhaver, Mort, 120
Copenhaver Castle, 120, **120–121**
Coronado, Francisco Vásquez de, 46–47
Courthouse Butte, 74
cow, dynamited, 25
cow skull–shaped restaurant, 145, **145**
Crater Range, 175
Culling's Well graves, 212, **212**
Cundiff, Earle and Louise, 226–227

D

Davis, Jefferson, 213
Deadman Gap, 175
Delgadillo, Juan, 102
Delgadillo's Snow Cap, 102
de Niza, Marcos, 47
Devil's Highway, 170–171, **171**
Diamondback Bridge, 143, **143**
diamonds, Cannon's caches of, 56
dinosaurs
    Flintstones Bedrock City, 158, **159**
    Holbrook, 160–162, **160, 161, 162, 163**
dog racing track, abandoned, 240,
    240–241, 242–243, **242–243**
Domes, The, **244**, 245, **245**, 246,
    246–247
Dragoon Mountains, Cochise's grave in,
    211, **211**
Dreamy Draw Dam, 69–71, **69, 70, 71**
Dunn, Jack, 99
Dunning, Linda, 170, 171

E–F

Earp, Morgan, 59–60
Earp, Warren, 200, **200**
Earp, Wyatt, 59–60
Eldredge, Dean, 188
elves, 84
Esenwein, Rattlesnake Bill, 99
fabled people and places, 44–63
    buried treasure, 56–58
    Canyon Diablo, 49–51, **49, 50, 51**
    Geronimo, 52–53, **52, 53**
    the Hydes, 61–63, **61, 63**
    Lost Dutchman Gold Mine, 54–55
    O.K. Corral, 59–60, **59, 60**
    Seven Cities of Gold, 46–47, **46, 47**
    Spider Rock, 48, **48**
Family Fun World, 234, **234**
Fantasma Colorado, 204–205, **205**
Finger Rock, 155, **155**
Flagstaff
    Museum Club, 188–189, **188, 189**
    sky ring over, 76–77, **76**
Flintstones Bedrock City, 158–159, **158,
    159**
Fort Huachuca, 193
Fort Yellowhorse, 166–167, **166, 167**
Franklin, Benjamin J., 211, **211**
Frontier Relics Museum, **112**, 113, **114**
Fuller, R. Buckminster, 28

G

Garden of Gethsemane, **118–119**, 119
Geronimo, 52–53, **52, 53**
Geronimo's Castle, 146, **147**
ghosts, 186–205. *See also* cemeteries
    and tombstones
    Acadia Ranch, 202, **202**
    Anthem Hitchhiker, 176, **176–177**
    Bird Cage Theatre, 190–192, **190–191,
    192**
    Brunckow's, 194–195, **195**
    Crater Range, 175
Fort Huachuca, 193
    Ghost Bus, 178–179, **179**
    La Llorona, **11**, 12–13, **13**
    Landmark Restaurant, 203, **203**
    Museum Club, 188–189, **188, 189**
    Oliver House, 198–199, **198, 199**
    Red Ghost, 204–205, **205**
    Saguaro Boulevard, 174, **174–175**
    stone-throwing poltergeist, 77
    in the Superstition Mountains, 24–25
    in Willcox, 200–201, **200, 201**
    Yuma Territory Prison, 196–197, **196, 197**
Giddings, Rimmy Jim, 100–101, **100, 101**
gold
    Coronado's search for, 46–47
    Lost Dutchman Gold Mine, 54–55
    waterfall of, 57–58
Goodyear giants, **137**, 138, **138–139**
Grand Canyon
    Beaver tombstone in, 216
    Hydes' disappearance in, 61–63, **61, 63**
    plane crash in, 217–219, **217, 218, 219**
    underground chambers around, 40–41,
    40–41
    waterfall of gold, 57–58
Gulley, Boyce, castle of, 122–123, **122, 123**

H

Hard Knocks High, 107
Heath, John, 98, **98**, 208
heroes and villains, 96–113
    Allen, A. A., 102
    Arpaio, Joe, 106–109, **106**
    Delgadillo, 102
    Mickens, Orville, **112**, 113
    Mother Goose, 110, **110**
    prairie dog Dr. Doolittle, 111
    Rattlesnake Bill, 99
    Rimmy Jim Giddings, 100–101, **100, 101**
    Santa Claus, death of, 103
    Tombstone's lynched man, 98, **98**
    Warren, George, 99

Wattron, Frank J., 104–105, **104**
Highway 93 ghost bus, 178–179, **179**
Hitchhiker, Anthem ghost, 176, **176–177**
Hobo Joe, 140–141, **140**
Hole in the Rock, 32–33, **32, 33**
Holliday, Doc, 59–60, **59, 60**, 208
Hoover, Herbert, 35
Hunt, George W. P., tomb of, 214, **214**
Hyde, Glen and Bessie, disappearance of, 61–63, **61, 63**

J–K

Jack Rabbit Trading Post, 144, **144**
Jail Tree, 150, **150**
JATO Impala, 19
Jerome, Sliding Jail in, 228, **228**
Johnson, George, 208, **208**
Kautza, Michael, 145
Kirlian, Semyon, 75
Kokopelli, world's largest, 141, **141**
Kolb, Emery, 62, 63
Kravetz, Robert, medical museum of, 134, **134, 135**

L

Lake Havasu City, London Bridge in, 172–173, **172–173**
Landmark Restaurant, 203, **203**
Launa's Canyon, 12. *See also* Llorona, La
LaVigne, Steve, 235, 236
Lee, Louis, 114, 116–117, **116, 117**
legends, local, 10–25
   Apache Leap, 14, **14**
   dynamited cow, 25
   El Tiradito, 18–19, **18**
   JATO Impala, 19
   La Llorona, **11**, 12–13, **13**
   Petrified Forest National Park, 15–16, **15, 16**
   San Xavier del Bac Mission, 20–21, **20, 21**
   Superstition Mountains, 22, **22, 23**, 24–25, **24**

tallest tree in Tucson, 17, **17**
   Window Rock, 21, **21**
Leslie, Frank, 208
Lewis, Chester, 148
Ley, Tim, 66–67
Llorona, La, **11**, 12–13, **13**
London Bridge, 172–173, **172–173**
Longhorn Grill, 145, **145**
Lost Dutchman Gold Mine, 22, 54–55
Lucero, Felix, 119
Luna, Adam, 160
lynching, in Tombstone, 98, **98**

M

Madden, Al, 130–131
magnetic phenomena
   Red Rock vortexes, 72–74, **72, 73, 74**
   in the Superstition Mountains, 24–25
Mainliner Vancouver, crash of, 217–219, **217, 218, 219**
Marion Hatch Dinosaur Park, 162
McLaury, Frank, 59–60, 208
McLaury, Tom, 59–60, 208
McPhee, John, 103
Mesa
   Landmark Restaurant in, 203, **203**
   Miranda in, 220–221, **220, 221**
   Meteor Crater, 36, **36–38**, 39, **39**, 56
Mickens, Orville, **112**, 113
milagros, 20–21
Miller, Harry "Indian," 226–227
miniature village, 133, **133**
Miracle Moon, 92
Miracle Valley, 102
Miranda, Ernesto, 220–221, **220, 221**
Mitchell, Jerry, 120
Model T, Plank Road and, 182, **182**
Mogollon Monster, 80–81
Montezuma Castle, 30–31, **30, 31**
Moore, Lester, 208, **208**
Mother Goose, 110, **110**
Museum Club, 188–189, **188, 189**

museums
   Frontier Relics Museum, **112**, 113, **114**
   Kravetz's medical, 134, **134, 135**
   Titan Missile, 151, **152, 153**, 154, **154**
mythology, 10. *See also* legends, local

N

Native American legends and sites
   Apache Leap, 14, **14**
   Casa Grande, **26–27**, 28, **29**
   Cochise's grave, 211, **211**
   Geronimo, 52–53, **52, 53**
   Grand Canyon underground chambers, 40–41, **40–41**
   Hole in the Rock, 32–33, **32, 33**
   Kokopelli, world's largest, 141, **141**
   lost Opata tomb, 58, **58**
   Montezuma Castle, 30–31, **30, 31**
   Signal Hill, 42–43, **42, 43**
   skinwalkers, **86–87**, 87
   small hominids, 84, **84, 85**
   Spider Rock, 48, **48**
   Sunset Crater, 34–35, **35**
   White Buffalo Calf Woman, 92, **92**
   Window Rock, 21, **21**
Ninimbe, 84

O–P

Oatman burros, 93, **93**
O.K. Corral, 59–60, **59, 60**
Oliveras, Juan, 18–19
Oliver House, 198–199, **198, 199**
Opata tomb, 58, **58**
Oracle Historical Society, 202, **202**
outhouse, wishing, 157, **157**
Palace of Montezuma, **26–27**, 28, **29**
Papago Park, 32–33, **32, 33**
Peak Trading Post, 233, **233**
Peralta Massacre, 54–55
Petrasch, Rhinehart, 55
Petrified Forest National Park, 15–16, **15, 16**
Petrified Rock Garden, 160–161, **160**

petroglyphs, Signal Hill, 42–43
Phoenix
    Hobo Joe, 140–141, **140**
    Hole in the Rock, 32–33, **32, 33**
    Hunt's tomb, 214, **214**
    Kravetz's medical museum, 134, **134, 135**
Poston tomb in, 215, **215**
UFO sightings in, 66–71, **66**
Picacho Peak, 233, **233**
Pinkley, Frank, 28
plane cemetery, 222–223, **222–223**
plane crashes, 217–219, **217, 218, 219**
Plank Road, 182, **182**
Poston, Charles, 57
Poston, Charles Debrille, 215, **215**
prairie dogs, language of, 111
Presley, Elvis, 106
Primrose Hill pyramid, 215, **215**
Prince, Thomas, 95
properties, personalized and experimental, 114–135
    Arcosanti, **124–125,** 125
    Biosphere 2, **126,** 127–129, **127, 129**
    Camelback Mountain castle, 120, **120–121**
    Garden of Gethsemane, **118–119,** 119
    Gulley's castle, 122–123, **122, 123**
    Kravetz's medical museum, 134, **134, 135**
    Lee's rock garden, 114, 116–117, **116, 117**
    miniature village, 133, **133**
    Quartzsite Yacht Club, 130–132, **131, 132**
pyramids, 213–215, **213, 214, 215**

Q–R
Quartzsite Yacht Club, 130–132, **131, 132**
radioactive buildings, 238, **238**
Ralston Rocket, 235–236, **235, 236–237**
Ramsey, Agnes, 202
Ransdell, Marvin, 140–141

rattlesnakes
    bridge shaped like, 143, **143**
    Rattlesnake Bill and, 99
Redford, Frank, 148
Red Ghost, 204–205, **205**
Red Rock vortexes, 72–74, **72, 73, 74**
religious sites
    Allen, A. A., and, 102
    El Tiradito, 18–19, **18**
    Rimmy Jim Giddings, 100–101, **100, 101**
    ring over Flagstaff, 76–77, **76**
roadside oddities, 136–167
    Arrow Tree, 151, **151**
    Bedrock City, 158–159, **158, 159**
    Cliff Jail, 149, **149**
    diamondback bridge, 143, **143**
    Finger Rock, 155, **155**
    Fort Yellowhorse, 166–167, **166, 167**
    Goodyear giants, **137,** 138, **138–139,**
    Hobo Joe, 140, **140**
    Holbrook dinosaurs, 160–162, **160, 161, 162, 163**
    Jack Rabbit Trading Post, 144, **144**
    Jail Tree, 150, **150**
    Kokopelli, world's largest, 141, **141**
    Longhorn Grill, 145, **145**
    Rocky the Frog, 156, **156**
    Skull Rock, 157, **157**
    sundial, world's largest, 142, **142**
    Teepee Cafe and Bar, 146, 147
    tiki sculptures, 164–165, **164, 165**
    Titan Missile Museum, 151, **152, 153,** 154, **154**
    Wigwam Village, 148, **148**
    wishing outhouse, 157, **157**
roads less traveled, 168–185
    alien abductions and, 180–181, **180, 181**
    Anthem Hitchhiker, 176, **176–177**
    Crater Range, 175
    Highway 93 ghost bus, 178–179, **179**
    London Bridge, 172–173, **172–173**
    Plank Road, 182, **182**

Route 66, 183–185, **183, 184, 185**
Route 666, 170–171, **171**
Saguaro Boulevard, 174, **174–175**
Rocky the Frog, 156, **156**
Root, Nile, 42–43
Route 66, 183–185, **183, 184, 185**
    Twin Arrows Trading Post, 232, **232**
Route 666, 170–171, **171**

S
Saguaro Boulevard, Fountain Hills, 174, **174–175**
Saguaro National Park West, 42–43, **42, 43**
Santa Claus, death of, 103
San Xavier del Bac Mission, 20–21, **20, 21**
Sasquatch, 80–81
Schnebly Hill, 74
Scott, Don and Thorna, 188–189
sculpture
    Garden of Gethsemane, **118–119,** 119
    tiki, 164–165, **164, 165**
Sedona
    aura photography in, 75, **75**
    vortexes in, 72–74, **72, 73, 74**
Seven Cities of Gold, 46–47, **46, 47**
Shaw, John, 210, **210**
Shoemaker, Eugene, 39
Signal Hill, 42–43, **42, 43**
silver, buried stashes of, 57, 58
Sipapu, 41
skinwalkers, **86–87,** 87
Skull Rock, 157, **157**
skull-shaped restaurant, 145, **145**
Sliding Jail, 228, **228**
Slobodchikoff, Constantine, 111
Smiley, George, 104–105, **105**
Snow Cap café, 102
Soleri Windbells, 125
Songers, Richard, 234
Speaking Rock, 48
Spider Woman, 48

Star of the Seine, crash of, 217–219, **217, 218, 219**
state seal, 99, **99**
Staveley, Gaylord, 216
Stevens, L. W., 80–81
Stewart's Petrified Wood, 162
stones and rock formations
    Finger Rock, 155, **155**
    Hole in the Rock, 32–33, **32, 33**
    Lee's rock garden, 114, 116–117, **116, 117**
    Petrified Forest National Park, 15–16, **15, 16**
    Rocky the Frog, 156, **156**
    Skull Rock, 157, **157**
    Spider Rock, 48, **48**
    Window Rock, 21, **21**
stone-throwing poltergeist, 77
Strom, Charlotte, 193
sundial, world's largest, 142, **142**
Sunset Crater, 34–35, **35**
Superstition Mountains, 22, **22, 23,** 24–25, **24**

T

Teepee Cafe and Bar, 146, **146, 147**
Tent City jail, 106, **107,** 109
Thing, The, 94–95, **95**
Thomas, Julia, 55
Thunderbird, 88–89, **89**
tiki sculptures, 164–165, **164, 165**
time, shifts in, 24
Tiradito, El, 18–19, **18**
Titan Missile Museum, 151, **152, 153,** 154, **154**
Tombstone
    Bird Cage Theatre, 190–192, **190–191, 192**

Boothill Graveyard, 208–209, **208, 209**
    lynching in, 98, **98**
    O.K. Corral, 59–60, **59, 60**
Townsend, Nancy, 110, **110**
treasure, buried, 56–58
trees, tallest in Tucson, 17, **17**
triangles, engraved in the earth, 239, **239**
Troup, Bobby, 183
Tucson
    Diamondback Bridge, 143, **143**
    El Tiradito, 18–19, **18**
    Garden of Gethsemane, **118–119,** 119
    La Llorona in, 13
    Signal Hill petroglyphs, 42–43, **42, 43**
    tallest tree in, 17, **17**
    Twin Arrows Trading Post, 232, **232**
    Two Guns, 226–227, **226, 227**

U

UFOs and aliens
    alien abductions, 180–181, **180, 181**
    Dreamy Draw Dam, 69–71, **69, 70, 71**
    Phoenix lights, 66–71, **66, 69**
    Red Rock vortexes and, 74
unexplained phenomena, 64–77
    aura photography, 75, **75**
    Red Rock vortexes, 72–74, **72, 73, 74**
    ring over Flagstaff, 76–77, **76**
    stone-throwing poltergeist, 77
UFOs, 66–71, **66, 69**
uranium mines, 238, **238**

V

village, miniature, 133, **133**
Vipinim, 84
volcanoes, 34–35, **35**
Volz, Fred, 50
vortexes, energy, 72–74, **72, 73, 74**
Vulture Mine and Vulture City, 229–231, **229, 230–231**

W

Walton, Travis, 180–181, **181**
Waltz, Jacob, 54–55, **55**
Warren, George, 99
water babies, 84
waterfall of gold, 57–58
Watson, "Long Tom," 57–58
Wattron, Frank J., 104–105, **104**
Weiser, Jacob, 54
White, Georgie, 63, 216, **216**
White Buffalo Calf Woman, 92, **92**
Wickenburg, Henry, 229
Wigwam Village, 148, **148**
Willcox ghosts, 200–201, **200, 201**
Window Rock, 21, **21**
wishing outhouse, 157, **157**
Wishing Shrine, 18–19, **18**
witches and witchcraft, 86–87, **87**
Wolf, Herman, 50
Wright, Frank Lloyd, 123

Y

Yellowhorse, Juan, 166–167, **166, 167**
Yuma Crossing State Historic Park, 182, **182**
Yuma Territory Prison, 196–197, **196, 197**

PICTURE CREDITS

All photos by the author or public domain except as listed below:

Page 2 bottom left © Ryan Doan (www.ryandoan.com), bottom right (prospector) © Lowell Georgia/CORBIS; **3** top right © Ron Niebrugge/Alamy; **4–5** © Ryan Doan; **7** © George Sozio; **11** © Cathy Wilkins, **13** © Ryan Doan; **18** © Catherine Karnow/CORBIS; **22** courtesy Astronomical Observatory of A. Mickiewicz University, Poznan, Poland; **24** © Lowell Georgia/CORBIS; **38** © Denis Scott/CORBIS; **40–41** © iStockphoto.com/Christophe Testi; **44–45** background © K. Parker, inset © Bettmann/CORBIS; **46** © NYPL Picture Collection; **47** © Kevin Fleming/CORBIS; **48** © K. Parker; **49** © Joseph Grumbo; **51, 52** center © CORBIS; **52** right, **53** Library of Congress; **56** © CORBIS; **57** © James Randklev/CORBIS; **58** © Bettmann/CORBIS; **60** top left © Peter Jordan/Alamy; **61, 63** courtesy Northern Arizona University/Cline Library; **64–65, 66** © Ryan Doan; **67** © iStockphoto.com/George Cairns; **69** © iStockphoto.com/Michael Knight; **72** © Linda Godfrey; **78, 79, 82** © Ryan Doan; **83** © Loston Wallace; **84** © Tim Cridland; **85, 86–87** © Ryan Doan; **89** © Ryan Doan; **91** © BananaStock/Alamy; **92** © Ryan Doan; **93** © Ron Niebrugge/Alamy; **96** © Lichtenstein Andrew/CORBIS SYGMA; **96–97** center courtesy Burton Frasher Sr./Pomona Public Library—The Frasher Foto Postcard Collection; **98** National Archives; **100–101** courtesy Burton Frasher Sr./Pomona Public Library—The Frasher Foto Postcard Collection; **103** © Annie Engel/zefa/Corbis; **104–105** courtesy of the Arizona Historical Society/Tucson; **106–107** courtesy Sheriff Joe Arpaio; **108** © Tore Bergsaker/CORBIS SYGMA; **122** © Linda Godfrey; **131, 132, 133** left © Mark Moran; **149** National Archives; **151** © Ingred Kaslik; **156, 157** left © Mark Moran; **158, 159** top left © Karen Christensen/karensoasis.com; **159** right top and bottom © Visions of America, LLC/Alamy; **166** top right © Dub Thomas; **168–169** © Ryan Doan; **171** © Troy Paiva; **174–177** © Heather Shade; **179** © Ryan Doan; **180** © iStockphoto.com/Manfred Karner; **181** © Michael H. Rogers; **183** © Bettmann/CORBIS; **184–186** © Troy Paiva; **196** © Donald W. Larson/timeoutofmind.com; **198–199** © Heather Shade; **202** courtesy Oracle Historical Society; **203** © Heather Shade; **205** © Ryan Doan; **212** © Kurt Wenner; **216** © Northern Arizona University, Cline Library, Special Collections and Archives, Joseph Muench Collection; **217** © David Muench/CORBIS; **219** bottom left © *The New York Times;* **220** © Arizona State Library, Archives and Public Records, History and Archives Division; **221** © Bettmann/CORBIS; **222–223** © Phil Buehler; **226** left courtesy Northern Arizona University, Cline Library, Special Collections and Archives; **228–231** © Trevor Freeman; **238** © iStockphoto.com/Randy Merrill; **240–243** © Trevor Freeman.

WEiRD ARiZONA

By

WESLEY TREAT

Executive Editors
Mark Sceurman and Mark Moran

CONTRIBUTING AUTHORS

Trevor Freeman is an Arizona native who enjoys exploring, photographing, and writing about abandoned and historic places in his spare time. He would like to thank Maggie, his family, and his friends for their love and support.

Heather Shade (known as Shady to her friends, and you can call her that too) was raised on a steady diet of ghost stories, Scooby Doo cartoons, treasure hunts, and horror flicks. She has been a lifelong addict of both the photography and exploration of all things strange and unusual. There's nothing she's more passionate about than exploring the Weird and capturing it all in